Treaties

ELEMENTS OF INTERNATIONAL LAW

Series Editors

Mark Janis is William F. Starr Professor of Law at the University of Connecticut.

Douglas Guilfoyle is Associate Professor of International and Security Law at UNSW Canberra.

Stephan Schill is Professor of International and Economic Law and Governance at the University of Amsterdam.

Bruno Simma is Professor of Law at the University of Michigan and a Judge at the Iran–US Claims Tribunal in The Hague.

Kimberley Trapp is Professor of Public International Law at University College London.

Elements of International Law represents a fresh approach in the literature of international law. It is a long series of short books. *Elements* adopts an objective approach to its subject matter, focusing on narrowly defined core topics in international law. Eventually, the series will offer a comprehensive treatment of the whole of the field. In this volume, Richard Gardiner explores the role of treaties in international law and the law which governs them.

Previously published titles in this series

The Law of International Financial Institutions
Daniel D. Bradlow

Occupation in International Law
Eliav Lieblich and Eyal Benvenisti

Arms Control and Disarmament Law
Stuart Casey-Maslen

International Law of Taxation
Peter Hongler

Jus Cogens
Dinah Shelton

The International Tribunal for the Law of the Sea
Kriangsak Kittichaisaree

International Law in the Russian Legal System
William E. Butler

The European Court of Human Rights
Angelika Nussberger

Treaties

Richard Gardiner

Great Clarendon Street, Oxford, OX2 6DP,
United Kingdom

Oxford University Press is a department of the University of Oxford.
It furthers the University's objective of excellence in research, scholarship,
and education by publishing worldwide. Oxford is a registered trade mark of
Oxford University Press in the UK and in certain other countries

© Richard Gardiner 2023

The moral rights of the author have been asserted

First Edition published in 2023

All rights reserved. No part of this publication may be reproduced, stored in
a retrieval system, or transmitted, in any form or by any means, without the
prior permission in writing of Oxford University Press, or as expressly permitted
by law, by licence or under terms agreed with the appropriate reprographics
rights organization. Enquiries concerning reproduction outside the scope of the
above should be sent to the Rights Department, Oxford University Press, at the
address above

You must not circulate this work in any other form
and you must impose this same condition on any acquirer

Public sector information reproduced under Open Government Licence v3.0
(http://www.nationalarchives.gov.uk/doc/open-government-licence/open-government-licence.htm)

Published in the United States of America by Oxford University Press
198 Madison Avenue, New York, NY 10016, United States of America

British Library Cataloguing in Publication Data

Data available

Library of Congress Control Number: 2023941723

ISBN 978-0-19-287207-4 (pbk.)
ISBN 978-0-19-287206-7 (hbk.)

DOI: 10.1093/law/9780192872067.001.0001

Printed and bound by
CPI Group (UK) Ltd, Croydon, CR0 4YY

Links to third party websites are provided by Oxford in good faith and
for information only. Oxford disclaims any responsibility for the materials
contained in any third party website referenced in this work.

Series Editors' Preface

Elements of International Law represents a fresh approach to the literature of international law. It is a long series of short books. Following the traditional path of an international law textbook, *Elements*, rather than treating the whole of the field in one heavy volume, focuses on more narrowly defined subject matters.

There is nothing like *Elements*. It treats particular topics of international law much more extensively and in significantly more depth than traditional international law texts or encyclopaedias. As each book in the *Elements* series has a relatively narrow focus, it provides a comprehensive treatment of a specialized subject matter, in comparison to the more limited treatment of the same subject matter in other general works.

Like a classic textbook, *Elements* aims to provide objective statements of the law. The series does not concern itself with the academic niches filled ably by doctoral theses, nor does it include works which take an argumentative point of view, already well done by the OUP *Monograph* series. Except in length and integration, *Elements* is for substantive topics comparable to OUP's *Commentary* series on individual treaties. Each book is exhaustively footnoted in respect of international legal practice and scholarship, including treaties, diplomatic practice, decisions by international and municipal courts and arbitral tribunals, resolutions and acts of international organizations, and commentary by the most authoritative jurists.

Elements adopts an objective, non-argumentative approach to its many subject matters and constitutes a reliable go-to source for practising international lawyers, judges, and arbitrators; government and military lawyers; and scholars, teachers, and students engaged in the discipline of international law.

Mark Janis
Douglas Guilfoyle
Stephan Schill
Bruno Simma
Kimberley Trapp

Acknowledgement

Some chapters of this book contain matter loosely based on revised material from R Gardiner, *International Law* (Longman 2003).

Contents

Table of Cases xv
Table of Treaties xxi
List of Abbreviations xxv

Introduction 1

1 Treaties in Modern Times 5
  I Introduction 5
      1 General Features of Treaties 5
      2 Treaties Set Out Obligations Binding in International Law 7
      3 Treaty Relations 8
      4 The Place of Treaties in International Law 9
      5 'Law of Treaties' Distinguished from 'Treaty Law' 11
  II Defining Treaties 13
      1 What Identifies an Instrument as a Treaty? 13
      2 Components of a Treaty 15
      3 Title not Conclusive of Status 15
      4 Recital of the Negotiating States 16
      5 Preamble, Statement of Agreement, and Provisions 16
      6 Final Clauses and Words of Conclusion ('Testimonium') 17
      7 'Mandatory' Language Combined with Formalities 18
  III Other Instruments and Engagements 20
      1 'Memorandum of Understanding' 20
      2 Miscellaneous Forms and Documents 22
      3 Unwritten International Agreements 24
  IV Parties to Treaties 26
  V Locating Treaties 27

2 Treaties in Development of International Law 30
  I How Treaties Can State Rules of Customary International Law 31
      1 The ILC and the ICJ's *North Sea Continental Shelf* Cases 31
      2 Codification, Crystallization, and Later Consolidation 33
      3 *North Sea Continental Shelf* Cases State Principles for Custom through Treaties 34

II	Codifying Treaties and Treaties Formulating Law	38
	1 Whether Codification or Progressive Development	38
	2 Codifying Instruments	39
III	Reducing Rules to Writing: Development of the 1969 Vienna Convention	42
	1 ILC's Preparatory Work	42
	2 The Vienna Conference 1968–1969	45
	(a) Reservations	45
	(b) Treaty interpretation	48
	(c) Peremptory norms (*jus cogens*)	49
	(d) Conclusion	51

3 How Treaties Are Made — 53

I	Introduction	53
II	Making a Treaty	56
	1 Negotiating Treaties	56
	2 'Concluding' a Treaty	58
	3 'Adoption' and 'Authentication' of a Text	59
	4 Proceedings at a Diplomatic Conference	60
	(a) Rules of procedure	60
	(b) Languages	61
	(c) Outcome of negotiations	62
	(d) Depositary functions	64
	5 Consenting to Be Bound by a Treaty	65
	(a) Decision to be bound	65
	(b) Signature as consent to be bound	66
	(c) Means of consent: ratification, accession etc.	67
	(d) Other forms of consent	68
III	Entry into Force	68
	1 Mechanisms for Start Up	68
	2 Time Factors	69

4 What the Treaty Means — 71

I	Interpretation and Its Rules	71
II	Elements of the General Rule	76
	1 Good Faith: VCLT Article 31(1)	76
	2 Ordinary Meaning, Context, Object, and Purpose: VCLT Article 31(1)	78
	3 Attribution of Meaning by the Parties	81
	(a) Agreements in connection with conclusion of a treaty: VCLT Article 31(2)(a)	83
	(b) Other instruments connected with conclusion: VCLT Article 31(2)(b)	83

	(c) Subsequent agreements: VCLT Article 31(3)(a)	85
	(d) Subsequent practice: VCLT Article 31(3)(b)	86
	4 Relevant Rules of International Law: VCLT Article 31(3)(c)	91
	5 Special Meanings: VCLT Article 31(4)	96
III	Supplementary Means of Interpretation: VCLT Article 32	97
	1 Preparatory Work and Circumstances of Conclusion	97
	2 Other Supplementary Means	101
IV	Languages: VCLT Article 33	102
V	Conclusion	103

5 Bringing Treaties Home — 105

I	Introduction	105
	1 General Considerations	105
	2 Treaties Require Good Faith Performance	106
	3 National Legal Systems: 'Monism' and 'Dualism'	107
II	International Law's Requirements	107
	1 International and Municipal Consequences of Treaties Distinguished	107
	2 A Treaty May Require Provisions in Municipal Law	111
	3 Monist and Dualist Approaches to Implementation	112
	4 More than Monism May Be Required	113
	5 'Self-executing' Provisions and 'Direct Applicability'	114
	6 Further Analysis of Treaty Obligations	115
III	National Requirements and Procedures	117
	1 Forms of Constitutional Implementation	117
	2 Distinguish Prior Authorization for Participation from Implementation	118
	3 Domestic Approval	119
	4 Implementing Treaties in a Dualist System	122
	(a) The United Kingdom as a paradigm	122
	(b) Reflecting obligations and reproducing provisions	125
	(c) Transforming treaty terms	126
	(d) Legislating the treaty's text	126
	(e) Consequence of differing legislative approaches	127
	(f) Considering treaties as aid to statute	128
	(g) Combined role of courts and Parliament	130
	(h) Function of courts in the United Kingdom	130
	(i) The court is not resolving an international dispute	132
	5 Implementing Treaties in a Civil Law System	132
	(a) France as a paradigm	132
	(b) The French constitution	133
	(c) The *Conseil Constitutionnel*	137
	(d) The *Conseil d'État* and the *Cour de Cassation*	142

xii Contents

      6 The European Union and Its Predecessors   146
         (a) Implementing the treaties establishing
            the European Union   146
         (b) Implementing treaties entered into by
            the European Union and its Member States   149
   IV Interpretation of Treaties in National Legal Systems   153
     1 Role of the Executive   154
     2 Role of Governments and Legislatures   155
     3 Role of Courts   155
       (a) General approach to Vienna rules   155
       (b) Interpretation in courts of states not parties to
          the Vienna Convention   158
       (c) Interpretation of treaties in courts in the United
          Kingdom and other 'common law' countries   162
       (d) Interpretation in courts of civil law jurisdictions   165
     4 Conclusion   170

6 Ensuring Treaties Work   172
   I Reciprocity and Diplomatic Action   173
     1 Simple Reciprocity   173
     2 Negotiated Arrangements   174
     3 Responding in Kind (*Exceptio Inadimplenti*)   175
   II Supervision by International Institutions   176
   III Resort to Arbitration, Courts, and Tribunals   178
   IV Suspension, Termination, and Other Responses to
     Breach of a Treaty   182
     1 Invalidity   182
     2 Suspension, Termination, and Countermeasures   183
   V Further Avenues for Dealing with Differences over
     Implementation   189

7 Treaties at the Heart of International Law   193
   I General International Law   193
     1 Scope   193
     2 War and Peace   194
     3 Statehood, State Immunity, and Diplomatic Relations   196
     4 Codification of International Law   198
     5 Law of Spaces   200
     6 Rights and Duties of Individuals   204
       (a) Consular law   205
       (b) Human rights   205
       (c) Investment law   207
       (d) International criminal law   207

II	International Organizations	208
	1 Historical Development	209
	2 The International Telecommunications Union	210
	3 Non-governmental Organizations	211
III	Specialist Areas	213
IV	Private International Law	216
V	Conclusion	218

Selective Bibliography   219
Index   221

Table of Cases

For the benefit of digital users, cases that are tabled as spanning two pages e.g., (52–53) may, on occasion, appear on only one of those pages.

INTERNATIONAL COURTS AND TRIBUNALS

Aerial Incident of 27 July 1955 (United States of America v. Bulgaria),
    Memorial of the USA, 2 December 1958...........................3n.3
Aguas del Tunari v Bolivia (ICSID ARB/02/03), Award of 21 October 2005...75n.8
Alabama Claims of the United States of America against Great Britain
    XXIX UNRIAA 125...105, 179
Applicability of the Obligation of the Arbitrate under section 21 of the
    United Nations Headquarters Agreement of 26 June 1947 (PLO
    Observer Mission Case) [1988] ICJ Rep 12........................105n.1
Application of the Convention on the Prevention and Punishment of the
    Crime of Genocide (Croatia v Serbia) [2015] ICJ Rep 3..............50n.52
Application of the International Convention on the Elimination of All Forms
    of Racial Discrimination (Georgia v. Russian Federation) (Preliminary
    Objections) [2011] ICJ Rep 70......................................174
Arbitral Award Made by the King of Spain on 23 December 1906 Judgment
    [1960] ICJ Rep 206...87n.41
Arbitration regarding the Iron Rhine ("IJzeren Rijn") Railway
    (Belgium/Netherlands) (2005) XXVII RIAA 35..............87n.43, 92–93
Armed Activities on the Territory of the Congo (Democratic Republic of the
    Congo v Uganda) ICJ Judgment of 9 February 2022..................44n.32
Armed Activities on the Territory of the Congo (New Application: 2002)
    (Democratic Republic of the Congo v Rwanda) (Jurisdiction and
    Admissibility) [2006] ICJ Rep 6...................................50n.52
Austro-German Customs Union [1931] PCIJ Series A/B 41.................17–18
Award of Arbitral Tribunal for the Agreement on German External Debt,
    (Belgium, France, Switzerland, UK and USA v Federal Republic of
    Germany) ('Young Loan' case, 1980) 59 ILR 495.................160n.153
Case Concerning the Air Services Agreement of 27 March 1946
    (USA v France) 54 ILR 304 (1978).............................188n.55
Case Concerning the Auditing of Accounts ... Convention on the Protection
    of the Rhine against Pollution by Chlorides of 3 December 1976
    (Netherlands v France), Arbitral Award of 12 March 2004,
    144 ILR 259...77n.13
Certain Expenses of the United Nations (Article 17, paragraph 2, of the
    Charter) (Advisory Opinion) [1962] ICJ Rep 157..................87n.41
Commission v Portugal Case C-84/98, judgment of 4 July 2000, [2000]
    ECR 1-5219...151

xvi Table of Cases

Corfu Channel (Merits) [1949] ICJ Rep 22 .... 87–88, 195–96
Costa v Ente Nazionale per l'Energia Elettrica (Enel)
   [1964] ECR 585. .... 147n.119, 148
Danube Dams case, see *Gabcíkovo-Nagymaros (Hungary/Slovakia)*
*Dispute Concerning Access to Information under Article 9 of the OSPAR
   Convention (Ireland v United Kingdom)* (2003) 42 ILM 1118 .... 19n.38
Diversion of Water from the Meuse [1937] PCIJ Series A/B, No. 70 .... 185n.46
Feldbrugge v Netherlands ECtHR case no 8/1984/80/127
   (Judgment of 23 April 1986) 88n.44
Gabcíkovo-Nagymaros (Hungary/Slovakia) (Danube Dams) [1997]
   ICJ Rep 7 185–88
Heathrow Airport User Charges Arbitration (United States–United Kingdom)
   (Award of 30 November 1992) XXIV UNRIAA 1 .... 21, 21n.44
Interpretation of Peace Treaties with Bulgaria, Hungary and Romania
   (Second Phase), Advisory Opinion [1950] ICJ Rep 221 .... 180n.23
*Interpretation of the Agreement of 25 March 1951 between the WHO and
   Egypt* [1980] ICJ Rep 73. .... 175n.8
Iron Rhine Arbitration see *Arbitration regarding the Iron Rhine ("IJzeren
   Rijn") Railway (Belgium/Netherlands)*
Island of Palmas case *(Netherlands, USA)* (1928) 2 RIAA 829 91
Jadhav (India v Pakistan) (Judgment), [2019] ICJ Rep 418 .... 205n.40
Jurisdictional Immunities of the State (Germany v Italy, Greece intervening)
   (Judgment) [2012] ICJ Rep 99 .... 197nn.11–12
Kasikili/Sedudu Island (Botswana/Namibia) [1999] ICJ Rep 1045 .... 87n.41
Kiliç v Turkmenistan ICSID Case No. ARB/10/1,
   Decision of 7 May 2012 .... 103n.81
LaGrand (Germany v USA) [2001] ICJ Rep 466 .... 43n.29, 78n.14,
                                                              103nn.83–84, 205
*Land and Maritime Boundary between Cameroon and Nigeria
   (Cameroon v. Nigeria: Equatorial Guinea intervening)* [2002]
   ICJ Rep 303 .... 65n.30
*Legal Consequence for States of the Continued Presence of South Africa in
   Namibia (South West Africa)* [1971] ICJ Rep 16 .... 89n.46, 91
Legal Status of Eastern Greenland (Denmark v Norway)
   PCIJ Series A/B, no. 53. 24
Legality of the Threat or Use of Nuclear Weapons [1966] ICJ Rep 226 .... 196n.6
Legality of the Use by a State of Nuclear Weapons in Armed Conflict
   (Advisory Opinion) [1996–I] ICJ Rep 66 .... 87n.41
Libyan Arab Jamahiriya/Chad, Territorial Dispute see *Territorial Dispute
   (Libyan Arab Jamahiriya/Chad)*
Maritime Delimitation and Territorial Questions (Qatar v Bahrain)
   (Jurisdiction and Admissibility) [1994] ICJ Rep 112 .... 25n.59, 181
*Maritime Delimitation and Territorial Questions between Qatar and Bahrain
   (Qatar v Bahrain) (Jurisdiction and Admissibility)* [1995] ICJ Rep 6 . . 77, 100–1
*Maritime Delimitation in the Area between Greenland and Jan Mayen, Case
   concerning (Denmark v Norway)* [1993] ICJ Rep 38. .... 86n.39
Maritime Delimitation in the Indian Ocean (Somalia v Kenya) (Preliminary
   Objections) [2017] ICJ Rep 3 21–22

Table of Cases **xvii**

*Military and Paramilitary Activities in and against Nicaragua (Nicaragua v
  United States of America)* (Jurisdiction and Admissibility) [1984]
  ICJ Rep 392 .... 9n.15, 87n.41
*Military and Paramilitary Activities in and against Nicaragua
  (Nicaragua v. United States of America)* [1986] ICJ Rep 14 37
Muhammet Çap v Turkmenistan ICSID Case No. ARB/12/6,
  13 February 2015 .... 103n.82
*N.V. Algemene Transport- en Expeditie Onderneming Van Gend en
  Loos v Neder-Landse Tariefcommissie* [1963] CMLR 105 147–48
*North Sea Continental Shelf (Federal Republic of Germany v
  Denmark and Netherlands)* [1969] ICJ Rep 3 ....31, 34–37
Oil Platforms (Islamic Republic of Iran v United States of America)
  (Merits) [2003] ICJ Rep 161 94–96
*Open Skies Agreements, Commission of the European Communities v UK,
  Germany, and others* (Cases C-466/98, C476/98 et al) 152n.131
*Prevention and Punishment of the Crime of Genocide, Application of
  the Convention on the (Bosnia and Herzegovina v Serbia and
  Montenegro)* [2007] ICJ Rep 43...................................50n.52
Pubblico Ministero v Tullio Ratti [1980] 1 CMLR 96....................149n.124
Rainbow Warrior (New Zealand/France) (1990)
  XX RIAA 251 .... 187–88, 187n.43–88
Reparation for Injuries Suffered in the Service of the United Nations
  (Advisory Opinion) [1949] ICJ Rep 174 .... 27n.64
*Reservations to the Convention on the Prevention and Punishment of the
  Crime of Genocide* (Advisory Opinion) [1951] ICJ Rep 15 .... 50n.52
Rhine Chlorides case, see *Case Concerning the Auditing of Accounts*
South China Sea Arbitration (Philippines v China) (Jurisdiction and
  Admissibility) (2015), PCA Case No 2013-19 .... 23, 23n.52
*Sovereign Rights and Maritime Spaces in the Caribbean Sea, Alleged
  Violations of (Nicaragua v Colombia)* ICJ Judgment of 21 April 2022 ... 44n.32
Temple of Preah Vihear (Merits) [1962] ICJ Rep 33 .... 87n.41
Territorial Dispute (Libyan Arab Jamahiriya/Chad) [1994] ICJ Rep 6 .... 87n.41
The 'Volga' (Russian Federation v Australia) (2003) 42 ILM 159 .... 79n.19
Trinidad Cement Ltd v Co-operative Republic of Guyana (Caribbean
  Court of Justice) (2009) 74 WIR 302 ....158n.143
United States Diplomatic and Consular Staff in Tehran (USA v Iran) [1980]
  1CJ Reports 31 .... 198n.15
United States—Import Prohibition of Certain Shrimp and Shrimp Products
  WTO Report of Appellate Board AB-1998-4, WT/DS58/AB/R, 12
  October 1998.. 77n.13
*United States—Measures Affecting the Cross-Border Supply of Gambling
  and Betting Services* WTO Appellate Body Report of 7 April 2005,
  WT/DS285/AB/R...99–100
Venezuelan Preferential Claims Case (1904) 1 HCR 55 76–77
Whaling in the Antarctic (Australia v Japan: New Zealand intervening)
  [2014] ICJ Rep 226... 81, 90
Witold Litwa v Poland ECtHR App no 26629/95, Judgment of
  4 April 2000.. 80, 99

xviii Table of Cases

AUSTRALIA

Commonwealth v Tasmania (The Tasmanian Dam) (1983) 158 CLR 1 165
Li v Zhou (Court of Appeal, New South Wales) [2014] NSWCA 176...........165
Minister of State for Immigration and Ethnic Affairs v Teoh [1995] HCA 20 125
QAAH v Minister for Immigration & Multicultural & Indigenous Affairs
  (1983) 158 CLR 1 165
Qenos Pty Ltd v Ship 'APL Sydney' [2009] FCA 1090 ....165n.174
Secretary, Department of Families, Housing, Community and Indigenous
  Affairs v Mahrous [2013] FCAFC 75 ....165n.174

BELGIUM

Cigna Insurance v Transport Nijs Cassation appeal, No C.97.0176.N,
  ILDC 38 (BE 2000), 30th March 2000 ....167n.184

CANADA

Crown Forest Industries Ltd v Canada [1995] 2 SCR 802 ....158n.143
Ezokola v Canada [2013] SCC 40 ....158n.143
Gulfmark Offshore N.S. Limited v Canada [2007] FCA 302...........157n.143–58
Peracomo Inc. v TELUS Communications Co. [2014] SCC 29 ....158n.143
Takeda Canada Inc. v Canada (Health) [2011] FC 1444 ....158n.143

FRANCE

Administration des Douanes v. Société Cafés Jacques Vabre Cour de
  Cassation, Chambre Mixte, du 24 mai 1975, 93 International Law
  Reports 240..142
Arrêt Nicolo, Conseil d'Etat, Assemblée, du 20 octobre 1989, 108243,
  publié au recueil Lebon 142
CETA, Decision no. 2017-749 DC of 31 July 2017 .... 137n.82, 139,
                                                               140–41, 140n.91
Cheriet-Benseghir Conseil d'État 09/07/2010, N° 317747................. 143n.103,
                                                               145, 145n.115
Chevrol v France (Application no. 49636/99), Judgment
  of 13 May 2003 144–45
Geoffrey F. and others Decision no. 2020-858/859 QPC of 2 October 2020......141
GISTI case Conseil d'Etat, Assemblée, du 29 juin 1990, 78519, publié au
  recueil Lebon 144n.110, 166–67, 167n.181
Loi relative à l'interruption volontaire de la grossesse Decision Number 74-54
  DC of 5 January 1975...138n.84
Mme Yamina Chevrol Conseil d'Etat, Assemblée, du 9 avril 1999,
  180277, Lebon..144–45
Re Société Schneider Electric 4 ITLR 1077 158–59
Voting Rights Décision n° 98-400 DC du 20 mai 1998 143–44
X and others Appeal judgment, no 13-84.778, ILDC 2376 (2014):
  Court of Cassation, Criminal Division 166n.177

GERMANY

Bundesrepublik Deutschland gegen Kanton Schaffhausen
  BGE 97 I 359 S. 359 .... 169n.193
Child Abduction case XII ZB 210/99, BGHZ 145, 97, 16 August 2000 ..... 158n.142
East German Expropriation Case (2004) BVerfGE 112, 1, ILDC 66 168
J (A Bosnian Serb) (Individual Constitutional Complaint)
  2 BvR 1290/99, ILDC 132 .... 168n.190
New Strategic Concept Case 2 BvE 6/99, ILDC 134 (2001) 168n.189
Tuition fees in Higher Education BVerwG 6 C 16.08, Judgment of
  29.04.2009, and ILDC 1556 (DE 2009) 167–68
Proceedings on The Constitutional Complaint BVerfG, 2 BvR
  1290/99 of 12/12/2000 .... 157–58n.142

INDIA

Jethmalani and others v Union of India (Supreme Court of India)
  14 ITLR 1 .... 159n.146

NORWAY

Sølvik v Staten v/Skatt Øst (Supreme Court of Norway) 11 ITLR 15 ...158n.146–59

UNITED KINGDOM

Ahmad and Aswat v USA [2006] EWHC 2927 .... 18n.36
Alize 1954 v Allianz Elementar Versicherungs AG [2021] UKSC 51 .... 164n.170
Anonymous v (Former) (Bitterfeld County, Order of Federal
  Administrative Court) 7 B 64.10, ILDC 2418 (DE 2010),
  NVwZ 2011, 752, 13th December 2010 .... 167n.185
Anson v Commissioners for Her Majesty's Revenue and Customs
  [2015] UKSC 44 .... 164n.169
Attorney-General v Zaoui [2006] 1 NZLR 289 .... 158n.143
Basfar v Wong [2022] UKSC 20 .... 164n.169, 165n.173
Belhaj v Straw [2017] UKSC 3 .... 124n.35
Ben Nevis (Holdings) Ltd v Revenue and Customs Commissioners [2013]
  EWCA Civ 578 .... 72n.3
Benkharbouche v Embassy of the Republic of Sudan [2017]
  UKSC 62 .... 130n.59, 132n.69
British Airways v Laker Airways [1985] 1 AC 58 131
Chloride Industrial Batteries v F & W Freight [1989] 1 WLR 823 .... 79n.18
Evergreen Marine (UK) Limited v Nautical Challenge Ltd
  [2021] UKSC 6 .... 164n.172
Fothergill v Monarch [1981] 2 AC 251 ...... 127n.48, 130n.59, 155n.135, 162n.162,
                                                          163–65, 169
Gard Marine and Energy Limited v China National Chartering
  Company Limited [2017] UKSC 35 .... 164n.171
Ghaidan v Godin-Mendoza [2004] UKHL 30 .... 129n.56

xx Table of Cases

Heathrow Airport Limited, and ors v Her Majesty's Treasury [2021]
  EWCA Civ 783 . . . . 118n.20
Hiscox v Outhwaite [1992] 1 AC 562 . . . . 129n.55, 155n.135
Home Secretary v GA and others [2021] EWCA Civ 1131 . . . . 116n.17
In Re Westinghouse [1978] AC 547 . . . . 131n.64, 131n.66
JH Rayner (Mincing Lane) Limited v Department for Trade and Industry
  [1990] 2AC 418 . . . . 118n.19, 123
Mandla v Dowell Lee [1983] 2 AC 548 . . . . 129, 130n.62
Moohan and another v The Lord Advocate [2014] UKSC 67 . . . . 164n.169
Pepper v Hart [1993] AC 593 . . . . 128n.51
R (Al-Jedda) v Secretary of State for Defence [2006] EWCA Civ 327 . . . . 124n.35
R (Bashir) v Secretary of State for the Home Department [2018] UKSC 45 . . . 124n.35
R (KTT) v Secretary of State for the Home Department [2021]
  EWHC 2722 (Admin) 123n.32
R (on the application of Miller and another) v Secretary of State for
  Exiting the European Union [2017] UKSC 5 . . . . 118n.20
R (SG and others) v Secretary of State for Work and Pensions [2015]
  UKSC 16 . . . . 125n.40
R v Immigration Officer at Prague Airport ex parte European Roma Rights
  Centre [2004] UKHL 55, [2005] 2 AC 1 . . . . 96n.64
R v Lyons [2002] UKHL 44 . . . . 162n.163
R v Reeves Taylor [2019] UKSC 51 . . . . 164n.169
R v Secretary of State ex parte Brind [1991] 1 AC 696 . . . . 128n.52
Re G (A Child) [2021] UKSC 9 . . . . 120n.30
Reyes v Al-Malki [2017] UKSC 61 . . . . 122n.35
Routier v Revenue and Customs Commissioners [2019] UKSC 43 . . . . 124n.35
Salomon v Commissioners of Customs & Excise
  [1967] 2 QB 116 . . . . 124n.34, 128n.50, 129n.53, 130n.63
Sepet v Secretary of State for the Home Department [2003] UKHL 15 . . . . . 164n.168
Trendtex Trading Corporation v Central Bank of Nigeria
  [1977] 1 QB 529 . . . . 122n.29
Warner v Scapa Flow Charters (Scotland) [2018] UKSC 52 . . . . 164n.170

UNITED STATES OF AMERICA

Abbott v Abbott 130 S.Ct. 1983 (2010) 160–61
BG Group Plc. v Argentina 134 S. Ct. 1198 (2014) 161
Chubb & Son, Inc v Asiana Airlines 214 F3d 301 (2d Cir 2000) 159n.149
Medellín v Texas 552 U.S. 491 (2008) 110–11
Sale v Haitian Centers Council 509 US 155 (1993) 96n.64, 159n.150
Weinberger v Rossi 456 US 25 (1982) 159n.150

Treaties

African Charter on Human and Peoples' Rights, Nairobi, 1981,
 1520 UNTS 217, no 26363. . . . . 206n.49
Agreement between the UK and USSR on Settlement of Mutual
 Financial and Property Claims Arising Before 1 January 1939',
 London, 1986 (UK Treaty Series No 65 (1986)) 14n.28
Air Navigation, International Convention relating to the Regulation of
 Aerial Navigation, 11 LNTS 173, no 297, [1922] Australian Treaty
 Series 6, ... 41, 201–2
Alaska, Convention ceding, Washington, 1867 (11 Bevans 1216) 14, 15
American Convention on Human Rights, San José, 1969,
 1144 UNTS 143, no 17955. 206
Apartheid, International Convention on the Suppression and Punishment
 of the Crime of, 1015 UNTS 243, no 14861. 51
Armed conflict, Geneva Conventions, 1949, and Additional Protocols,
 1977, 75 UNTS 31, 85, 135, 287, nos 970–3 and 1125 UNTS 3, 609,
 nos 17512–3 . . . . 36 , 51
Aviation sabotage, Convention for the Suppression of Unlawful Acts
 against the Safety of Civil Aviation, Montreal, 1971, 974 UNTS 177,
 no 14118, revised at Beijing, 2010 . . . . 111, 202
Biological Diversity, Convention on the Conservation of, Rio de Janeiro,
 1992, 1760 UNTS 79, no 30619. 215
Bribery, OECD Convention on Combating Bribery of Foreign Public
 Officials in International Business Transactions, Paris 1997, 2802
 UNTS p 225 No 49274. . . . . 113n.10, 178, 207–8
Charter of the United Nations, https://treaties.un.org/doc/Publication/
 UNTS/No%20Volume/Part/un_charter.pdf 9, 9n.13, 19, 42, 51, 64, 89,
                                                        90, 91, 110, 173, 176, 184–85,
                                                        188–89, 194–95, 205–6,
                                                        207–8, 208n.58
Chicago Convention *see* International Civil Aviation, Convention on,
Child Abduction, Convention on the Civil Aspects of International,
 The Hague, 1980, 1343 UNTS 97, no 22514. . . . . 101–2, 122n.30, 157–58,
                                                              160, 217
Child, UN Convention on the Rights of the, 1989,
 1577 UNTS 3, 27531 . . . . .125, 130n.63–31, 145, 206
Code of Conduct for Liner Conferences, Convention on a, Geneva,
 1974, 1334 UNTS 15, no 22380. . . . . 42n.29–43
Continental Shelf, Convention on, Geneva, 1958, United Nations,
 499 UNTS 311, no 7302. . . . . 34, 42

xxii Treaties

Convention for the Unification of Certain Rules for International
  Carriage by Air, Montreal, 1999, 2242 UNTS 309,
  no 39917 ....53n.1, 114, 202, 216
Convention for the Unification of certain Rules relating to International
  Carriage by Air (with Additional Protocol), Warsaw, 1929, 137
  LNTS 11, no 3145 and various amending Protocols ...114, 163n.165, 202, 216
Convention on Jurisdiction, Applicable Law, Recognition, Enforcement
  and Co-operation in Respect of Parental Responsibility and
  Measures for the Protection of Children, The Hague, 1996, 2204
  UNTS 503, no 39130 ....116n.17
Convention on the Rights and Duties of States, Montevideo, 1933,
  165 LNTS 19, no 3802 ....196n.8
Convention on the Settlement of Investment Disputes between States
  and Nationals of Other States (ICSID), Washington, 1965,
  575 UNTS 159, no 8359..............................83n.29, 207, 213–14
Convention relating to the Status of Refugees, Geneva, 1951, 189 UNTS
  150, no 2545 and amending Protocol, New York, 1967, 606 UNTS
  267, no 8791 .... 11–12, 96, 124, 130, 164
Covenant of the League of Nations (Part I of Treaty of Versailles),
  Australian Treaty Series 1920, no 1 ....85, 91–92
Elimination of All Forms of Racial Discrimination, International
  Convention on the, New York, 1966, 660 UNTS 195,
  no 9464 ....51, 129, 174n.5
European Convention for the Protection of Human Rights and Fundamental
  Freedoms, Rome, 1950, 213 UNTS 221, no 2889 .... 80, 129, 141, 143,
                                                              144–45, 206–7
European Convention on State Immunity, Basel, 1972, (ETS) No 74...........197
European Economic Community, Treaty of Rome establishing the, 1957,
  294 UNTS 3, no 4300.......................................142, 147, 151
European Union, Treaty on, Lisbon, 2007 (TEU), *Official Journal of the
  European Union* (7 June 2016) C202/13...........................140, 147
Functioning of the European Union, Treaty on the, Lisbon, 2007
  (TFEU) *Official Journal of the European Union*
  (7 June 2016) C202/47 .... 147, 148, 149–50, 151n.128
Fur Seals, Convention for the Preservation and Protection of,
  Washington, 1911, Treaty Series, No 5648 214
General Agreement on Tariffs and Trade, Protocol of Provisional
  Application of the, Geneva, 1947, 55 UNTS 308, no 814...... 69, 150, 213–14
Genocide, Convention on the Prevention and Punishment of the Crime of,
  78 UNTS 277, no 1021............. 45, 50, 50n.52, 51, 157–58n.142, 168–69
Hijacking, Convention for the Suppression of Unlawful Seizure of Aircraft,
  The Hague, 1970, 860 UNTS 105, no 12325 202
ICSID *see* Convention on the Settlement of Investment Disputes
International Civil Aviation, Convention on, Chicago, 1944,
  15 UNTS 295 no 1021 ....31n.3, 201–2, 215
International Civil Aviation, Protocol Relating to an Amendment to the
  Convention on International Civil Aviation, Montreal, 1984, 2122
  UNTS 337, no 36983 ....31n.3

International Convention for the Safety of Life at Sea, London, 1974
and amendments, 1184 UNTS 2, no 18961...........................200
International Convention for the Unification of Certain Rules relating to
the Immunity of State-owned Vessels, Brussels, 1926 and Additional
Protocol, Brussels, 1934, 176 LNTS 199, no 4062.............63n.22, 196–97
International Covenant on Civil and Political Rights, 1966, 999 UNTS
171, no 14668 .... 177, 206, 206n.50
International Interests in Mobile Equipment, Convention on,
Cape Town, 2001, 2307 UNTS 285, no 41143..........................217
International Telecommunications Union, Constitution and Convention of
the, Geneva, 1992, 1825 UN Treaty Series 3, No 31251 .... 5–6, 23n.51
International Liability for Damage Caused by Space Objects, Convention
on, London, Moscow and Washington, 1971, 961 UNTS 187,
no 13810 202–3
Jay Treaty, Treaty of Amity Commerce and Navigation between Great
Britain and USA, London, 1794, https://avalon.law.yale.edu/18th_
century/jay.asp.. 120, 178–79
Kellogg–Briand Pact *see* Treaty for Renunciation of War
Montevideo Convention *see* Convention on the Rights and Duties of States
Offences and certain other acts committed on board aircraft, Convention
on, Tokyo, 1961, 704 UNTS 219, no 10106 .... 202n.30
Outer Space Treaty 1967, 610 UNTS No 8843...........................39–41
Pact of Paris *see* Treaty for Renunciation of War
Paris Convention for the Protection of Industrial Property of March 20,
1883, as revised at Brussels on December 14, 1900, at Washington on
June 2, 1911, at The Hague on November 6, 1925, at London on June 2,
1934, at Lisbon on October 31, 1958, and at Stockholm on July 14 1967,
828 UNTS 305, no 11851............. 14, 60–61, 147, 191, 209, 211n.64, 216
Peace, Treaty of Peace between Israel and Jordan, Arava, 1994,
2042 UNTS p 351, No 35325.....................................109n.6
Prevention of Marine Pollution by Dumping of Wastes and other Matter,
Convention on the, London, 1972, 1046 UNTS 120, no 15749 215
Prevention of Pollution from Ships, 1973, International Convention for the,
as modified by the Protocol, London, 1978, and later amendments,
1340 UNTS 61, no 22484..215
Prevention of Pollution of the Sea by Oil, International Convention for the,
London, 1954, 327 UNTS 3, no 4714................................215
Protection of the Ozone Layer, Convention for the, Vienna, 1985,
1513 UNTS 293, no 26164......................................215n.79
Protocol on Aircraft Equipment, Cape Town, 2001, UK Treaty Series
No 32 (2015), Cm 9155 217
Protocol on Substances that Deplete the Ozone Layer, Montreal, 1987,
1522 UNTS 3, no 26369...215
Recognition and Enforcement of Foreign Arbitral Awards, Convention
on the, New York, 1958, 330 UNTS 3, no 4739............. 126, 207, 217–18
Refugees *see* Convention relating to the Status of Refugees
Registration of Objects Launched into Outer Space, Convention on,
New York, 1974, 1023 UNTS 15, no 15020 202–3

Rescue of Astronauts, the Return of Astronauts and the Return of Objects
  Launched into Outer Space, Agreement on the, London, Moscow and
  Washington, 1968, 672 UNTS 119, no 9574 202–3
Slavery Convention, Geneva, 1926, (1927) 60 LNTS 253, no 1414..............51
Statute of the International Court of Justice *see* Charter of the United Nations
Taking of Evidence Abroad in Civil or Commercial Matters, Convention on
  the, The Hague, 1970, 847 UNTS 240 no 12140 .... 114n.12, 131n.66
Territorial Sea and Contiguous Zone, Conventions on, Geneva,
  1958, 516 UNTS 205, no 7477....................................44n.32
Torture and Other Cruel, Inhuman or Degrading Treatment or Punishment,
  Convention against, New York, 1984, 1465 UNTS no 24841 ....51, 206
Transboundary Movement of Hazardous Wastes, Convention on the,
  Basel, 1989, 1672 UNTS 57, no 28911 215
Treaty for the Renunciation of War, General Treaty for Renunciation of
  War as an Instrument of National Policy, Paris, 1928,
  94 LNTS 54, no 2137 ....84, 109–10
Treaty on the Protection of the Olympic Symbol, Nairobi, 1981,
  1863 UNTS 367, no 31732...................................211–12n.64
Tzarist Assets *see* Agreement between the UK and USSR on Settlement of
  Mutual Financial and Property Claims
Ukraine, Memorandum on Security Assurances in connection with
  Ukraine's accession to the Treaty on the Non-Proliferation of
  Nuclear Weapons', Budapest, 1994, 3007 UNTS 167, no 52241 24
UN Charter *see* Charter of the United Nations
UN Convention on the Law of the Sea, 1982, 1833 UNTS 3,
  no 31363 ....62n.21, 113–14, 201, 215
United Nations Convention on Jurisdictional Immunities of States and
  Their Property, New York, 2004, General Assembly Resolution
  A/59/38 of 2 December 2004 197
United Nations, Agreement regarding the Headquarters of the,
  Lake Success, 1947, 11 UNTS 11, no 147...........................105n.1
Vienna Convention on Consular Relations, 1963, 596 UNTS 261,
  no 8638 .... 10, 42, 110–11, 126–27n.43, 198, 205
Vienna Convention on Diplomatic Relations, 1961,
  500 UNTS 95, no 7310................................ 33, 173–74, 198
Vienna Convention on the Law of Treaties between States and International
  Organizations or between International Organizations, 1986, Docs vol
  II, A/CONF.129/15...7
Warsaw Convention *see* Convention for the Unification of certain Rules
  relating to International Carriage by Air
Whaling Convention, Geneva, 1931, 155 LNTS 349 ....81, 90, 214
World Intellectual Property Organization, Convention establishing
  the, Stockholm, 14 July 1967, 828 UNTS 3, no 11846 14

Abbreviations

AJIL	*American Journal of International Law*
ATS	Australian Treaty Series
BYIL	*British Yearbook of International Law*
CJEU	Court of Justice of the European Union
CLP	*Current Legal Problems*
ECJ	European Court of Justice (now CJEU qv)
ECOSOC	Economic and Social Council (UN)
EEZ	exclusive economic zone
EHHR	European Human Rights Reports
EJIL	*European Journal of International Law*
ESA	European Space Agency
ETS	European Treaty Series
ICAO	International Civil Aviation Organization
ICC	International Criminal Court
ICJ	International Court of Justice
ICLQ	*International and Comparative Law Quarterly*
ICRC	International Committee of the Red Cross/Crescent
ICSID	International Centre for the Settlement of Investment Disputes
ILC	International Law Commission
ILDC	International Law in Domestic Courts at Oxford Reports on International Law (online)
ILM	*International Legal Materials*
ILO	International Labour Organization
ILR	International Law Reports
IMCO	Inter-governmental Maritime Consultative Organization (now IMO)
IMF	International Monetary Fund
IMO	International Maritime Organization
IMSO	International Mobile Satellite Organization (formerly the International Maritime Satellite Organization)
ITU	International Telecommunications Union
LNTS	League of Nations Treaty Series
MOU	Memorandum of Understanding
MPEPIL	*Max Planck Encyclopedia of Public International Law*

PCA	Permanent Court of Arbitration
PCIJ	Permanent Court of International Justice
RdC	Recueil des Cours, Hague Academy
RIAA	Reports of International Arbitral Awards (United Nations)
UKTS	United Kingdom Treaty Series
UNCITRAL	United Nations Commission on International Trade Law
UNCLOS	United Nations Convention on the Law of the Sea
UNEP	United Nations Environment Programme
UNHCR	United Nations High Commissioner for Refugees
UNRIAA	(see RIAA above)
UNTS	United Nations Treaty Series (Volume and Treaty number, unless page indicated)
UPU	Universal Postal Union
VCLT	Vienna Convention on the Law of Treaties 1969
WHO	World Health Organization
WIPO	World Intellectual Property Organization
WTO	World Trade Organization
ZaöRV	Zeitschrift für ausländisches öffentliches Recht und Völkerrecht

Introduction

Lawyers are increasingly likely these days to encounter one of the several types of international agreement that constitute treaties. Yet many practitioners and others may not have had the opportunity to study public international law, and even law courses on this subject may have included only a small component specifically on treaties. This book aims to provide an account of the role of treaties as a key element of modern international law, to give the background to this key element, and to provide a brief outline of the law of treaties for those who need an overview of it.

In practice, most modern applications of international law are likely to involve a treaty in some way. Much of general international law has been codified through treaties. Specialist areas of law have been established by treaties. The jurisdiction of international courts and tribunals depends on treaties. International organizations derive their legal personality, competence, and functionality from treaties. Treaties are also increasingly applied in national systems of law, something which provides a further major element for attention.

The law governing how treaties are negotiated, joined by prospective parties, brought into force, interpreted and applied, and suspended or terminated is largely codified in a treaty named the Vienna Convention on the Law of Treaties 1969. The law of treaties is an extensive subject. The number of treaties is now vast. So is the literature about them and their governing law. One of the commentaries on the 1969 Vienna Convention runs to two large volumes, while numerous books and academic articles address particular aspects of the subject.[1] An overview of the area of law which the Vienna Convention covers forms a substantial part of this book. Being itself of relatively short compass, this book is intended to offer a gateway to more detailed study of the role of treaties in international law and the law of treaties. However, it also aims to provide much of the essential ancillary knowledge for understanding and applying treaties.

---

[1] O Corten and P Klein (eds), *The Vienna Conventions on the Law of Treaties: A Commentary* (OUP 2011); see further the selective bibliography at 219 below.

2 Introduction

Part of this understanding requires grasping the terminology, form, and functioning of treaties. This is not just a matter of diplomatic niceties. Identifying what is a treaty and what is merely a political commitment has become more difficult with the proliferation of instruments of a less formal character than agreements negotiated through traditional diplomatic processes. Further, there are sometimes misunderstandings as to which states are bound by a particular instrument. Countless are the occasions when the term 'signatory' is misused to denote a 'party' to a treaty (signature commonly being only a step towards ratification), while the term 'ratification' itself, which in international law is the formal international confirmation of a state's acceptance to being bound by a treaty, is sometimes confused with the national legislative or other domestic processes leading up to implementation of the treaty. Such basic terms are explained in the early chapters of this book.

The way in which treaties contribute rules to international law (specifically addressed in Chapter 2) is a pervasive consideration, while the history of the development of the law of treaties and the typology of treaties are mainly for background consideration; but these latter matters also provide signposts to some essential material and touch on some of the more controversial aspects of the subject. The way in which treaties are made (Chapter 3) may seem more of interest to those who are likely to be involved in negotiating treaties, but this is in fact of considerable potential significance to most lawyers who encounter treaties. Both for a full understanding of a treaty and when interpreting it, what constitutes the records of negotiations (the preparatory work), how these records can be located, and what role they play in interpretation and application of a treaty can be useful, and sometimes key, considerations.

Interpreting a treaty is the activity which most lawyers who encounter a treaty are likely to be required to undertake (Chapter 4). The codified principles for treaty interpretation are very brief and deceptively simple. They are, however, accompanied by less obvious background considerations and by a wealth of practice and guidance. Proper application of the rules of treaty interpretation requires that the interpreter be informed by an understanding of these considerations, practice, and guidance.

While some treaties affect only the international relations of their parties, more and more treaties have effect in whole or in part within national legal systems (Chapter 5). Some have obvious and significant effects for individuals. Others provide substance and content for laws on specific matters, a particular example being where there are international standards such as safety requirements for products and activities, uniform definitions of crimes, rules for use of sea and air space, etc. Treaties that take effect in whole or in part through national law are legion. Whether a treaty's text is incorporated directly into national law by the constitution of a state or its terms are brought into the national legal system by legislation, a treaty demands effective compliance with its obligations in whatever manner this is accomplished. Thus, the relationship of treaties to national law is often a central consideration.

A legal regime for treaties cannot guarantee that they will be effectively implemented, but the law of treaties does include some specific measures to assist in this direction (Chapter 6). If there are problems, a treaty may need amendment or revision. In addition to regulating these possibilities and their consequences, the law of treaties takes some account of the possibility of non-compliance. While the law on state responsibility and liability for breach of treaties is mainly the province of general international law, suspension or termination of rights and obligations following a breach is part of the law of treaties.

Finally, there are the specialist areas of international law, some of which present different issues from the mainstream law of treaties (Chapter 7). Treaties which directly affect private individuals or corporate bodies established by national laws have some distinctive features. While they are instruments governed by international law and take effect in relations between international legal persons (states and international organizations), they establish institutions to which there is direct access by non-state actors. Prime examples are human rights treaties which establish courts and commissions, bilateral investment treaties which give investors access to international arbitral tribunals, and treaties establishing international criminal law.

There are also some treaties which give specific roles or rights to non-governmental bodies, such as the humanitarian law treaties which involve the Red Cross or Red Crescent institutions, or the Nairobi Treaty on the Protection of the Olympic Symbol 1981, which ascribes rights and powers to the International Olympic Committee. There is also an increasing blurring of the boundary between public and private international law (also described as the 'conflict of laws'), with treaties being the means by which private international law is harmonized.

A short account of the present kind cannot provide an answer based on theory or philosophy to the question of whether treaties constitute 'law' but can, it is hoped, show that treaties constitute a key element of international law and have an important function in the international rule of law.

1
Treaties in Modern Times

> Of international law as it is, the principal part of the matter is composed of treaties between State and State; of what it is supposed to be, the matter is composed of deductions from these *written instruments*.
>
> Jeremy Bentham[1]

I Introduction

1 General Features of Treaties

For many people the word 'treaty' may bring up recollections of treaties met when studying history, such as a peace treaty or a treaty of alliance. In modern international law, however, the term covers much more than those types of treaty. Nowadays, a treaty can be loosely described as any agreement between states which is governed by international law.[2] Treaties concern all manner of human activities, but they tend to stay largely in the background. Without treaties your mobile or cell phone might suffer from radio interference and your imported fruit might not reach you before it rots. The phones that we carry, the sat-navs in cars, and radio and television broadcasting, all depend on use of wavelengths or frequencies whose

---

[1] Letter to Jabez Henry (15 January 1830) in John Bowring (ed), *The Works of Jeremy Bentham*, vol 11 (William Tait 1838–1843) 34. <The Works of Jeremy Bentham, vol. 11 (Memoirs of Bentham Part II and Analytical Index) | Online Library of Liberty (libertyfund.org)> (original emphasis).

[2] The definition of 'treaty' and entities which can be parties to treaties, including international organizations, are considered further below, where other terms used in titles to treaties (such as 'convention', 'pact', 'protocol', etc.) are also addressed.

freedom from obstructive or harmful interference is achieved through regulations of an international organization established by treaty.[3]

The ships and aircraft which are responsible for much of the world's trade generally avoid collisions by following international rules drawn up in or under treaties. They are also regulated by treaties concerned with safe construction and use, as well as being affected by those establishing uniform rules on bills of lading, contracts of carriage, and so on.[4] Almost every area of law, many within national legal systems, ranging widely from adoptions and child custody to jurisdiction over contracts between people in different countries, assisting implementation of criminal law, or regulation of food standards and medicines, can be affected in some instances and in some measure by treaties.

Every modern specialist area of international law is based on, or features, one or more treaties. Such specialist areas include human rights, trade and transport, economic law, environmental law, humanitarian law in armed conflict, international criminal law, investment law, and intellectual property.[5] With the considerable expansion in the number of states in the second half of the twentieth century such treaties have a great many parties (hence termed 'multilateral'). This has not, however, eclipsed treaties between pairs of states ('bilateral'), which were the prevalent type in earlier times. Bilateral treaties cover an almost unlimited range of topics, from individual transactions—such as an aid project, exploitation of a particular resource, or some form of military cooperation—to recognizably common form ones, such as avoidance of double taxation, consular agreements, extradition, or investment treaties.

---

[3] Constitution and Convention of the International Telecommunications Union (Geneva 1992) 1825 UNTS 3, no 31251 (as successor to the International Telegraphic Union established by the Convention télégraphique internationale (Paris 1865). See https://treaties.un.org.

[4] Convention on the International Regulations for Preventing Collisions at Sea (1972, and later amendments), 1050 UNTS 16, no 15824; Convention on International Civil Aviation 1944 15 UNTS 295 no 102, Annex 2: 'The Rules of the Air'. Some idea of the proliferation of treaties can be had from noting that the treaty under which the rules of the air are adopted (Convention on International Civil Aviation 1944) was registered as treaty number 102 at the United Nations in 1948, while the treaty establishing a new constitution for the International Telecommunications Union (whose earliest predecessor is cited in n 3 above and whose radio regulations are mentioned in the text above) was number 31251 when registered in 1994.

[5] An overview of the treaties in these areas is given in the final chapter of this book.

2 Treaties Set Out Obligations Binding in International Law

The fundamental principle of international law applicable to all treaties is that once a treaty has entered into force it is legally binding. The parties must comply with the obligations which it creates. This is enshrined in the treaty which codifies the law of treaties—the Vienna Convention on the Law of Treaties 1969 (VCLT) in the words: 'Every treaty in force is binding upon the parties to it and must be performed by them in good faith.'[6]

In the Convention ('convention' being used in its international law sense as a synonym for 'treaty'), this principle is set out under its rather more concise Latin version *pacta sunt servanda*.[7] The same provision is in the Vienna Convention on the Law of Treaties between States and International Organizations or between International Organizations 1986.[8]

A concomitant of this provision states: 'A party may not invoke the provisions of its internal law as justification for its failure to perform a treaty.'[9] Taken together, these two provisions show that a state is bound by treaties to which it is a party and is under an international law obligation to make any adjustments to its own laws that are necessary to achieve compliance with its treaty commitments.[10]

---

[6] See VCLT 1969, art 26; the full text of the Vienna Convention on the Law of Treaties, signed at Vienna (23 May 1969) is in 1155 UNTS 331; UK Treaty Series 58 (1980), Cmnd 7964; [1974] Australian TS No 2; (1969) 8 ILM 679; the text used in this book is from the UN print of 2005 at https://legal.un.org/ilc/texts/instruments/english/conventions/1_1_1969.pdf.

[7] This use of 'convention' is long-established in diplomatic practice (see Oxford English Dictionary). Usage in this sense is not to be taken as diluted in legal effect by one of its other OED common meanings as 'practice based upon general consent, or accepted and upheld by society at large'. While 'convention' is most commonly used for multilateral treaties, it is also sometimes seen in the title of bilateral ones.

[8] Also art 26; the VCLT 1986 substantially parallels the VCLT 1969, but with adjustments to fit the role of international organizations; concluded at Vienna on 21 March 1986, the Convention has not yet come into force (as at 11 June 2023), but this does not prejudice the application of the customary international law of treaties to international organizations; the text is at UN Conference on the Law of Treaties between States and International Organizations or between International Organizations 1986, Docs vol II, A/CONF.129/15, and in UN print 2005 at https://legal.un.org/ilc/texts/instruments/english/conventions/1_2_1986.pdf. Note that the VCLT 1986 applies to treaties to which one or more international organizations are parties; it does not, therefore, apply to treaties between states providing constitutions of international organizations, art 5 of the 1969 VCLT specifically applying that Convention to 'any treaty which is the constituent instrument of an international organization and to any treaty adopted within an international organization without prejudice to any relevant rules of the organization'.

[9] VCLT, art 27.

[10] Implementation of treaties in national legal systems is the subject of ch 5 below.

3 Treaty Relations

Treaties are binding in international law, but it must be stressed that their obligations are only assumed by consent of states choosing to become parties to them. In the law of treaties, the core legal effect of this is creation of 'treaty relations'. Obligations established by treaty are dependent on the relationship created. Even treaty obligations in multilateral treaties are essentially relational, unlike customary international law or general principles of law which apply to all states. Thus 'treaty relations' is a more specific concept than the general principle of *pacta sunt servanda*. 'Treaty relations' denotes the full extent of the particular obligations established by a treaty in force as between any two parties to it. This goes beyond simply identifying whether a state has consented to be bound by a treaty to which another state (or international organization) has similarly consented to be bound. That is an essential element of treaty relations, but also relevant is that particular obligations are in force as between the parties at the relevant time. Although often to a considerable extent reciprocal, treaty obligations may not be exactly concordant. For example, obligations of one state may be affected by a 'reservation' which it has made to a particular provision (where such reservation is permitted or not excluded), or there may be a distinction between the territory in respect of which a state is bound as a matter of its treaty relations and territory which is within the scope of application of substantive provisions of the treaty.[11]

Treaty relations are established when more than one state has become a 'party' to a treaty and the treaty has entered into force. To become a party requires definitive consent to be bound. This is achieved most commonly, particularly in the case of multilateral treaties, by ratification or accession.[12] Signature may sometimes amount to definitive consent (more often in the case of bilateral treaties), but is commonly only an indication of conclusion of negotiations on a final text and is subject to ratification. These processes are indicated in the final clauses at the end of each treaty.

---

[11] Reservations and territorial application are considered in ch 2, section III.2(a) below. The residual rule on territorial application in the Vienna Convention is that: 'Unless a different intention appears from the treaty or is otherwise established, a treaty is binding upon each party in respect of its entire territory' (article 29) below.

[12] Definitions of 'party', 'ratification', etc. are in art 2 of the Vienna Convention and see further below on final clauses and ch 3 below on processes of treaty-making.

4 The Place of Treaties in International Law

Analogies with legislated national law, and with contracts made under those laws, are dangerous because treaties are not directly parallel to either, but they have the capacity to produce legal effects somewhat comparable to both. Because treaties depend on consent in order to become binding, their potential for a role in establishing general rules of customary international law or setting out obligations owed to all (*erga omnes*) is less obvious. In the absence of an international legislature, consensual agreement between states can only constitute a quasi-legislative means of making law applicable to all states, either by identifying rules which are binding as custom or by the widespread acceptance of particular treaties. The International Law Commission (ILC) has a major role in drawing up treaties which state customary rules or whose provisions come to be regarded as propositions of customary international law.[13] Its role in developing the drafts of the 1969 Vienna Convention is considered in the next chapter.

Treaties are often described as a 'source' of international law, this being deduced from the Statute of the International Court of Justice (ICJ) annexed to the Charter of the United Nations. The Statute prescribes that the Court, in exercise of its function of deciding disputes in accordance with international law, is to apply 'international conventions, whether general or particular, establishing rules expressly recognized by the contesting states'.[14] In referring to recognition by 'the contesting states', however, this more closely reflects the nature of treaties as being a source of rights and obligations for particular states rather than as general international law.

Nevertheless, provisions in treaties can codify or state rules of general applicability, these being binding on all states as customary international law. In this case, parties to the treaty are bound by both their treaty obligations and customary international law in parallel, while non-party states are only bound by the latter.[15] Further, even where a treaty provision does not codify an existing rule, it may crystallize a nascent rule or lead to a general practice accepted as law and hence a new rule. How this works is considered in more detail in Chapter 2 below.

---

[13] The International Law Commission was set up by the UN General Assembly to fulfil its mandate in the UN Charter (art 13) 'to initiate studies and make recommendations for the purpose of ... encouraging the progressive development of international law and its codification'.

[14] Statute of the ICJ, art 38.

[15] See *Military and Paramilitary Activities in and against Nicaragua (Nicaragua v United States of America)* (Jurisdiction and Admissibility) [1984] ICJ Rep 392, 424, para 73.

Although treaties are essentially commitments by states entered into in their relations with one another, there are some ways in which the legal relations which they establish are more extensive than that. The Vienna Convention includes specific provisions for treaties and a state which is not a party (defined in Article 2(h) as a 'third State') in its Articles 34–38. These provide that a treaty does not create obligations or rights for a third state without its consent. Such obligations can be achieved if shown to be intended by the parties and accepted in writing by the third state. A similar arrangement applies to grant of rights except that Article 36 spells out the possible intent of the parties to accord a right 'either to the third State, or to a group of States to which it belongs, or to all States', and the third state's assent can be presumed so long as the contrary is not indicated, unless the treaty otherwise provides.[16] Article 38 indicates that nothing in these treaty provisions 'precludes a rule set forth in a treaty from becoming binding upon a third State as a customary rule of international law, recognized as such'. This may have particular resonance in the case of international crimes where a number of states are not parties to the Rome Statute setting up the International Criminal Court, but several of the crimes which it identifies are international crimes whoever commits them. Thus treaties may state obligations owed to all other states (*erga omnes*).

While international criminal law demonstrates how treaties confirm or create international obligations which can apply directly to individuals, it is only in more recent times that treaties have directly given to individuals, and corporate entities established in domestic law, rights regulated by international law. Individuals can acquire such rights in two ways. First, some treaties allow direct access to independent tribunals established by the treaties. Leading examples are access by individuals to international courts and tribunals having jurisdiction over human rights and access to international law remedies through international arbitration as, for example, in investment arbitrations. The latter remedies are most commonly sought by corporate legal persons. Second, in much more limited circumstances, it has been recognized that rights can be attributed to individuals directly under international law. This has been held to be so by the ICJ in cases about the right of individuals arrested in states parties to the Vienna Convention on Consular Relations 1963 to be informed that they have a right of access to the consular services of their state of nationality.[17]

---

[16] Further provisions detail modalities of exercise, revocation, and modification of rights and obligations of third states.
[17] See ch 7 below, text to n 40.

5 'Law of Treaties' Distinguished from 'Treaty Law'

A distinction is to be drawn between those treaties which address the making and implementation of instruments governed by international law—such as the Vienna Conventions on the Law of Treaties of 1969 and 1986—and those whose content prescribes the rules to regulate a particular area of activity or individuals' lives—such as the Convention on the International Regulations for Preventing Collisions at Sea 1972 or the Convention Relating to the Status of Refugees 1951. The following chapters are much concerned with the former type of treaties but have the main aim of assisting access to treaties of the latter characterization. The former class is usually known as 'the law of treaties', while the content of the latter type is 'treaty law' (although there is no authoritative definition of these terms and this useful distinction is not universally observed).

The difference can be shown by considering the United Nations Convention on Refugees.[18] This defines who is a refugee, what rights such a person has in countries outside that of their origin, how they are to be treated in a state party in which they are present, and so on. Such rules are part of the substance of refugee law binding upon the parties. They are therefore 'treaty law'. The 'final clauses'—those at the end of the Convention—in common with other treaties, set out the procedures by which states become parties to it, can cease to be parties ('denunciation' or 'termination'), how it comes into force, can be amended, how differences over interpretation and application are to be resolved, etc. These latter provisions are ancillary to the substantive terms of the treaty but are essential to establishment of treaty relations, thus giving the Convention effect. Although the final clauses of a treaty are tailored to that particular treaty, they apply in the context of general international law rules regulating procedural aspects of making and implementing treaties.[19] These rules constitute 'the law of treaties'. The

---

[18] Convention Relating to the Status of Refugees (adopted 28 July 1951, entered into force 22 April 1954) 189 UNTS 137 (Refugee Convention) and amending Protocol of 31 January 1967, 606 UNTS 267.

[19] 'General international law' is used here, and throughout this book unless otherwise indicated, to refer to rules of public international law which apply to all states as distinct from rules which apply solely by reason of treaty relations. The term is used in arts 53, 64, and 71 of the VCLT but without definition; and see ILC, 'Report of the Study Group on Fragmentation of International Law: Difficulties arising from the Diversification and Expansion of International Law', finalized by Martti Koskenniemi, UN Docs (2006) A/CN.4/L.682 and A/CN.4/L.682/Corr.1, 254–56.

VCLT 1969 codifies most of these rules or provides residual rules if the parties to a treaty do not make specific provisions instead.[20]

The law of treaties does not deal extensively with enforcement of treaties which in many instances is largely dependent on states' acceptance of, and respect for, the value of an international system of law and, more specifically, on reciprocity and the self-interest.[21] Responsibility or liability for breach of a treaty is addressed by the law of treaties in the context of international law only to the extent of providing certain rights to suspend or terminate treaties if a breach occurs.[22] State responsibility for breaches of international obligations is a separate subject from the law of treaties.[23] This distinction is considered further in chapter 6 below.

The law of treaties is the gateway to understanding and using the treaties which provide the substance of almost all the specialist areas of international law. Hence it is the law of treaties which is a major focus of most of the following chapters in this book, except for an account of the relationship of treaties with national law in Chapter 5 below and an overview of functional areas of treaty law in the final chapter. This first chapter aims to give a general description of a typical treaty, with some definitions and explanations of key terms in the law of treaties. The Vienna Convention includes definitions of key terms in its Article 2. Although those definitions are only applicable for the purposes of that treaty, they are useful guidance generally and are taken up in this book at the appropriate points. Also essential for lawyers working with treaties is knowledge of how to find authentic texts of treaties and records of the preparatory work leading to the conclusion of treaties. How treaties are made is described in Chapter 3, how they are interpreted and applied internationally in Chapter 4, and how they are implemented in national systems of law in Chapter 5.

---

[20] Citation of sources for the full text of the VCLT are given in n 6 above. Major commentaries on the VCLT are O Corten and P Klein (eds), *The Vienna Conventions on the Law of Treaties: A Commentary* (OUP 2011), O Dörr and K Schmalenbach (eds), *The Vienna Convention on the Law of Treaties: A Commentary* (2nd edn, Springer 2018); and ME Villiger, *Commentary on the 1969 Vienna Convention on the Law of Treaties* (Martinus Nijhoff 2009). Multi-authored works addressing particular aspects of the law of treaties include E Cannizzaro, *The Law of Treaties Beyond the Vienna Convention* (OUP 2011); DB Hollis (ed), *The Oxford Guide to Treaties* (2nd edn, OUP 2020); MJ Bowman and D Kritsiotis (eds), *Conceptual and Contextual Perspectives on the Modern Law of Treaties* (CUP 2018).
[21] See further ch 6 below.
[22] VCLT 1969 (n 6) art 60.
[23] See ILC, 'Draft Articles on Responsibility of States for Internationally Wrongful Acts, with commentaries' [2001-II(2)] Yearbook of the ILC 20, UN Doc A/56/10 https://legal.un.org/ilc/texts/instruments/english/commentaries/9_6_2001.pdf.

II Defining Treaties

1 What Identifies an Instrument as a Treaty?

In most instances there will be little scope for doubt whether an instrument is a treaty. Title, form, content, concluding provisions, registration with the United Nations, and inclusion in official publications of treaties may provide a strong indication of this. However, sometimes some of these features are absent or ambiguous. Further, in more recent times, less formal memoranda, minutes, letters, and other documents may contain treaties of an atypical character. The 1969 Vienna Convention defines 'treaty' as:

> [A]n international agreement concluded between States in written form and governed by international law, whether embodied in a single instrument or in two or more related instruments and whatever its particular designation.[24]

A more cynical definition is that by Philip Allott, who has defined a treaty as 'a disagreement reduced to writing'.[25] While this is essentially a reflection on the process of negotiation of a treaty, the underlying point takes on a particular significance when considering the role of records of negotiation of a treaty in interpreting its terms, a matter considered in Chapter 4. Professor McDougal of Yale University took a rather different line, which emphasized the establishment and continuity of treaty relations as something projecting forwards into the life of a treaty:

> The most comprehensive and realistic conception of an international agreement ... is ... not that of a mere collocation of words or signs on a parchment, but rather that of a continuing process of communication and collaboration between the parties in the shaping and sharing of demanded values.[26]

---

[24] VCLT, art 2; some oral agreements or statements have been held to constitute treaties, but even these have been evidenced in writing. See also J Klabbers, *The Concept of Treaty in International Law* (Kluwer Law International 1996).
[25] P Allott, 'The Concept of International Law' (1999) 10 EJIL 31, 43.
[26] MS McDougal, HD Lasswell, and JC Miller, *The Interpretation of International Agreements and World Public Order: Principles of Content and Procedure* (Yale UP 1967, reprinted 1994) xxiii.

This is apt to describe the development of law in widely accepted treaties that have endured for decades or more. For example, the Paris Convention of 1883 on industrial property, which has been developed through several revisions, signalled the start of a family of treaties on intellectual property and was the progenitor of international institutions leading to the founding of the World Intellectual Property Organization.[27] Countless other treaties, ranging from those on access to international waterways to world trade, and in particular those that fall in the orbit of international organizations, involve the 'continuing process of communication and collaboration' which Professor McDougal envisaged.

There are, however, other treaties which provide for single transactions or short-term projects. These, when fulfilled, require no continuing process for 'shaping and sharing demanded values'. Examples of single transactions are settlements of territorial claims or boundaries, such as the 'Alaska Purchase' treaty by which the USA paid a stated sum for cession of specified land by Russia, or settlement of international claims for specific sums of money, such as the 1986 agreement on final settlement of mutual financial and property claims between the United Kingdom and the then Soviet Union, claims dating back to the period between the 1917 Russian revolution and 1939.[28]

It will be seen, however, that the VCLT definition is not entirely helpful in practical terms, particularly as it is somewhat circular in its use of the test of whether the agreement is governed by international law. This is both a qualification for being a treaty and a consequence of an agreement being a treaty. How, then, is an instrument to be identified as a treaty? There are a number of identifiers which, taken together, will, in the typical case, make the nature of the instrument clear. Where the title includes the term 'Treaty', 'Agreement', or 'Convention', what follows will usually be a treaty and will contain provisions having the effect of being binding under international law.[29] To confirm this, and in cases where the title does not provide such a

---

[27] Paris Convention for the Protection of Industrial Property of 20 March 1883, as revised at Brussels on 14 December 1900, at Washington on 2 June 1911, at The Hague on 6 November 1925, at London on 2 June 1934, at Lisbon on 31 October 1958, and at Stockholm on 14 July 1967, 828 UNTS 305, no 11851 and Convention establishing the World Intellectual Property Organization, Stockholm (14 July 1967) 828 UNTS 3, no 11846.
[28] See US Treaties in Force (2020) 'Convention ceding Alaska', Washington, 1867 (11 Bevans 1216), and 'Agreement between the UK and USSR on Settlement of Mutual Financial and Property Claims Arising Before 1 January 1939' UK Treaty Series No 65 (1986).
[29] DP Myers, 'The Names and Scope of Treaties' (1957) 51 AJIL 575.

clear indication, cumulative evidence from all the components of an instrument should resolve doubts in all but the most difficult instances.

2 Components of a Treaty

There is no set form for a treaty and no minimum or required components. There are, however, generally recognizable features to be found in most treaties, although recently documents of a less formal nature than traditional instruments have been acknowledged as treaties. Typical components of more traditional treaties are: a title, recital of the negotiating states, preamble, substantive provisions, final clauses, concluding words, and signature block (the *testimonium*), plus any annexes or appendices.

3 Title not Conclusive of Status

Formal reference to a treaty is by title, followed by place and date of signature, but shorter forms may be used (as in the footnotes here) if giving a source for a text where the formal details are shown. One exception is the VCLT where the 1969 conference at which the treaty was adopted voted to name it 'the Vienna Convention on the Law of Treaties', obviating the need to mention the place of conclusion after the title. However, the title and designation (whether a 'treaty', 'agreement', 'convention', 'protocol'. or whatever) are not always specifically decided in the course of negotiations, and may look as if they have been added as an afterthought. Sometimes the title is simply extracted from a preambular statement such as 'Desiring to conclude a treaty on sale of wet fish', which would attract the title of 'Treaty on the Sale of Wet Fish'. In the case of the Alaska Purchase mentioned above, one US source describes the instrument as 'Cession of Alaska', another as 'Treaty concerning the Cession of the Russian Possessions in North America', while yet another calls it 'Convention ceding Alaska'.[30] The difference in designation is not material to the legal status of the instrument, but nor is inclusion of a term such as 'agreement' in the designation conclusive.

---

[30] See n 28 above, 11 Bevans 1216, 15 Stat 539, and US Treaties in Force, respectively.

4 Recital of the Negotiating States

The opening words of a typical treaty list the states whose representatives have negotiated its terms. This may be a list of the heads of the states, the names of the states, the governments of the states, other descriptive lists such as the members of an international organization, or simply some phrase such as 'The States parties to this Convention'. The latter formulation gives no indication which states are actually parties, but even where states or governments are named, the list cannot be viewed as reliable evidence of which states are parties to the treaty, which is to say those that are bound by it. Not all negotiating states will necessarily become parties, particularly if signature of it is subject to ratification and a state's authorities decline to ratify it. Nor is any list necessarily complete as states which have not participated in the negotiations may be able to become a party later by 'accession'.[31] The point to note, however, is that even if the treaty lists heads of states or governments, it is states themselves which are bound by treaties so that a change in head of state or government of a state party to a treaty does not mean that the treaty ceases to be binding.

5 Preamble, Statement of Agreement, and Provisions

A preamble recites the considerations motivating the terms of the treaty and the objectives. This is optional but is sometimes useful if issues of interpretation arise.[32] This opening is followed by words of agreement, which should provide a clear indication that the parties are concluding an instrument whose terms are binding. At its simplest the words of agreement are set out, often in a bold form: '[The negotiating states] … HAVE AGREED AS FOLLOWS:'. Such words of agreement are a strong indication that the instrument actually is a treaty, but not invariably. Following these words of agreement, the articles comprising the substance of the treaty are set out.

---

[31] Accession is equivalent to ratification but by a state which has not signed a treaty: see further ch 3, section II.5 below.
[32] See ch 4 below.

6 Final Clauses and Words of Conclusion ('Testimonium')

At the end of a treaty are the 'final clauses'. These set out the procedures by which states become parties to the treaty, whether ratification is required, how and when the treaty is to be brought into force, whether reservations are permitted or limited, how the treaty may be amended and terminated, and any other procedural considerations.[33] There may also be indications of the treaty's relationship with other treaties and of the temporal and territorial scope of its application. These are the provisions which particularize the application of the law of treaties to the treaty in which they appear.

The most common words of conclusion (the 'testimonium') at the end are: 'DONE at [place] on [date]', followed by indications on the document or documents of the number of original copies and the languages used, and then a list of signature blocks where the parties' authorized representatives are to sign. As indicated above, the place and date of signature are appended to the treaty's title when citing it formally. Because signature is often subject to ratification, and therefore not a commitment by a signatory state to be bound by the treaty there and then, ascribing the term 'conclusion' to this stage in treaty-making is not free from all uncertainty. In the VCLT there are indications that in some contexts 'conclusion' of a treaty is a process of the various stages from finalization of text, or from signature, and preceding entry into force, while in other contexts conclusion refers to an act or moment (typically symbolized by the word 'Done').[34] Either way, the fact that the VCLT's definition of a treaty refers to an agreement being 'concluded' clearly points to there being some formality in the way in which an instrument is turned into a treaty. A testimonium meets this requirement but is not irrefutable evidence. Bilateral treaties will usually be signed in duplicate so that each party may retain one of the pair. The original signed print of a multilateral treaty is lodged with a 'depositary' which may be a state or an international organization.[35]

Bilateral treaties may also take the same general form as typical multilateral treaties. However, a frequently found alternative, which is mainly used for less extensive treaties, is the 'Exchange of Notes' or 'Exchange of

---

[33] For more on ratification, reservations, and other procedural matters see ch 3 below.
[34] See ch 3, section II.2 below and R Gardiner, *Treaty Interpretation* (2nd edn, OUP 2015) ch 6, section 2.1.
[35] See further ch 3 below.

Letters'. These exchanges are established through the diplomatic channel. The ambassador of one party writes to the Foreign Minister of the state to which he or she is accredited setting out the proposed terms of the agreement and ending along the lines that they 'have the honour to propose that this Note [Letter] and your reply to that effect, shall constitute an Agreement between our two Governments which shall enter into force on the date of your reply'. The reply sets out the identical terms of the proposing Note/Letter, indicates that these are acceptable and confirms that the proposing Note/Letter and the Reply together constitute an agreement between the two governments.

Such formalities may seem a bit of a diplomatic rigmarole. They do, however, make it clear when an Exchange of Notes or Letters is intended to produce a binding agreement, that is a treaty. Ordinary diplomatic exchanges commonly take the form of notes or letters but do not normally amount to treaties.[36] As becomes increasingly clear, however, the boundary between what is a binding instrument and what is a political statement or record of discussions is increasingly blurred. The notion of 'agreements in simplified form', mooted by the ILC in its work preparing drafts for the Vienna Convention, has taken on a wider potential perhaps than that envisaged by the ILC.[37]

7 'Mandatory' Language Combined with Formalities

Where the title or such other formal pointers are not entirely clear (and in any event), the substance of the provisions is the best indication of an intention to create legal obligations and successful accomplishment of that objective. Hence the general practice in English versions of treaties is to use

---

[36] For a more detailed account and examples, see I Roberts (ed), *Satow's Diplomatic Practice* (7th edn at 661–63); and cf *Ahmad and Aswat v USA* [2006] EWHC 2927, where a court in the UK viewed a diplomatic note as binding because 'exchanges of notes' were in a list of forms of international 'engagements' in a PCIJ Advisory Opinion on *Austro-German Customs Union* [1931] PCIJ Series A/B 41, 47—in fact, the notes in the English case may have been binding by estoppel, but lacked the normal formalities of agreement to constitute a treaty.

[37] M Fitzmaurice, 'Concept of a Treaty in Decisions of International Courts and Tribunals' (2018) 20 Intl Community LR 137, 146–47; see also use of the concept in connection with the French constitutional arrangements for international agreements ch 5, section III.5 below, and for an example of minutes of a meeting constituting an agreement see text to n 59 below.

the mandatory form 'shall' in place of the simple future tense and to use other accepted words of obligation such as 'agree' or 'undertake to'.[38]

All treaties made after the establishment of the United Nations must be registered with the UN Secretariat and are published in the UN Treaty Series.[39] Hence this is a good source for finding authoritative texts of treaties, though the huge number of treaties and the time it may take for treaties to be registered and published may mean that a search does not necessarily produce a result. Registration is not, however, conclusive evidence that an instrument is a treaty. Other sources are collections made by specialist international organizations of treaties in their fields of competence and national publications by states of treaties to which they are parties.

Further indications that an instrument is a treaty are, in the case of a multilateral treaty, nomination of a 'depositary' (usually a government or international organization's secretariat charged with collecting and disseminating notifications and information concerning the treaty), and explicit acknowledgement by parties that their practices are in performance of the obligations which the treaty sets out. These may not be sufficient individually to establish the status of an instrument as a treaty, registration (for example) notoriously being commonly at the instigation of one state alone.[40] It is the combined effect of form, substance, procedure, and, at a later stage, practical implementation which enables a treaty to be clearly identified as such.

In contrast, the converse of the same elements, or absence of forms and procedures, can lead to a conclusion that there was no intention on the part of the negotiators or the states which they represent to be bound by what has been recorded in writing. To exclude legally binding commitments, introductory words and substantive provisions may avoid formalities and pointers of the kind described. Instead of referring to states or governments as being 'parties' to a concluded agreement, the document may simply refer to delegations having reached 'the following understandings' which are then set out in words that do not suggest a commitment intended to bind states under international law. Such words may include 'intend to', 'will' or 'expect to' and similar non-mandatory formulations. Equally, final

---

[38] On 'mandatory language' see arbitral award in *Dispute Concerning Access to Information under Article 9 of the OSPAR Convention (Ireland v United Kingdom)* (2003) 42 ILM 1118, 1142, paras 129–30; and *LaGrand Case (Germany v USA)* [2001] ICJ Rep 466, paras 99–109.
[39] See Charter of the United Nations, art 102.
[40] See DN Hutchinson, 'The Significance of Registration or Non-registration of an International Agreement in Determining Whether or Not it Is a Treaty' (1993) 46 CLP 257.

clauses in the manner of a treaty will be omitted, along with subsequent formalities of the kind described. In some instances the document may deliberately be kept off the public record (a 'Confidential Memorandum of Understanding'), or simply be kept by the respective government departments in their archives without being published.[41]

III Other Instruments and Engagements

1 'Memorandum of Understanding'

Probably the most indeterminate usage of titles of instruments found in international relations is the 'memorandum of understanding' (MOU). This is not a term which has any agreed usage and is generally unhelpful in ascertaining an instrument's legal effect. Sometimes a MOU is just what those words indicate—a written record of understandings. Thus, one view is that it is the written embodiment of what used to be known as 'a gentlemen's agreement', a term now disfavoured and replaced by 'a political agreement'.[42] Based on the idea that once an 'understanding' had been reached—traditionally symbolized by a handshake, decent behaviour did not require the backing of law. An MOU would, on the basis of this approach, be like those memoranda in domestic law which might record matters essentially agreed, but not put into binding form. Such an MOU would have the advantage of not requiring all the formalities of a treaty (of which more later) and could be most readily replaced by fresh understandings.[43] The utility of MOUs, side letters, operating protocols, guidance, and so on is evidenced by their ubiquity, though not by their visibility.

One area, for example, where memoranda of understandings have been commonly used is in conjunction with air transport treaties, though these memoranda are not easily accessible. The treaties, until recently usually bilateral, set out the principles for operating air services, but the details (such as frequency of flights, capacity in terms of seat numbers etc.) were

---

[41] See A Aust, 'The Theory and Practice of Informal International Instruments' (1986) 35 ICLQ 787.
[42] OED: 'gentlemen's agreement n. (also gentleman's agreement) originally U.S. an arrangement or understanding which is based upon the trust of both or all parties, rather than being legally binding.'
[43] OED: understanding 'A mutual arrangement or agreement of an informal but more or less explicit nature.'

set out for each treaty in a memorandum of understanding (or sometimes 'Confidential Memorandum of Understanding') which were documents distinct from the treaties.[44] Aeronautical authorities could agree changes in the details of implementation of the treaties as new aircraft types came into use, new passenger flows and operational characteristics arose (and so on), by reaching new understandings between themselves and without altering the provisions in the bilateral treaties.

In contrast, however, the form and content of some instruments headed 'Memorandum of Understanding' are such that they are clearly treaties. They are formulated in the same way as other treaties, with the same words of agreement, provisions denoting obligations and final clauses. Others are hybrids, with tops and tails that look like treaties but with contents formulated to look as if not intended to be binding and sometimes expressly stated not to be so. There is no obvious advantage in uprating the idea of an 'understanding' to the same status as a formal agreement, and there is the considerable disadvantage that blurring the established treaty form leaves it unclear what is intended *not* to be a binding instrument. It is all the more important, therefore, when the title is unhelpful, to be able to identify what is a treaty from all the relevant factors.

There have been a few cases in which the status of an instrument such as a memorandum of understanding, or something similar, has been considered by an international court or tribunal. In the *London Heathrow User Charges* arbitration, an arbitral tribunal found that an inter-governmental MOU, which had not been registered with the UN as a treaty, constituted 'consensual subsequent practice' of the two states but did not establish obligations, hence not being a treaty. The tribunal indicated: 'The MOU is therefore available to the Tribunal as a potentially important aid to interpretation but is not a source of independent legal rights and duties capable of enforcement in the present Arbitration.'[45]

In direct contrast, in *Somalia v Kenya* the International Court of Justice considered a short document whose title began 'Memorandum of Understanding between the Government of' but whose main features were clearly those of a treaty while the terms included some explicit words

---

[44] The legal status of these memoranda was nevertheless not free from difference of opinion: see *United States—United Kingdom Heathrow Airport User Charges Arbitration* (Award of 30 November 1992) XXIV UNRIAA (electronic) 1, 131; the complete text of the MOU is set out in Appendix 4 to the Award, ibid 332–34.

[45] See n 44 above.

of agreement or of mandatory character.[46] The MOU was registered with the UN at Kenya's request, though after registration the Prime Minister of Somalia wrote to the UN Secretary General requesting that the MOU be treated as 'non-actionable' after its rejection by the Somali parliament. In further evidence that the instrument was binding, the Court noted that the Prime Minister of Somalia had given 'full powers' (authorization) to the minister who signed it and that it included a provision for 'entry into force' on signature. Thus, the Court concluded that it was a treaty.[47]

2 Miscellaneous Forms and Documents

An example of an instrument which shows evidence of a deliberate avoidance of creating treaty relations is the Final Act of the Conference on Security and Co-operation in Europe (Helsinki 1975).[48] A 'final act' is usually the record drawn up at the end of a diplomatic conference giving a brief factual account of the proceedings of the conference, with lists of those forming committees, resolutions it adopted, and sometimes annexing a treaty opened for signature at the conference. The Helsinki Final Act leads on from the details of the proceedings to recitals (as if in a treaty) and then the substantive paragraphs with: 'The High Representatives of the participating States have solemnly adopted the following: … '. The substantive components of the Final Act are formulated in language close to 'treaty language', but also much like a resolution of an international organization. Evidence that non-binding status was intended for the instrument is the statement:

> The participating States, paying due regard to the principles above and, in particular, to the first sentence of the tenth principle, 'Fulfilment in good faith of obligations under international law', note that the present Declaration does not affect their rights and obligations, nor the corresponding treaties and other agreements and arrangements.[49]

---

[46] *Maritime Delimitation in the Indian Ocean (Somalia v Kenya)* (Preliminary Objections) [2017] ICJ Rep 3; the text of the MOU is set out in para 37 of the judgment.
[47] ibid paras 47 and 50.
[48] (1975) 14 ILM 1292.
[49] The non-binding status of the Declaration in the Helsinki Final Act did not prevent the arrangements becoming the basis for a fully-fledged international organization, the Organisation for Security and Cooperation in Europe (OSCE), with many operational features.

III Other Instruments and Engagements 23

Thus, this is one of a growing number of documents which constitute what has been dubbed 'soft law', used by states to record political commitments, common policies, or goals in their international relations.[50] This is not completely new. The Final Act of the International Meridian Conference, Washington DC, October 1884, records resolutions accepting the Greenwich meridian for use as a common zero of longitude and standard of time-reckoning throughout the world. Although the instrument recording the arrangements that were then adopted did not have the status of a treaty, the effect of these arrangements as 'norms' has been quite far reaching.[51]

Because of the failure of states in recent times to adopt a clear distinction in both the form and the expressions to be used in documents that are intended *not* to be treaties, it is becoming increasingly difficult to predict what will be regarded by a court or tribunal as a treaty or as simply a document recording 'political commitments'. Thus, for example, in the *South China Seas Arbitration* one issue was whether a '2002 Declaration on the Conduct of Parties in the South China Sea' (abbreviated as the DOC) constituted an agreement to reach a settlement through negotiations and thereby excluded arbitration.[52] The DOC had the 'shape' of a treaty, that is it recited the prospective parties, set out preambular paragraphs, etc. and included phrases such as 'the Parties undertake', ending with a formal signature block ('testimonium') after 'Done', and the dates. However, as the tribunal stated:

> To constitute a binding agreement, an instrument must evince a clear intention to establish rights and obligations between the parties. Such clear intention is determined by reference to the instrument's actual terms and the particular circumstances of its adoption. The subsequent conduct of the parties to an instrument may also assist in determining its nature.[53]

---

[50] A Boyle, 'Some Reflections on the Relationship of Treaties and Soft Law' (1999) 48 ICLQ 901.

[51] The Meridian retains its function for longitude and demarcation of time zones, but Greenwich Mean Time has largely been replaced by 'Coordinated Universal Time' ('UTC', a neutral acronym chosen because agreement could not be reached on whether to use the English CUT or French TUC sequence of initial letters): UTC is now supervised by the Bureau International des Poids et Mesures (set up by the Treaty of the Metre 1875) and endorsed by ITU Recommendation ITU-R TF.460-6 (2002) as incorporated in ITU Radio Regulations which are binding under arts 4 and 54 of the Constitution and Convention of the International Telecommunication Union 1992: 1825 UNTS 330, no 31251.

[52] *South China Sea Arbitration (Philippines v China)* (Jurisdiction and Admissibility) (2015), PCA Case No 2013-19, paras 212 ff.

[53] ibid para 213.

Acknowledging that the form or designation of an instrument is not decisive of its status as an agreement, that the DOC shared some hallmarks of a treaty, and that some of the terms used (such as 'undertake') were suggestive of the existence of an agreement, the tribunal nevertheless found it apparent that the DOC was not intended by its drafters to be a legally binding document, but rather 'an aspirational political document'. This conclusion was based on much of the content being a reaffirmation of existing obligations while other terms were of a provisional or permissive character.[54] The tribunal found this conclusion reinforced by evidence of the purpose and circumstances surrounding the DOC's adoption, as well as in subsequent treatment by the parties.

3 Unwritten International Agreements

The requirement in the VCLT's definition of a treaty that the agreement be in written form is for the purposes of the VCLT only. The VCLT specifically allows for unwritten agreements, stating that the fact that the VCLT does not apply to international agreements not in written form is not to affect their legal force or the application to them of any of the rules in the VCLT to which they would be subject under international law independently of the Convention.[55] The classic case of what is said by some to have constituted an unwritten treaty is the oral statement by M. Ihlen, the Norwegian Foreign Minister (known as 'the Ihlen declaration') in response to the Danish Foreign Minister in discussions concerning Spitzbergen and Greenland.[56] The Permanent Court of International Justice (PCIJ) stated:

> The Court considers it beyond all dispute that a reply of this nature given by the Minister for Foreign Affairs on behalf of his Government in response to a request by the diplomatic representative of a foreign Power, in regard to a question falling within his province, is binding upon the country to which the Minister belongs.[57]

---

[54] ibid para 215; but cf 'Memorandum on Security Assurances in connection with Ukraine's accession to the Treaty on the Non-Proliferation of Nuclear Weapons' 1994, whose substantive provisions are all reaffirmations of existing obligations (save for a consultation commitment), but which was nevertheless registered with the UN at 3007 UNTS 167, no 52241; see also R Müllerson, 'NATO Enlargement and the NATO-Russian Founding Act: The Interplay of Law and Politics' (1998) 47 ICLQ 192, 197–201, and n 40 above.
[55] See art 3.
[56] *Legal Status of Eastern Greenland (Denmark v Norway)* PCIJ Series A/B, no 53, 22.
[57] ibid 71.

III Other Instruments and Engagements

The Ihlen declaration was recorded in M Ihlen's own minutes of the meeting, although Norway later declined to give Denmark confirmation of the declaration. Not much turns on whether the upshot could be described as an unwritten treaty. There was clear, written evidence of a commitment given in an international exchange which the PCIJ held to be binding, though not specifically designated as a treaty.[58] A somewhat similar approach, but with stronger evidence of a mutual recognition of agreement and express reference to the definition of 'treaty' in the VCLT, has been adopted by the ICJ in holding minutes of a meeting to constitute a binding agreement, even though the minutes were not formulated in line with the other common characteristics of a treaty.[59]

What is the significance of the discussion of the possibility of unwritten treaties and the growing recognition of less formal instruments as treaties? First, it is really a question of identifying what evidence there is of agreement between representatives of states who are authorized to commit their states. Heads of states, heads of government and ministers of foreign affairs are recognized as having power to bind their states without further formalities.[60] Where any of these have made an agreement some form of written record could be expected to be kept, and it is a matter of interpretation whether it amounts to an agreement within the understanding of what is a treaty. Observance of the described formalities helps to make it clearer that an agreement is a treaty. Second, even if there is no clear treaty, records of discussions may indicate some form of agreement relevant for legal purposes, particularly if touching on issues of interpretation. Third, unilateral declarations or statements may bind the maker's state, even if such declarations or statements are not to be classed as indicating an agreement amounting to a treaty.[61]

---

[58] See further ILC, 'Eighth report on unilateral acts of States' (Cedeño, Special Rapporteur), UN Doc (2005) A/CN.4/557.
[59] *Maritime Delimitation and Territorial Questions (Qatar v Bahrain)* (Jurisdiction and Admissibility) [1994] ICJ Rep 112.
[60] VCLT, art 7(2)(a) and see further ch 3, section II.1 below on authorization of representatives.
[61] For further details see ILC's Guiding Principles applicable to unilateral declarations of States capable of creating legal obligations, with commentaries thereto, 2006, endorsed by UN General Assembly Resolution 61/34 of 4 December 2006. Some declarations, although ostensibly unilateral, which are part of a treaty procedure are accepted by the UN for registration as treaties: see eg entries 1–3 in UNTS vol 1, Declarations by the United Kingdom, Netherlands, and the USA (recognizing compulsory jurisdiction of ICJ pursuant to art 36 of the ICJ Statute).

IV Parties to Treaties

The VCLT 1969 applies to treaties between states, while the VCLT 1986 applies to treaties between a state or states and an international organization or organizations, and treaties between international organizations. Both define a treaty in terms of an international agreement 'governed by international law'. To be a party to a treaty, therefore, an entity needs a capacity to enter into relations governed by international law.[62] Until relatively recently sovereigns, and subsequently states, were the only entities whose relations were governed by international law and which entered into engagements with other sovereigns or states by treaty. They could, of course, voluntarily subject themselves to a national system of law, such as by entering into a contract with a specific choice of such a law, but between themselves sovereigns and states were, and are, in principle only subject to international law.

International organizations came on to the world stage around the second half of the nineteenth century, but initially mostly in the form of functional unions of states assisted by small international secretariats. When such organizations became more numerous they acquired differentiated organs and increasingly autonomous roles. With permanent headquarters, secretariats, and continuous functioning, international organizations acquired capacity and status akin to corporate entities of an international character. When the ICJ examined the status of the United Nations it came to the conclusion that it was 'an international person'.[63] Setting the framework for subsequent understanding of the legal status of international organizations, the Court continued:

> That is not the same thing as saying that it is a State, which it certainly is not, or that its legal personality and rights and duties are the same as those of a State ... It does not even imply that all its rights and duties must be upon the international plane, any more than all the rights and duties of a State must be upon that plane. What it does mean is that it is

---

[62] VCLT, art 5 recognizes the capacity of states to conclude treaties. A proposed provision for recognition of capacity of members of federal unions was rejected on the basis that this aspect of capacity was an internal aspect of statehood: O Corten and P Klein (eds), *The Vienna Conventions on the Law of Treaties: A Commentary*, vol 1 (OUP 2011) 108–12; there have, however, been occasions when components of states have been accepted by other parties to treaties as authorized to negotiate and conclude treaties.

[63] *Reparation for Injuries Suffered in the Service of the United Nations* (Advisory Opinion) [1949] ICJ Rep 174 at 179; see further E Lauterpacht, 'Development of the Law of International Organisations by the Decisions of International Tribunals' (1976) 152 RdC 377.

a subject of international law and capable of possessing international rights and duties.[64]

Thus, not only are treaties involved in the establishment of international organizations—their constitutions being typically established in this form—but a consequence of their international legal personality is that they have capacity to enter into treaties. On institutional matters, the most common ones are headquarters agreements with host states, while operationally agreements of all kinds are made by international organizations with individual states as required.

V Locating Treaties

An original of a treaty may be difficult to locate and access. It is usually possible, however, to find an authentic text without tracking down the original. Signed multilateral treaties are kept by a 'depositary', along with instruments of ratification where required and other communications by signatories and parties.[65] Traditionally, the depositary tended to be the Ministry of Foreign Affairs of the state in which the diplomatic conference which drew up the treaty had been held. With the proliferation of states and international organizations, the latter have increasingly been the home for originals of treaties and for handling matters connected with them. Bilateral instruments are usually retained by the foreign ministry of each party.

Where, then, can authentic texts be found for general use? In principle, every treaty and every international agreement entered into by any member of the United Nations since the organization was established is registered as indicated above and published by the Secretariat of the UN.[66] Hence treaties entered into after World War II should all be found in the United Nations Treaty Series (UNTS).[67] However, not all states are assiduous in registering treaties, and it may take some time before a treaty is published by the Secretariat.[68] It should be noted that the UN also acts as depositary for

---

[64] *Reparation for Injuries Suffered in the Service of the United Nations* (Advisory Opinion) (n 63).
[65] The functions of a depositary are examined in more detail in ch 3 below.
[66] See text to n 39 above.
[67] https://treaties.un.org.
[68] 3110 UNTS, listed as the latest volume in June 2023, published treaties registered in February 2016 (Nos 53473–85).

over 500 treaties, a different function from registration and publication of treaties deposited elsewhere.

Choice of language or languages can feature as an element in the negotiation of treaties, though in most cases precedent and practice make clear which languages are to be used for the final text, the normal practice being for the text to indicate in which languages the treaty has been concluded. The difficulty is ensuring that the treaty means the same thing in each authentic language. In some treaties a particular language is designated as the authoritative one in the case of divergence. Comparison of provisions in the different authentic languages sometimes becomes necessary if there is a difference between parties over interpretation of the treaty.[69] The UN Treaty Series sets out the text of each treaty in all its authentic languages, with translations into English and French if either or both of these are not specified as authentic languages.

Many international organizations publish texts of treaties in their areas of interest. For example, the Hague Conference on Private International Law publishes an online list and texts of treaties and other documents in whose creation the organization has been instrumental.[70] Similarly, the Council of Europe publishes texts on free, open access of all the treaties in its treaty series, currently numbering over 200.[71] Several states also publish treaty series, some with full texts online, such as the Australian Treaty Series, though these are usually only treaties to which the state is a party or potential party.[72]

In addition to finding a complete and authentic text of a treaty, those working with treaties may need to find how the treaty came to be as it is—sometimes described as the 'legislative history', but in the Vienna Convention 'the preparatory work'. This is commonly referred to in international practice by its French soubriquet *travaux préparatoires* or just 'the *travaux*'. There is no defining authority for the form, content, extent, or location of the preparatory work of a treaty.[73] Where a treaty is drawn up under the aegis of an international organization the modern practice is for the secretariat to arrange for publication of the records of the diplomatic

---

[69] VCLT, art 33 makes provision for this and is considered in ch 4 below.
[70] See list of conventions, protocols, and principles at https://www.hcch.net/en/instruments/conventions.
[71] See complete list at https://www.coe.int/en/web/conventions/full-list.
[72] See Australian Treaties Database https://www.info.dfat.gov.au/treaties. The US State Department periodically publishes a list of *Treaties in Force*, with supplements, where citations are given for locating texts: https://www.state.gov/treaties-in-force/.
[73] See further ch 3 below.

conference at which the treaty was negotiated, which in the documents circulated to the participants may include reports of such bodies as preparatory commissions and working parties. A good example is the two-stage conference which produced the Vienna Convention. The UN published the Official Records of the Conference, which included in the Final Act (and elsewhere) reference to the preparatory work done by the International Law Commission, preparatory work which has been cited by the ICJ (among many others) in interpreting the VCLT.[74]

---

[74] See https://legal.un.org/diplomaticconferences/1968_lot/; see also D Azaria, '"Codification by Interpretation": The International Law Commission as an Interpreter of International Law' (2020) 31 EJIL 171, 173, citing 32 decisions in which the ICJ has expressly relied on work of the ILC.

2
Treaties in Development of International Law

> From the period of Customary Law we come to another sharply defined epoch in the history of jurisprudence. We arrive at the era of Codes.[1]

The fundamental rule of the law of treaties—that every treaty in force is binding upon the parties to it and must be performed by them in good faith (which was examined in Chapter 1), is a rule of customary international law. As such, the rule binds all states. That is not controversial, but many rules of customary international law are more difficult to identify and formulate with precision. The trend has therefore been towards codification of the rules. The main means of attempting this, although not the only one, has been the conclusion of treaties. This is an imperfect solution because of the consensual nature of treaty relations and the need to be able to identify which propositions in a treaty state rules of customary law and are therefore applicable to all states regardless of whether a state is a party to the treaty. This is the focus of this chapter, which uses the development of the law of treaties as one of the prime examples of codification.

---

[1] H Maine, *Ancient Law* (Henry Holt and Company 1861) https://oll.libertyfund.org/title/pollock-ancient-law, 13 and on the relationship between treaties and customary international law see Y Dinstein, 'The Interaction Between Customary International Law and Treaties' (2006) 322 RdC 243.

I How Treaties Can State Rules of Customary International Law

1 The ILC and the ICJ's *North Sea Continental Shelf* Cases

Under the heading 'Two Constituent Elements' the ILC concluded that: 'To determine the existence and content of a rule of customary international law, it is necessary to ascertain whether there is a general practice that is accepted as law (*opinio juris*).'[2] Treaties have provided a significant aid to ascertaining the presence of these elements when identifying a rule of customary international law. This contribution has been particularly in the formulation of rules, the evidence of general practice accepted as law being more likely to be found elsewhere in the preparatory work or history of a treaty provision.[3] The judgments of the ICJ in the *North Sea Continental Shelf* cases set the foundational analysis for the potential of treaties to identify or contribute to formation of rules of customary international law in an approach which has been confirmed by the ILC.[4] One of the ILC's conclusions gives a summary of the three ways in which treaties may provide evidence of custom:

---

[2] International Law Commission (ILC), 'Draft Conclusions on Identification of Customary International Law, with Commentaries' (2018) Annual Report, UN Doc A/73/10, 121: Conclusion 2 https://legal.un.org/ilc/texts/1_13.shtml. The Draft Conclusions were endorsed by the UN General Assembly in Resolution 73/203 of 20 December 2018.

[3] An example of a comprehensive case being made out to demonstrate the existence of a rule of customary international law is in the written proceedings at ICJ, *Aerial Incident of 27 July 1955 (United States of America v Bulgaria)* (Memorial of the USA (2 December 1958) 212–27, showing that the use of weapons against a civil aircraft in flight is not allowed and that there is an affirmative obligation to assist such an aircraft that has been forced off course by bad weather. That this was an existing rule of customary international law was shown by its formulation in a treaty: 'The contracting States *recognize* that every State must refrain from resorting to the use of weapons against civil aircraft in flight' (emphasis added), Protocol Relating to an Amendment to the Convention on International Civil Aviation, Montreal 1984, 2122 UNTS 337, 36983, inserting art 3 bis into the Chicago Convention on International Civil Aviation (Chicago 1944).

[4] *North Sea Continental Shelf (Federal Republic of Germany v Denmark and Netherlands)* (Judgment) [1969] ICJ Rep 3.

A rule set forth in a treaty may reflect a rule of customary international law if it is established that the treaty rule:
(a) codified a rule of customary international law existing at the time when the treaty was concluded;
(b) has led to the crystallization of a rule of customary international law that had started to emerge prior to the conclusion of the treaty; or
(c) has given rise to a general practice that is accepted as law (opinio juris), thus generating a new rule of customary international law.[5]

The ILC's full conclusions, and in particular its commentaries, offer practical guidance on how the existence of rules of customary international law, and their content, are to be determined.[6] The conclusions were endorsed by resolution of the UN General Assembly.[7] Whether a particular treaty provision constitutes a codification is not always easy to identify; nor are crystallization and inception of a new rule of customary law furnished with clear signposts. Sometimes, if the treaty is the product of the work of the ILC, its commentaries may offer guidance. However, the mandate of the ILC is both codification and 'progressive development' of international law. Thus, even in treaties which are generally held to be codifications there may be elements of progressive development. The 1969 Vienna Convention is a prime example of a treaty formulated by the work of the ILC as essentially a codification but which has some provisions only later accepted as codification (for example the rules on treaty interpretation in Articles 31–33 of the VCLT) or which developed new rules (such as Articles 53 and 64 on 'peremptory norms of general international law', also known in the VCLT by the shorter soubriquet *jus cogens*).[8] This is considered in section III of this chapter.

---

[5] ILC (n 2) Conclusion 11, 121.
[6] Further detail can be found in the Reports of the ILC's Special Rapporteur (Sir Michael Wood), which guided the work of the ILC on this topic. For his bibliography see Annex II to the Fifth Report (2018) UN Doc A/CN.4/717/Add.1—an addendum separate from the Report N1817653.pdf (un.org).
[7] Resolution 73/203 of 20 December 2018 N1845741.pdf (un.org).
[8] Treaty interpretation is the subject of ch 4 below; for details of *jus cogens* see D Shelton, *Jus Cogens: Elements of International Law* (OUP 2021), and for current work of the ILC on this topic see its analytical guide https://legal.un.org/ilc/guide/1_14.shtml#top.

2 Codification, Crystallization, and Later Consolidation

The first two propositions of the ICJ as affirmed by the ILC ((a) and (b) above) can be summarized in the single terms 'codification' and 'crystallization'. The third does not so readily attract a label but it amounts to a treaty provision defining a rule which becomes established by subsequent consolidation of practice. These terms are not defined by international law, but the first two are in common use. Codification is stating in a treaty rules of customary law which were already established before the treaty was made. Crystallization signifies the case where the act of making the treaty fixes a proposition sufficiently for it to become a rule of customary law at the moment of conclusion of the treaty, some variance of practice or divergence of *opinio* having prevented its earlier emergence. In effect, this is consolidation at the very point of adoption or conclusion of the treaty.

The third situation is where practice and *opinio* converge upon a treaty provision *after* the treaty has been concluded. At some point the treaty provision is accepted as encapsulating the law on that point. 'Later consolidation' (a term used here as a convenient label, but not as a term of art) does not describe the process alone but also the result: a potential or nascent rule solidifies or becomes firm at a later date than conclusion of the treaty in which it is located. The obvious difficulty is identifying when this has occurred, but this is equally the case with crystallization.

Whatever labels are given to the three processes, they may help analysis even if they are not always readily separated in practice. Codification has already been mentioned here several times, particularly in the context of the work of the International Law Commission (ILC). In drawing up treaties, such as the Vienna Conventions on the Law of Treaties and on diplomatic relations, it fulfils its mandate of codification and progressive development of international law. Treaty provisions which codify could more properly be described as 'law-stating' rather than 'law-making'. In strict analysis, provisions of the former kind identify customary rules applying to all states, while the latter apply only to parties to the treaty unless the second or third process takes place.

3 *North Sea Continental Shelf* Cases State Principles for Custom through Treaties

The *North Sea Continental Shelf* cases concerned determination of the extent of the continental shelves of Germany, Denmark, and the Netherlands. The German coast fronting the North Sea is a concave stretch (in the shape of a great bay), set between the coasts of Denmark and the Netherlands. For such a situation, Article 6(2) of the Convention on the Continental Shelf (Geneva, 1958) provided:

> Where the same continental shelf is adjacent to the territories of two adjacent States, the boundary of the continental shelf shall be determined by agreement between them. In the absence of agreement, and unless another boundary line is justified by special circumstances, the boundary shall be determined by application of the principle of equidistance from the nearest points of the baselines from which the breadth of the territorial sea of each State is measured.

The core elements of this provision are agreement or, in the absence of agreement, an equidistance principle to define boundary lines. However, the then Federal Republic of Germany was not a party to the treaty and this provision was not therefore 'opposable' to it (capable of being relied on by a party to the treaty as binding Germany). Had it applied, Germany would have had a much-reduced area of continental shelf, as two equidistance lines drawn out from the frontier points on the coast would be pulled together by the effect of the coast being indented. Denmark and the Netherlands argued that the equidistance principle was customary international law. However, it was clear from the work of the ILC in preparing the Convention, and from the Geneva Conference, that the treaty was not a codification of existing rules.

Denmark and the Netherlands therefore argued that the second process ('crystallization') had taken place. What crystallization involves, however, is somewhat uncertain and imprecise. When suggested in the *North Sea Continental Shelf* cases, the ICJ found that it had not taken place in the particular circumstances; but the Court accepted that it could occur. The issues arose because Denmark and the Netherlands argued that:

> '[a]lthough prior to the Conference, continental shelf law was only in the formative stage, and State practice lacked uniformity, yet 'the process

of the definition and consolidation of the emerging customary law took place through the work of the International Law Commission, the reaction of governments to that work and the proceedings of the Geneva Conference'; and this emerging customary law became 'crystallized in the adoption of the Continental Shelf Convention by the Conference'.[9]

The Court found that the history of Article 6 of the Convention showed that its original proponents, the ILC, had put it forward 'with considerable hesitation, somewhat on an experimental basis', and that this was 'clearly not the sort of foundation on which Article 6 of the Convention could be said to have reflected or crystallized such a rule'. The Court further mentioned 'crystallization' when it found confirmation of its view of Article 6:

> The foregoing conclusion receives significant confirmation from the fact that Article 6 is one of those in respect of which, under the reservations article of the Convention (Article 12) reservations may be made by any State on signing, ratifying or acceding—for, speaking generally, it is a characteristic of purely conventional rules and obligations that, in regard to them, some faculty of making unilateral reservations may, within certain limits, be admitted; whereas this cannot be so in the case of general or customary law rules and obligations which, by their very nature, must have equal force for all members of the international community, and cannot therefore be the subject of any right of unilateral exclusion exercisable at will by any one of them in its own favour. Consequently, it is to be expected that when, for whatever reason, rules or obligations of this order are embodied, or are intended to be reflected in certain provisions of a convention, such provisions will figure amongst those in respect of which a right of unilateral reservation is not conferred, or is excluded. This expectation is, in principle, fulfilled by Article 12 of the Geneva Continental Shelf Convention, which permits reservations to be made to all the articles of the Convention 'other than to Articles 1 to 3 inclusive'—these three Articles being the ones which, it is clear, were then regarded as reflecting, or as crystallizing, received or at least emergent rules of customary international law relative to the continental shelf.[10]

---

[9] [1969] ICJ Rep 3, 38, para 61.
[10] ibid 38, para 63.

In its reference to reflecting or crystallizing received or emergent rules, the ICJ confirms the analysis that there is a distinction between codification and crystallization, but offers little to help in defining the latter. The Court then considered the third possibility, that is (as argued by Denmark and the Netherlands) that:

> [e]ven if there was at the date of the Geneva Convention no rule of customary international law in favour of the equidistance principle, and no such rule was crystallized in Article 6 of the Convention, nevertheless such a rule has come into being since the Convention, partly because of its own impact, partly on the basis of subsequent state practice – and that this rule, being now a rule of customary international law [is] binding on all States ... [T]his contention ... involves treating that Article as a norm-creating provision which has constituted the foundation of, or has generated a rule which, while only conventional or contractual in its origin, has since passed into the general *corpus* of international law, and is now accepted as such by the *opinio juris*, so as to have become binding even for countries which have never, and do not, become parties to the Convention. There is no doubt that this process is a perfectly possible one and does from time to time occur: it constitutes indeed one of the recognized methods by which new rules of customary international law may be formed.[11]

The Court found that for this process of 'impact' and subsequent practice (consolidation) to have occurred, it was necessary to show that the provision in issue was formulated in such a way as to be capable of constituting a general rule as well as meeting the requirements of practice and *opinio* common to the identification of customary rules. In the instant case, there were three contra-indications. The equidistance principle was secondary in Article 6 to the requirement of that provision to settle the boundary by negotiation. Second, it was qualified by the requirement to consider 'special circumstances' which might modify application of the principle. Third, as previously noted by the Court, it was subject to the possibility of reservation. Hence, these factors, taken with lack of practice, showed that the equidistance principle had not become a general or customary rule.

---

[11] ibid 41, paras 70–71.

In the *North Sea Continental Shelf* cases the ICJ provides an analysis which offers a theoretical view of the relationship between treaties and customary laws in terms of those categories, codification, crystallization, and subsequent consolidation. Although the Court gives pointers to when these processes may be viewed as having taken place, that is a far cry from providing a formula of ready application. Without the Court's specific guidance on a particular rule, or overwhelming evidence of long standing, identification of customary rules remains a somewhat mystical art. The lawyer's task is to marshal coherent evidence, a task made simpler if there is a treaty formulation which can be made the focus of consideration.

A further indication of the relationship between customary law and treaties is found in the judgment of the ICJ in the *Nicaragua* case.[12] There, the ICJ addressed the parallel existence of customary rules and their embodiment in treaties:

> The existence of identical rules in international treaty law and customary law has been clearly recognized by the Court in the *North Sea Continental Shelf* cases. To a large extent, those cases turned on the question whether a rule enshrined in a treaty also existed as a customary rule, either because the treaty had merely codified the custom, or caused it to 'crystallize', or because it had influenced its subsequent adoption. The Court found that this identity of content in treaty law and in customary international law did not exist in the case of the rule invoked, which appeared in one article of the treaty, but did not suggest that such identity was debarred as a matter of principle: on the contrary, it considered it to be clear that certain other articles of the treaty in question 'were ... regarded as reflecting, or as crystallizing, received or at least emergent rules of customary international law' ([1969] ICJ Rep 39, para 63).[13]

---

[12] *Military and Paramilitary Activities in and against Nicaragua (Nicaragua v United States of America)* [1986] ICJ Rep 14.
[13] ibid 95, para 177.

II Codifying Treaties and Treaties Formulating Law

1 Whether Codification or Progressive Development

As noted above, it is not always easy to draw a line between what is a statement of an existing rule and what is progressive development. The Statute of the ILC provides that, in that instrument:

> [T]he expression 'progressive development of international law' is used for convenience as meaning the preparation of draft conventions on subjects which have not yet been regulated by international law or in regard to which the law has not yet been sufficiently developed in the practice of States. Similarly, the expression 'codification of international law' is used for convenience as meaning the more precise formulation and systematization of rules of international law in fields where there already has been extensive State practice, precedent and doctrine.[14]

This differentiation, the separate grouping of articles in the Statute on progressive development and codification, and the distinct procedures specified in the Statute, make it appear that a line can be drawn between the two functions. In practice, however, the ILC tackles both together and does not systematically draw a distinction between drafts constituting codification and those amounting to progressive development. That progressive development includes matters regarding which the law has not yet been sufficiently developed in the practice of states supports the observation of Professor Gaja that '[t]here is in fact a continuum between progressive development and codification.'[15]

Although the Statute does not prescribe a treaty as the only outcome of the work of the ILC, it implies this as a prime possibility. In the case of codification, the ILC is to prepare its drafts in the form of articles, with an accompanying report, and may recommend the drafts to the UN General

---

[14] ILC Statute adopted by the General Assembly in Resolution 174 (II) of 21 November 1947 (as amended 1950, 1955, and 1981) art 15 https://legal.un.org/ilc/texts/instruments/english/statute/statute.pdf.

[15] G Gaja, 'The Place of Treaties in the Codification and Progressive Development of International Law' in S Chesterman, DM Malone, and S Villalpando (eds), *The Oxford Handbook of United Nations Treaties* (OUP 2019) 88.

Assembly with a view to concluding a convention or convoking a conference to do so.[16] The ILC may equally recommend that the Assembly simply take note of, or adopt, its report by resolution and in more recent times there have been several instances where the Assembly has done so with a recommendation to states to take note of the conclusions of the ILC.

These variable practices lead to the question of whether adopting a treaty is the best way of identifying and formulating rules of international law. The nature of customary international law being a distillation of rules from practice and *opinio juris*, the key utility of any instrument in this regard is that it reduces these elements to writing. Drawing up a treaty does, however, also have the advantage that where its provisions contain progressive development of the law, those states which wish to have clarity in identifying these provisions as obligations can do so without having to rely on producing evidence of 'crystallization' or subsequent consolidation into a rule through practice, at least as regards others who become parties to the treaty. The counterbalancing disadvantage of a treaty is that if there are provisions in the instrument which may be either codification or progressive development, a paucity of states becoming a party to the treaty may offer an indication of doubt whether the provisions are binding under either classification.

2 Codifying Instruments

An example of the difficulty of assessing the weight to be attached to differing forms of instrument for identifying rules of international law can be seen from the sequence of events leading to the Outer Space Treaty 1967.[17] Although use of outer space was in its early days, two of the treaty's provisions give examples of rules which were already of potentially wide significance. These are the rule prohibiting national appropriation of outer space 'by claim of sovereignty, by means of use or occupation, or by any other means' (which has precluded claims by equatorial states to the geostationary/geosynchronous orbit where location of satellites is favoured), and the undertaking 'not to place in orbit around the earth any objects carrying nuclear weapons or any other kinds of weapons of mass destruction'.[18]

---

[16] ILC Statute (n 14) art 17.
[17] 610 UNTS 8843; 112 states parties as at 1 January 2022.
[18] ibid arts II, IV.

The Outer Space Treaty put into a treaty the substantive provisions of two 1963 resolutions of the UN General Assembly, both adopted unanimously, as is recounted in the preamble to the treaty.[19] Adoption of the resolutions was accompanied by discussion of whether their content could be regarded as stating rules of international law. The longer resolution, the one dealing with matters other than weapons, was headed 'Declaration of Legal Principles Governing the Activities of States in the Exploration and Use of Outer Space'.[20] On the use of the term 'Declaration', the UN Office of Legal Affairs had furnished the UN Commission on Human Rights in the previous year with a memorandum including the indication that:

> [T]here is probably no difference between a 'recommendation' or a 'declaration' in United Nations practice as far as strict legal principle is concerned. A 'declaration' or a 'recommendation' is adopted by resolution of a United Nations organ. As such it cannot be made binding upon Member States, in the sense that a treaty or convention is binding upon the parties to it, purely by the device of terming it a 'declaration' rather than a 'recommendation'. However, in view of the greater solemnity and significance of a 'declaration', it may be considered to impart, on behalf of the organ adopting it, a strong expectation that Members of the international community will abide by it. Consequently, in so far as the expectation is gradually justified by State practice, a declaration may by custom become recognized as laying down rules binding upon States.[21]

In the debates surrounding adoption of this Declaration, some states came near to expressing the view that if all members of the UN considered a proposition to be a rule of international law, it should be viewed as such. This posed the question of whether there could be 'instant customary law' established by the unanimous opinion of states without there being any actual practice to support the propositions. Professor Cheng investigated this question.[22] His main conclusion was that the constitutive element of international customary law (or as he described general international law being 'the unwritten rules of international law applicable *erga omnes* minus

---

[19] Resolutions 1962 (XVIII) and 1884 (XVIII).
[20] Resolution 1962 (XVIII).
[21] UN Doc E/CN.4/L.6l0 (2 April 1962).
[22] B Cheng, *Studies in International Space Law* (OUP 1997) ch 7: 'United Nations Resolutions on Outer Space: "Instant" International Customary Law?', first published in (1965) 5 Indian JIL 23.

the general principles of law') requires only the *opinio juris* of states, but that usage or practice instead of being a constitutive and indispensable element merely provides evidence of the existence and contents of the underlying rule and of the requisite *opinio juris*.

Cheng's argument, although extensively discussed (and sometimes misrepresented), has not prevailed.[23] However, it is important to record that he carefully noted a number of considerations and qualifications, including that in the particular instance the wording of the space resolutions fell short of what was required for law-finding resolutions and that some states supporting the Declaration had indicated that they did not regard it as binding. This was before the *North Sea Continental Shelf* cases, and many decades before the ILC's conclusions on the formation of customary law. His assessment of these resolutions was also made before their incorporation into the 1967 treaty, which was clearly designed to ensure legal effects. That a treaty was considered necessary so soon after resolutions in the same terms suggests that the treaty form has been considered to be the best way of setting the foundations for a specialist code of international law.

The role for treaties in rapidly confirming an international law proposition which has received recognition by general acceptance without long years of practice was shown earlier by the rule on extent of sovereignty over air space. In 1910, at a conference in Paris, there had been disagreement on this, a strong body of opinion holding that, by analogy with the territorial sea, states should be allowed to claim sovereignty only to some limited height, such as 1,500 metres. The evidence which the First World War provided of the significance of airspace for defence of the state led to swift general acceptance that states should have sovereignty over the complete airspace above their territory. Thus, the first codification of air law in 1919 opened with 'recognition' of this: 'The High Contracting Parties *recognise* that every Power has complete and exclusive sovereignty over the air space above its territory.'[24] In other words, that a customary rule had arisen between 1910 and 1919 was evidenced by a treaty provision reflecting the opinion of states as to its emergence.

---

[23] See M Wood (ILC Special Rapporteur), 'Third Report on Identification of Customary International Law' UN Doc A/CN.4/682 (27 March 2015) 31–41; DG Mejía-Lemos, 'Some Considerations Regarding "Instant" International Customary Law, Fifty Years Later' (2015) 55 Indian JIL 85.

[24] Convention Relating to the Regulation of Aerial Navigation 1919 (the Paris Convention of 1919) (signed at Paris on 13 October 1919, entered into force 29 March 1922) 11 LNTS 173, art 1 (emphasis added).

III Reducing Rules to Writing: Development of the 1969 Vienna Convention

1 ILC's Preparatory Work

The history of the 1969 Vienna Convention provides a useful example of the development of a codification treaty and how such a treaty may come to state international law. Although there were established practices for making treaties over the centuries, a first attempt at formulation of a comprehensive set of rules for the modern era came as part of the Harvard research project on international law, resulting in a set of draft articles on the law of treaties in 1935.[25] This formed one of the starting points of the work of the ILC on treaties.

In 1947, UN General Assembly Resolution 174 (II) had established the ILC and approved its Statute. This was in implementation of Article 13(1)(a) of the Charter of the UN requiring the Assembly 'to initiate studies and make recommendations for the purpose of ... encouraging the progressive development of international law and its codification'. Of the twenty-five topics considered by the Commission, from which fourteen were selected for codification at its first session in 1949, the law of treaties was the first of the three to which the Commission decided to give priority in its work programme (the second and third being arbitral procedure and the law of the high seas).[26]

Although work on draft articles started immediately, progress on the law of treaties was slow and its codification was overtaken by other items. The initial efforts may have been hampered in part by their being begun at an early stage of the Commission's life when its aims and practices had not assumed a mature form. By the time the ILC's draft articles were ready for consideration at the 1968–1969 Vienna Conference, the ILC's work had already led to significant codifications in treaty form, in 1958 on the law of the sea and in 1961 and 1963 on diplomatic and consular law.[27]

Four Special Rapporteurs of the ILC successively tackled the law of treaties. That the work on the law of treaties took so long may also have

---

[25] (1935) 29 AJIL Supp 653; for an assessment see A Aust, 'Law of Treaties' in JP Grant and JC Barker (eds), *The Harvard Research in International Law: Contemporary Analysis and Appraisal* (WS Hein 2007) ch 11.
[26] 'ILC Report to the General Assembly' [1949] Yearbook of the ILC 277, 280–81.
[27] For a brief history of development of the Vienna Convention see ME Villiger, *Commentary on the 1969 Vienna Convention on the Law of Treaties* (Nijhoff 2009) 28–38.

also been because the second and third Rapporteurs each had a truncated innings as a result of their translation to being judges at the ICJ. The third Special Rapporteur, Fitzmaurice, paid particular attention to the form of the intended product, steering towards a sui generis code. The most important point concerning the character of treaties to emerge from the first report by Fitzmaurice, although not stated in these terms, was that the essence of treaties is statements of rights and obligations.[28] Treaties are not appropriate repositories of exhortations, observations, recommendations, or other non-binding considerations. Inclusion of such items actually detracts from the principle *pacta sunt servanda* because it points to some substance of a treaty being optional. Yet, sadly and unhelpfully, such dilution of legal certainty can be found in the content and wording of some treaties with hybrid provisions leading to confusion as to whether the instrument, or particular provisions in it, are binding agreements.[29]

As regards the law of treaties, Fitzmaurice considered it inappropriate that a code on the law of treaties should itself be a treaty, and he felt that it would better stand outside that form. Further, he noted:

> [M]uch of the law relating to treaties is not especially suitable for framing in conventional form. It consists of enunciations of principles and abstract rules, most easily stated in the form of a code; and this also has the advantage of rendering permissible the inclusion of a certain amount of declaratory and explanatory material in the body of the code, in a way that would not be possible if this had to be confined to a strict statement of obligation. Such material has considerable utility in making clear, on the face of the code itself, the legal concepts or reasoning on which the various provisions are based.[30]

Although the Commission later decided that it should propose a treaty, Fitzmaurice's considerations favouring explanation of the legal concepts and reasoning underlying the law of treaties have proved justified to some degree. The Convention which eventually emerged reduced the rules

---

[28] Sir Gerald Fitzmaurice, 'Report on the Law of Treaties' [1956-II] Yearbook of the ILC 104.
[29] For an example of a mixture of mandatory ('shall') and exhortatory ('should') terms see the Convention on a Code of Conduct for Liner Conferences, Geneva, 1974, 1334 UNTS 15, No 22380, arts 12–19; on the potential for different uses of mandatory and exhortatory words in a treaty provision in different languages see *LaGrand (Germany v USA)* (Judgment) [2001] ICJ Rep 466, 502, para 101.
[30] Fitzmaurice (n 28) 107.

governing treaties to rather terse propositions without the accompanying declaratory and explanatory material often necessary for their effective application. However, that deficiency has in some measure been made up by liberal reference to the ILC's explanations of the legal concepts and reasoning on which the Convention's provisions are based, particularly those in the commentary on the draft articles.[31] Professor Azaria notes how many times the ICJ has expressly relied on the ILC's work in its decisions.[32]

The fourth special rapporteur, Waldock, endorsed the view in the Commission that one of the attractions of drafting provisions for a treaty was that the large number of then newly independent states would have a chance to participate in the formulation of the law at a diplomatic conference. Such involvement would enhance the chance of the outcome of a diplomatic conference being generally acceptable.[33]

A further means of increasing the likelihood of acceptability of a treaty which combines codification with progressive development is the interaction between the ILC and the Sixth (Legal) Committee of the UN General Assembly on which all member states are represented. The established practice is that after a report by a Special Rapporteur has been debated in the ILC, and any draft articles have been refined and reworked by the Commission, it includes the outcome in its annual report to the General Assembly. In the debate on the ILC's annual report, states have the opportunity to comment on the drafts and are sometimes asked to respond to questionnaires on their practices. The Special Rapporteur can then take account of the Sixth Committee's input and reactions when the draft articles are before the Commission for further consideration.

Waldock, effectively the architect of the draft convention on the law of treaties, had some other sources of inspiration in addition to the Harvard draft articles. For example, in offering formulations for the articles on treaty interpretation, he referred to draft provisions in a resolution of the

---

[31] [1966-II] Yearbook of the ILC 187.
[32] Professor Azaria cites twenty-three decisions in contentious cases up to 31 January 2020: D Azaria, '"Codification by Interpretation": The International Law Commission as an Interpreter of International Law' (2020) 31 EJIL 171, 173; since then, the ICJ has referred to the ILC's commentary on its 'Articles on Responsibility of States for Internationally Wrongful Acts' in its judgment of 9 February 2022 in *Armed Activities on the Territory of the Congo (Democratic Republic of the Congo v Uganda)* (Judgment of 9 February 2022) (icj-cij.org), and the ILC's preparatory work on the Geneva Convention on the Territorial Sea and the Contiguous Zone 1958 and its commentary on the Articles on State Responsibility in its judgment of 21 April 2022 in *Alleged Violations of Sovereign Rights and Maritime Spaces in the Caribbean Sea (Nicaragua v Colombia)* (Judgment of 21 April 2022) (icj-cij.org).
[33] 'ILC Summary Records' [1961-I] Yearbook of the ILC 252.

Institut de Droit International and to an analysis of the ICJ's case law made by Fitzmaurice, his predecessor.[34] The utility and widespread acceptance of most of the Vienna Convention's provisions, in their application and invocation even by states not parties to the treaty, derive mainly from the detailed studies in the six reports by Waldock and the conversion by the ILC of his proposals into draft articles likely to be acceptable to all states.

2 The Vienna Conference 1968–1969

Although the two sessions of the 1968–1969 Vienna Conference delved into detail, with some lively debates, few matters came up that were likely to prove deal-breakers. Those that were controversial are the ones which are most worth examining here. Three topics which Sinclair, a delegate to the conference, subsequently described as having given rise to extended debate were:

(a) reservations to multilateral conventions;
(b) treaty interpretation; and
(c) the concept of *jus cogens* as invalidating a treaty.[35]

A preliminary point to note is that the procedure at a diplomatic conference can have a powerful impact on the outcome and hence adoption of rules of procedure is typically one of the earliest agenda items.[36] The law of treaties Vienna Conference was perhaps unusual in that, rather than dividing work on the substantial provisions between two or more committees to prepare what is the equivalent of a second reading of drafts by many legislatures, the conference proceeded with a single 'Committee of the Whole', with the consequence that all could participate in all of the debates and thus contribute to the development of the text—a further enhancement of the prospect of general acceptability.

(a) Reservations

The term 'reservation' came to be defined as:

---

[34] Institut Resolution of 19 April 1956 which is translated in [1964-II] Yearbook of the ILC 55, where Waldock also cites G Fitzmaurice, 'The Law and Procedure of the International Court of Justice 1951–1954: Treaty Interpretation and Other Points' (1957) 33 BYBIL 203.

[35] IM Sinclair, 'Vienna Conference on the Law of Treaties' (1970) 19 ICLQ 47.

[36] For further details of treaty-making procedures see ch 3 below.

a unilateral statement, however phrased or named, made by a State, when signing, ratifying, accepting, approving or acceding to a treaty, whereby it purports to exclude or to modify the legal effect of certain provisions of the treaty in their application to that State.[37]

The debate on reservations at the Vienna Conference had its origins in the ICJ's advisory opinion in the *Reservations to the Genocide Convention* case.[38] That opinion intimated a shift from an established rule requiring that any reservation be unanimously accepted by all states having an interest in the relevant treaty to a consideration of whether a proposed reservation was compatible with the object and purpose of the treaty.[39] Underlying the opposing sides in the debate at the Vienna Conference was the notion, on the one hand, that sovereign states have a right to shape and identify the specific terms which they are prepared to accept in an international agreement and, on the other hand, the concept that a multilateral international agreement should not lose its integrity by different parties agreeing to different commitments.

The principle underlying the first of these approaches was respected in Article 19 of the Vienna Convention by acknowledging that a state has a right, when signing, ratifying, accepting, approving, or acceding to a treaty, to formulate a reservation unless the reservation is prohibited by the treaty, unless the latter provides for only specified reservations not including the reservation in question or, in any other case, where the reservation is incompatible with the object and purpose of the treaty.

To compensate for departure from the historic requirement of unanimous acceptance of a reservation, the second approach (integrity of the treaty) was respected by inclusion in the Vienna Convention of the provision that:

> When it appears from the limited number of the negotiating States and the object and purpose of a treaty that the application of the treaty in its entirety between all the parties is an essential condition of the consent

---

[37] VCLT, art 2(1)(d).
[38] *Reservations to the Convention on the Prevention and Punishment of the Crime of Genocide* (Advisory Opinion) [1951] ICJ Rep 15. That case concerned a multilateral treaty, as does most consideration of issues connected with reservations since, in practical terms, negotiation of different terms is the simpler resolution of one side's reservations in bilateral negotiations.
[39] For further use of object and purpose in the VCLT, see ch 4, section II.2 below.

of each one to be bound by the treaty, a reservation requires acceptance by all the parties.[40]

While expressly permitted reservations do not require acceptance, in other cases (bar the one just described) the Vienna scheme provides that acceptance by a contracting state of a reservation constitutes the reserving state a party in relation to the accepting state when the treaty is in force for those states, but an objection by a contracting state does not preclude the entry into force of the treaty as between the objecting and reserving states unless a contrary intention is expressed by the objecting state.[41] A reservation is deemed accepted by any state which has raised no objection by the end of twelve months from being notified of the reservation or by the date on which it consented to be bound by the treaty, whichever is later.[42]

Reservations which are permitted have the effect of reciprocally modifying treaty relations between the parties or likewise, where subject to acceptance, between reserving and accepting states.[43] If an objecting state has not opposed the entry into force of the treaty between itself and a reserving state, the Vienna Convention holds that the 'provisions to which the reservation relates do not apply as between the two States to the extent of the reservation'.[44]

The ILC Special Rapporteur (Pellet), appointed when reservations came before the Commission again nearly twenty five years after the Vienna Convention was concluded, characterized its provisions as the outcome of 'lively differences of opinion ... settled only by means of compromises based on judicious ambiguities'.[45] It would be an over-simplification to sum up the main contest as between 'permissibility' (the question of whether a reservation is intrinsically permitted) and 'opposability' (whether a reservation is subject to acceptance and can be defeated by objection). That the ILC's product after nearly twenty years was a 630-page 'Guide to Practice on Reservations to Treaties' is evidence enough that multiple issues had to be addressed.[46]

[40] VCLT, art 20.
[41] ibid.
[42] ibid.
[43] ibid art 21.
[44] ibid.
[45] Alain Pellet, 'First Report on the Law and Practice Relating to Reservations to Treaties' [1995-II(1)] Yearbook of the ILC 136, para 61.
[46] Addendum to Report of the International Law Commission, Sixty-third session (2011), UN General Assembly Official Records, Sixty-sixth Session, Supplement No 10, A/66/10/Add.1, http://legal.un.org/ilc/reports/2011/english/addendum.pdf.

The points to note here, however, are that the Vienna provisions on reservations remain unamended but that they require a great deal of background and amplification for practical application. The same may be said of much of the codification in the Vienna Convention. Many a treaty sets a framework of legal rules but often these are too concise for clear application in practical situations. Customary rules need the accompanying declaratory and explanatory material of which Fitzmaurice had given forewarning, such as is found in the preparatory work of the treaty, in subsequent ILC conclusions, or other sources of an authoritative character (such as judgments and opinions of the ICJ). The massive 'Guide to Practice on Reservations to Treaties' stands as evidence of this.

(b) Treaty interpretation

Although Sinclair noted treaty interpretation as the second topic which gave rise to extensive debate at the Vienna Conference, there was really only one issue which exercised the conference on this topic. This was whether the articles proposed by the ILC were unduly restrictive in confining use of preparatory work and other supplementary means of interpretation to the roles of confirming a meaning of a treaty's terms achieved by applying a general rule of interpretation or determining the meaning only in defined circumstances.[47] Although there was a debate over a proposal advanced by the USA to merge the two separate articles constituting a general rule of interpretation and supplementary means, this proposal was decisively rejected.

The interpretation provisions were ultimately adopted without dissenting vote and with little amendment beyond an addition to Article 33 on the use of different languages.[48] What is of significance here is that, despite uncertainty in the debate as to whether there were or should be rules of interpretation, and whether the proposed text accurately recounted past practice, correctly indicated the then present state of the law on interpretation, or established a new code for the future, the Vienna Convention rules of interpretation have become universally recognized as customary international law, applying even to treaties pre-dating the Vienna Convention and to treaties between states not parties to that Convention. On the face of it, application of the Vienna rules on interpretation to treaties pre-dating the Vienna Convention is remarkable. Article 4 of the Vienna Convention

---

[47] Treaty interpretation is the subject of ch 4 below.
[48] See further ch 4, section IV below.

provides that it applies only to treaties which are concluded after its entry into force, albeit without prejudice to application of rules of international law which would apply to treaties independently of the Convention. Article 28 establishes a residual general principle of non-retroactivity of treaties, although this may be counter-indicated.

In the light of this subsequent history, it is difficult to tell whether complete acceptance of the rules of interpretation is because the treaty did codify international law, crystallized the rules upon unanimous adoption, or led to consolidation of opinion that the new rules constitute customary international law. The latter seems best to accord with the steady and incremental acceptance of the rules in practice and in the work of courts and tribunals. This means that no precise date can been attributed to this acceptance; but this does not appear to have thrown up major difficulties, perhaps because the rules of interpretation, although controversial at the time of their reduction to writing, have not been shown to diverge from earlier practice and are not restrictive in their application to treaties of differing kinds and on greatly different subjects.

(c) Peremptory norms (*jus cogens*)

Of the third area which he addressed in his report on the Vienna conference (peremptory norms or *jus cogens*), Sinclair wrote that this was 'unquestionably one of the most crucial and controversial issues debated at the conference, namely, the concept, reflected in Article 50 of the ILC draft articles [Article 53 in the eventual Convention], that a treaty is void if it conflicts with a peremptory norm of general international law from which no derogation is permitted'.[49] In the present context, the significance of this is how the Vienna Convention as a treaty has established the concept of peremptory norms as a feature of international law. Professor Shelton notes: 'Peremptory norms/*jus cogens* entered positive law with the Vienna treaties on treaties.'[50]

Article 53 defines a peremptory norm for the purposes of the Vienna Convention as 'a norm accepted and recognized by the international community of States as a whole as a norm from which no derogation is permitted and which can be modified only by a subsequent norm of general international law having the same character'. Article 64 similarly invalidates any treaty if it conflicts with 'new peremptory norm of general

---

[49] Sinclair (n 35) 66.
[50] Shelton (n 8) 13.

international law'. In response to the concerns over inclusion of these provisions on peremptory norms, and in order to sweeten their acceptability, specific provision was made in Article 66 for dealing with disputes concerning application or interpretation of Article 53 or Article 64. If a dispute remained unresolved twelve months after objection to validity of a treaty on the ground of conflict with a peremptory norm, any party to the dispute may submit it to the ICJ, unless the parties by common consent agree to arbitration.

A whole panoply of issues surrounds the identification, modalities of generation, and effects of peremptory norms.[51] What is now beyond question is that the concept of a peremptory norm is an element of international law. This has been recognized by the ICJ and by other international courts and tribunals.[52] An example of explicit recognition by the Court as a peremptory norm is the prohibition of genocide.[53] The Court worked its way to such recognition via the analysis that the Genocide Convention contains obligations owed to the international community generally (*erga omnes*). Peremptory norms are a distinct and higher category of obligations owed to the international community so that all peremptory norms are owed *erga omnes* but not all *erga omnes* obligations are peremptory norms.

Professor Shelton notes that the ILC has considered peremptory norms when working on other topics, instancing Article 26 of the Draft Articles on State Responsibility (for which the commentary offers a non-exhaustive list of *jus cogens* norms) and the 'Guide to Practice on Reservations' (which includes examination of effects of *jus cogens* on permissibility and consequences of reservations).[54] More directly, the ILC has been working on draft articles on peremptory norms of general international law, reporting in 2016 that its draft conclusions would 'concern the way in which *jus cogens* rules are to be identified, and the legal consequences flowing from them'.[55]

---

[51] ibid *passim*; and JA Green, *The Persistent Objector Rule in International Law* (OUP 2016) 189 ff.
[52] *Armed Activities on the Territory of the Congo (New Application: 2002) (Democratic Republic of the Congo v Rwanda)* (Judgment) [2006] ICJ Rep 6, 31–22, para 64, reaffirmed in *Application of the Convention on the Prevention and Punishment of the Crime of Genocide (Bosnia and Herzegovina v Serbia and Montenegro)* (Judgment) [2007] ICJ Rep 43, 110–11, para 161 and *Application of the Convention on the Prevention and Punishment of the Crime of Genocide (Croatia v Serbia)* (Judgment) [2015] ICJ Rep 3, 47, para 88; see also Shelton (n 8) ch 5, ss 5.2 'International Jurisprudence' and 5.3 'National Legislation and Jurisprudence'.
[53] See the three cases cited in n 52 above. See also JA Frowein, 'Obligations erga omnes' in *Max Planck Encyclopedia of Public International Law* (MPEPIL) (update of December 2008).
[54] Shelton (n 8) 17–18.
[55] ILC Report on the work of the sixty-eighth session (2016) A/71/10, 299, para 110, fn 1296.

III Development of the 1969 Vienna Convention 51

The ILC draft conclusions set out a non-exhaustive list of norms it regards as having the status of peremptory norms of general international law (*jus cogens*):

(a) the prohibition of aggression;
(b) the prohibition of genocide;
(c) the prohibition of crimes against humanity;
(d) the basic rules of international humanitarian law;
(e) the prohibition of racial discrimination and apartheid;
(f) the prohibition of slavery;
(g) the prohibition of torture;
(h) the right of self-determination.[56]

These can be matched with formulations in treaties where their content is stated:

(a) UN Charter, Article 2(4);
(b) Genocide Convention, Paris 1948;
(c) Rome Statute 1998;
(d) Geneva Conventions 1949, and Additional Protocols 1977;
(e) Elimination of Racial Discrimination and of Apartheid Conventions;
(f) Slavery Convention, Geneva, 1926 (1927) 60 LNTS 253, 1414;
(g) Convention against Torture and Other Cruel, Inhuman or Degrading Treatment or Punishment, New York 1984, 1465 UNTS 24841;
(h) UN Charter, Article 1(2).[57]

(d) Conclusion

Thus, in conclusion, for each of the three areas of international law which Sinclair identified as controversial at the 1968–1969 Vienna Conference,

---

[56] Text adopted by the ILC, Report of the International Law Commission, Seventy-third session (2022), A/77/10, Chapter IV, conclusion 23 and Annex.

[57] Well-known treaties are here given short titles; full citations for items (e) International Convention on the Elimination of All Forms of Racial Discrimination, New York 1966, 660 UNTS 9464 and International Convention on the Suppression and Punishment of the Crime of Apartheid 1015 UNTS 243, 14861; (f) Slavery Convention 1926 (1927) 60 LNTS 253, 1414; (g) Convention against Torture and Other Cruel, Inhuman or Degrading Treatment or Punishment 1984, 1465 UNTS 24841.

the articles of the Vienna Convention formed part of the foundation of establishment and development of the law. Each has been the subject of further work by the ILC, but this has not resulted in proposals for amendment of the Vienna Convention. The rules for treaty interpretation have become firmly established as of general application, albeit with a need for deeper understanding and amplification of how they apply. The regime for reservations has proved more controversial in some respects but is now accompanied by a detailed Guide from the ILC with potential to lead to more consistent outcomes. Peremptory norms still form the least certain code of the three, but their treaty-based recognition in the 1969 Convention is playing some part in the work of both international and national courts and tribunals, even if not specifically in the matter of treaties being invalid for violations of peremptory norms.

3
How Treaties Are Made

I Introduction

In his book *Peacemaking, 1919*, Harold Nicolson recounts meeting Marcel Proust at dinner during the Paris conference that led to the Treaty of Versailles. Proust asked how the conference's committees worked. Nicolson started to reply 'Well, we generally meet at 10.0, there are secretaries behind …'. Proust cut him short, demanding much more detail—from the journey to the Quai d'Orsay, going up the steps, and entering the conference room. 'So I tell him everything. The sham cordiality of it all: the handshakes: the maps: the rustle of papers: the tea in the next room: the macaroons. He listens enthralled, interrupting from time to time—'*Mais précisez, mon cher monsieur, n'allez pas trop vite.*"[1]

Proust, in demanding more detail and asking Nicolson to slow down, was correct in suspecting that much of the key negotiation of a major multilateral treaty may take place outside the formal stages of a diplomatic conference. Many of the necessary compromises and deals are made in small groups over coffee breaks or in private huddles in the corridors. The official records of a diplomatic conference typically show something like a parliamentary process with working papers, proposals, and plenary debates fed by committees and working groups.[2] Where the world's community of states is involved, the sheer number and variety of states makes even the

---

[1] *Peacemaking, 1919* (Faber & Faber 2013, originally published 1933) 224, diary entry for 2 March 1919. On making international law by treaties see K Schmalenbach, 'Lawmaking by Treaty: Negotiation of Agreements and Adoption of Treaty Texts' and D Costelloe and M Fitzmaurice, 'Lawmaking by Treaty: Conclusion of Treaties and Evolution of Treaty Regimes in Practice', chs 5 and 6 in C Brölmann and Y Radi (eds), *Research Handbook on the Theory and Practice of International Lawmaking* (Edward Elgar Publishing 2016); and J Barrett and RC Beckman, *Handbook on Good Treaty Practice* (CUP 2020).

[2] An example of the informal being made formal was the establishment of a 'Friends of the Chairman Group' to conduct extensive behind the scenes negotiations at the conference producing a supposedly new Convention for the Unification of Certain Rules for International Carriage by Air 1999, the members of this group being listed in the Final Act of the International Conference on Air Law held under the auspices of the International Civil Aviation Organization at Montreal from 10 to 28 May 1999, DOC 9775-DC/2, 437 at 440–41.

committee system unwieldy so that blocks of like-minded or geographically proximate states tend to work in groups. Whereas major diplomatic conferences used to be hosted by a single state which provided the venue and facilities, multilateral treaties are increasingly worked up under the aegis of international organizations.

The importance for lawyers of how treaties are made is twofold. The key stages of treaty-making are relevant for identifying the points at which the treaty text becomes final, how states become parties to it, and when the treaty enters into force both initially and for any states which later become parties to it. Second, the records of the preparatory work and the indications of the circumstances in which a treaty has been concluded have a role to play in its interpretation.

The Vienna Convention sets out the procedures by which a treaty is made. It does not set out to explain how treaties are instigated or prepared. Multilateral treaties increasingly constitute the building blocks of international law. The work programme for the International Law Commission (ILC) on codification and progressive development, described in the previous chapter and leading in many instances to provisions in treaties, is set by agreement between the ILC and the UN General Assembly. If the outcome is to be a treaty, the General Assembly and the UN Secretariat will arrange for the appropriate negotiations to achieve conclusion.

More generally, however, the impetus for drawing up a multilateral treaty can come from a wide range of sources. Although it is open to an interested state to gather together other similarly concerned states, call a diplomatic conference to agree a text, and to produce a treaty by that means, the more common way nowadays is through the machinery of an international organization. The United Nations, its specialized agencies and many regional organizations have developed numerous treaties either through standing machinery or by calling special diplomatic conferences. Random examples of other organizations which have produced great collections of treaties are the Council of Europe, the Hague Conference on Private International Law, and UNIDROIT.[3]

---

[3] The International Institute for the Unification of Private Law (UNIDROIT) has drawn up treaties of a unifying character on several areas of private law with quite a number on commercial law. The Council of Europe lists 224 treaties, several on human rights but many on diverse subjects ranging from social and scientific topics to contemporary criminal matters such as money laundering, cybercrime, and insider trading: https://www.coe.int/en/web/conventions/full-list. The Hague Conference has also produced treaties on a range of private law matters, particularly in the area of family law and commercial law, such as international sale of goods: https://www.hcch.net/en/instruments/conventions.

International organizations tend to have several advantages over individual states as midwives for assisting in the production of treaties. Their secretariats may have specialist knowledge to assist in the preparation of drafts, they can provide administrative support, and can conveniently circulate necessary documents. Suitably large facilities for conferences may be found at some headquarters of international organizations. Details, such as simultaneous interpretation, may be simplified if an international organization is involved, and the organization can handle subsequent formalities, such as receiving deposits of instruments of ratification and circulating treaty information. Nevertheless, a diplomatic conference may still be held at the invitation of a particular state, although, as with the conference culminating in the 1969 Vienna Convention, the preliminary work, publication of records, and subsequent handling of stages necessary to bring the treaty into effect are increasingly likely to be accomplished by the relevant organization.[4]

'Bilateral' treaties are negotiated as and when the need arises to regulate relations between the two states concerned on a particular matter. This is usually initiated through diplomatic contacts. Commonly, drafts and written preparatory material are exchanged. Formal negotiations by delegations representing the two sides may take two or more rounds of meetings. These are often held in alternating capital cities. The negotiations will be finished by the leaders of the delegations initialling a text for referral to their respective authorities. It is a matter of choice and constitutional requirements whether signature is then sufficient to indicate commitment to be bound by the treaty, whether this is subject to ratification, or some other formality is required such as respective completion of necessary formalities. For short treaties, a formal exchange of notes is very common.[5]

---

[4] On international conferences see I Roberts (ed), *Satow's Diplomatic Practice* (7th edn, OUP 2017) ch 30, and on the shared role of the UN and Austria in holding the Vienna Conference see Final Act of the UN Conference on the Law of Treaties 1969, Doc A/CONF.39/26 https://legal.un.org/diplomaticconferences/1968_lot/docs.shtml (accessed 18 July 2022).

[5] See ch 1, section II.6. On making treaties see *UN Treaty Handbook* (2012) https://treaties.un.org/doc/source/publications/THB/English.pdf; and J Barrett and RC Beckman, *Handbook on Good Treaty Practice* (CUP 2020).

II Making a Treaty

1 Negotiating Treaties

The part of the Vienna Convention which covers what it describes as 'Conclusion and Entry into Force of Treaties' opens with a general proposition that: 'Every State possesses capacity to conclude treaties.'[6] This, when combined with the definition of 'party' and the obligation of faithful performance, reminds those dealing with treaties that whether a treaty is expressed in its opening words as being between heads of states, states, or governments, if the instrument is a treaty it binds the state, that is each state party to it regardless of change of head of state or government.[7] While that is a key factor in the law of treaties, for practical purposes in treaty-making it is necessary to identify who has the power to negotiate a treaty and to engage the state in binding commitments.

The Vienna Convention identifies a person as verifiably representing a state for the purpose of adopting or authenticating the text of a treaty, or for the purpose of expressing the consent of the state to be bound by a treaty, if he or she produces a document described as 'full powers'.[8] This is defined as:

> [a] document emanating from the competent authority of a State designating a person or persons to represent the State for negotiating, adopting or authenticating the text of a treaty, for expressing the consent of the State to be bound by a treaty, or for accomplishing any other act with respect to a treaty.[9]

However, the Convention does allow for deviation from this formality 'if it appears from the practice of the States concerned or from other circumstances that their intention was to consider that person as representing the State for such purposes and to dispense with full powers'.[10] Bilateral negotiations are often set up through diplomatic channels and the identity of the negotiator or members of the negotiating team will be communicated

---

[6] VCLT, art 6.
[7] See ibid art 2(1)(g): ' "party" means a State which has consented to be bound by the treaty and for which the treaty is in force'; and art 26: 'Every treaty in force is binding upon the parties to it and must be performed by them in good faith.'
[8] ibid art 7.
[9] ibid art 2(1)(c).
[10] ibid art 7(b).

in the same way, without the need therefore for a formal document of full powers.

There is also dispensation for those sometimes described as 'the big three' (heads of state, heads of government, and ministers for foreign affairs), for heads of mission (ambassadors, for treaties between their sending state and the receiving state), and for those accredited to international conferences and organizations for treaties being drawn up within the conference or organization.[11] Typically, at a diplomatic conference a 'credentials committee' will be set up to check powers of representatives. While the leader of a delegation may be equipped with full powers to sign if a satisfactory text emerges, further members of the delegation are likely to simply be notified as such to the host state or organization by the Ministry of Foreign Affairs of the sending state.

The entity which the person with full powers represents is termed in the Convention a 'negotiating state' which it identifies as one 'which took part in the drawing up and adoption of the text of the treaty'.[12] The significance of this definition mainly arises when it comes to becoming bound by a treaty and interpreting it. Negotiating states traditionally were present to sign the text at conclusion of a conference and later become bound by ratification, while other eligible states would become bound following accession. Particularly with older treaties where preparatory work was not always published, a state which had not participated in negotiations might not have all the back history of a treaty. In the case of modern multilateral treaties the records are more generally available. However, there are often many more states attending the diplomatic conference, at which key obstacles to agreement must ultimately be resolved, than there are participants in working groups or preparatory commissions drawing up the early drafts. As well as the obvious possibility of influencing the content of a treaty through participation in its negotiation, involvement in the final stage of its adoption will also enable a state to have an input into the interpretative material which surrounds adoption of a treaty, such as resolutions in the Final Act of the conference.

---

[11] ibid art 7(2).
[12] ibid art 2(1)(e).

2 'Concluding' a Treaty

The Vienna Convention refers several times to 'conclusion' of a treaty, but without indicating exactly when this is achieved.[13] For identification of a treaty it is regarded as concluded when it is signed. As previously noted, the accepted manner of citing a treaty is to couple its name with the place and date of signature. This tends to suggest that 'conclusion' matches the moment recorded in the word often put in capital letters in the testimonium, as in the Vienna Convention: 'DONE at Vienna, this twenty-third day of May, One thousand nine hundred and sixty-nine.'[14]

In some provisions of the Convention, however, 'conclusion' clearly has a broader meaning. Provisions under the Convention's heading of Part II ('Conclusion and Entry into Force of Treaties'), and of section 1 ('Conclusion of Treaties') relate not only to drawing up a treaty, its authentication, and signature, but also to how states are to consent to be bound. This goes well beyond the stage of signature and, via ratification, accession, etc., up to the stage of entry into force.

This all suggest that 'conclusion' is a process. Yet some provisions of the section (Articles 11–17) refer to different means of 'consent to be bound by a treaty', thus presupposing existence of a treaty. 'Treaty' is defined in the Convention as an 'international agreement *concluded* etc.'.[15] This suggests that by the time of the procedures in these articles, conclusion has already taken place, assuming a concluded agreement is a synonym for a treaty. The switch from reference to 'text of a treaty'—the phrase used in articles covering development of the treaty text, to reference to 'treaty' *(tout court)* comes between Article 10 (authentication of the text) and Article 11 (means of expressing consent); but this is not sufficient evidence to pinpoint this as the moment of conclusion for all purposes. Broadly, therefore, the various provisions in the Vienna Convention referring to conclusion embrace two notions, one being that conclusion occurs at a particular moment, the other being that it is a process. The context is the best guide for deciding which meaning applies.[16]

---

[13] See EW Vierdag, 'The Time of the "Conclusion" of a Multilateral Treaty: Article 30 of the Vienna Convention and Related Provisions' (1988) 59 BYBIL 75.
[14] United Nations Conference on the Law of Treaties, Official Records, Documents 301.
[15] VCLT, art 2(1)(a) (emphasis added).
[16] See further Vierdag (n 13); and R Gardiner, *Treaty Interpretation* (2nd edn, OUP 2015) 232–35.

3 'Adoption' and 'Authentication' of a Text

'Adoption' of the text of a treaty is viewed in the Vienna Convention as different from 'authentication'. The former refers to the vote (or consensus), at the end of a conference, agreeing on the text of the treaty. The latter denotes the physical evidence that the text is in final form. Thus the Convention provides that, unless otherwise agreed:

> The text of a treaty is established as authentic and definitive ... by the signature, signature *ad referendum* or initialling by the representatives of those States of the text of the treaty or of the Final Act of a conference incorporating the text.[17]

None of the steps described represents any commitment on behalf of the negotiators to bind the states which they represent. This is explicit in the term 'signature *ad referendum*', where a state's representative signs on the express understanding that the text will need to be referred to the authorities of the sending state. This notion applies to the other forms of authentication, except where signature is definitive (mostly nowadays in bilateral treaties).

In earlier times, an ambassador or delegation sent to a diplomatic conference would not have had the benefit of instantaneous methods of communication, but only the set of instructions taken to the negotiations. Those instructions would be unlikely to cover every eventuality. In such circumstances, the negotiating authority would extend to signing a treaty whose terms came sufficiently close to the instructions for the ambassador to be reasonably confident that the treaty should prove acceptable, but the state represented would not be bound until his signature was ratified after study of the text in the sending state and completion of constitutional processes there. If such study and processes required changes, it might be possible to achieve this by the inclusion of reservations (considered further below) in the instrument of ratification. Otherwise, if there were fundamental difficulties, no ratification would be forthcoming.

---

[17] VCLT, art 10.

4 Proceedings at a Diplomatic Conference

(a) Rules of procedure

The Convention sets out unanimity as the default position for adoption of a treaty text, with an alternative default of a two-thirds majority of those states present and voting at a diplomatic conference unless by the same majority they adopt a different rule.[18] This is a very rough and ready approximation to a general practice but does not amount to a rule of customary law. Given that only about half of the world's community of states are parties to the Vienna Convention, diplomatic conferences commonly adopt a complete set of rules akin to the standing orders of a parliamentary or legislative body.

Frequently, a conference will act rather in the same way as such a body, with a plenary gathering, that is all representatives meeting as required to parcel out work to committees, to receive and adopt (or amend) the committees' efforts, and to vote on a first, second, and final reading of the full text. The object of this procedure is to ensure that any text ultimately adopted is likely to receive widespread acceptance. That this is not always the result is confirmed by a number of multilateral treaties that have not come into force or received widespread participation. This may be because there is a democratic deficit in treaty-making in that foreign relations of states are conducted by governments, whereas final acceptance or approval of treaties generally involves legislatures which may be less willing to accept the compromises necessary to achieve the agreement of large numbers of states.

At a diplomatic conference, adoption of the rules of procedure will be one of the early agenda items. These commonly specify the voting majorities required at the various stages of the work of the conference. The importance of rules of procedure may not be immediately obvious. Their effect on treaties can be dramatic because of the distribution of power that they reflect and produce. Were Article 9 of the Vienna Convention a firm rule, greater regard would be paid to the notional sovereign equality of states. One example showing that this is not the case is the development of treaties for the protection of intellectual property rights, in particular the rights of inventors, authors, composers, artists and others. A long-established 'parent' treaty, widely known as 'the Paris Convention' of 1883,

---

[18] ibid art 9.

provided a rudimentary scheme for international protection in the sense of non-discrimination and other very basic rules. Early amendments up until about 1910 required unanimity for amending protocols to come into force. Once participation in the Paris Convention had become very widespread the unanimity rule for amendments was dropped, and successive treaties ('Acts' in the system's terminology) came into force for those states parties to them after a specified number had ratified the amending treaty.

However, when attempts were made in the early 1980s to revise the Paris Convention, partly to include certain advantages for developing countries, the first of four sessions of a diplomatic conference was effectively blocked by the USA's opposition to rules of procedure which would have allowed adoption of a new treaty by less than a unanimous vote.[19] A hugely expensive diplomatic conference lay largely idle for two weeks. Note that even without a unanimity rule, the USA would not have been bound by new measures unless it ratified any resulting revised Act or amending Protocol; but it did not want new measures to which it did not agree to come into force even among other states. While complete consensus at a diplomatic conference is desirable, particularly when considering treaties whose aim is a uniform regime, the large number of states in the international community may make such consensus unrealistic. However, the underlying political dynamics will tend to triumph in international law making by treaty. Revision of the Paris Convention was never achieved and much of the attention to intellectual property became the province of the World Trade Organization.

(b) Languages

A further important element in a diplomatic conference is deciding on languages. This is not just a matter of the languages to be used for negotiating but, more importantly, for the text of the treaty. Simultaneous interpretation deals with the former, but achieving precisely that same import in different languages is more exacting. In major diplomatic conferences issues over alignment of languages commonly arise in a drafting committee but there is no certainty that the representatives will always achieve concordant meanings. One of the main functions of the drafting committee is to fine tune the text, to ensure consistency and coherence. Where negotiations have worked on drafts in a limited number of languages, production of the final wording

---

[19] WE Schuyler, 'Paris Convention for the Protection of Industrial Property: A View of the Proposed Revisions' (1982) 8 North Carolina J Intl L & Com Reg 155, 159.

of the treaty in all authentic languages may not be accomplished until a late stage. With the aid of the secretariat, where the conference is backed by an international organization, this task is sometimes described as part of the *toilette finale*.[20]

Article 33 of the Vienna Convention (on interpretation of treaties authenticated in more than one language) was negotiated against a background of concerns that the provision should reflect that a treaty is a single agreement expressed in different languages. Hence its first paragraph refers to the case 'where a treaty has been authenticated in two or more languages' and prescribes that 'the text is equally authoritative in each language', referring to the treaty and text in the singular. However, the wording then departs from the notion of a single text by adding the rider 'unless the treaty provides or the parties agree that, in case of divergence, a particular text shall prevail'. The rest of the article accepts that 'texts' can be authenticated in different languages, but 'versions' (typically so-called 'official' translations promulgated by states in their own languages) are only authentic if so agreed by the parties.

(c) Outcome of negotiations

The classic outcome of a diplomatic conference is that an authenticated text is 'opened for signature' and a record of the conference is produced as a 'final act'. Unless the treaty provides for states to become parties to it by signature alone, opening for signature usually provides an opportunity for states to sign subject to later ratification. Reservations and interpretative declarations may be formulated at this stage and appended to signature, but these should be re-stated at ratification to indicate that they are maintained. As explained above in the context of the term 'authentication', the effect of such signature is to indicate acceptance of the finality of negotiations and an intention to ratify later. Signature used to take place on a single day only, but in several more recent treaties provision is made for the treaty to be open for signature for a specified period, and sometimes at different places.[21]

---

[20] DB Hollis (ed), *The Oxford Guide to Treaties* (2nd edn, OUP 2020) 690, fn 43.
[21] See eg UN Convention on the Law of the Sea, signed 10 December 1982, which provided in art 305 that the Convention would remain open for signature until 9 December 1984 at the Ministry of Foreign Affairs of Jamaica, and also from 1 July 1983 until 9 December 1984, at UN Headquarters in New York; another example is the Treaty on the Non-Proliferation of Nuclear Weapons (London, Moscow, and Washington, 1 July 1968) which provided in art IX for signature by any state at one of the three depositary locations until its entry into force after which a state could accede to it at any time.

Signature in these circumstances is only a very loose indication of expected ratification. Sometimes ratification is significantly delayed, possibly for decades.[22] The further effects of such signature may be difficult to identify. According to the Vienna Convention signature engages an obligation 'to refrain from acts which would defeat the object and purpose of a treaty' until ratification or until the signatory state 'shall have made its intention clear not to become a party to the treaty'.[23] Acts which would defeat the object and purpose of a treaty are nowhere authoritatively listed. The clear example would be where a state had signed a treaty agreeing to transfer territory or some item to another state and before ratification, and without any notice or indication that it was resiling from its signature, it transferred the territory or item to a third state.

Other situations may be less clear, but there is certainly no obligation to implement the substantive provisions of the treaty unless there is an indication in the treaty or elsewhere that signature triggers provisional application (considered further below). There is, however, scope for a signatory state to be involved in stages which lead up to entry into force, such as involvement in preparatory conferences or to be engaged in interaction over reservations formulated by other potential parties. Further, the provisions of a treaty regulating the authentication of its text, how states to be bound, when and how it comes into force, reservations, the functions of the depositary, and in the words of the Vienna Convention 'other matters' arising necessarily before the entry into force, apply from the time of the adoption of its text.[24] Accepting the operation of these provisions is a necessary concomitant of signature.

It may have been a misunderstanding about the nature of signature of a treaty that instigated or contributed to the furore which arose when President Bush was reported as wanting to 'unsign' the Rome Statute establishing the International Criminal Court, which had been signed for the USA under the instructions of his predecessor, President Clinton. There is, however, no procedure for 'unsigning' a treaty, nor need there be as a

---

[22] See International Convention for the Unification of Certain Rules relating to the Immunity of State-owned Vessels (Brussels, 10 April 1926) CLXXVI LNTS 199, no 4062, which Poland and the United Kingdom signed on 10 April 1926 but only ratified in 1976 and 1979, respectively; for two examples of the USA not ratifying treaties for decades see CA Bradley, 'Unratified Treaties, Domestic Politics, and the U.S. Constitution' (2007) 48 Harv Intl LJ 307, 309–10.
[23] VCLT, art 18.
[24] ibid art 24(4).

clear indication of an intention not to proceed to ratification is all that is required.[25]

(d) Depositary functions

Bilateral treaties are most commonly drawn up in the languages of the two parties. They each retain an executed text and can communicate with each other over the modalities of bringing the treaty into force and its implementation. A multilateral treaty needs a guardian, described in treaty practice as the 'depositary'. The depositary is nominated in the treaty or elsewhere by the negotiating states. Traditionally, this has been the host state of the conference at which the treaty was adopted, whose ministry of foreign affairs retains the treaty and records of the conference. With the increase in number of multilateral treaties the scope for nominating depositaries has grown. The Vienna Convention recognizes as possible depositaries one or more states, an international organization or the chief administrative officer of an organization.[26] The Convention also acknowledges the importance of the depositary by including quite detailed provisions, while noting that: 'The functions of the depositary of a treaty are international in character and the depositary is under an obligation to act impartially in their performance.'[27] This applies irrespective of whether the treaty is in force or only in force for some parties, actual or potential.

From the Convention's long list of depositary functions, there are some to which attention should be particularly drawn.[28] The depositary is responsible for providing certified copies of the treaty to the parties and states entitled to become parties. This does not directly enable the public to obtain authentic copies, but the depositary is required to register the treaty with the Secretariat of the United Nations. The Convention reiterates the obligation in the UN Charter to transmit treaties after entry into force for registration, or for filing and recording, and for publication.[29] Hence the public should have access to an authoritative text of a treaty in the UN Treaty Series, albeit with considerable delay in many instances.

---

[25] In the case of the USA and the Rome Statute this was a letter to the UN Secretary-General: for text see LA McLaurin, 'Can the President Unsign a Treaty: A Constitutional Inquiry' (2006) 84 Wash U L Rev 1941, fn 6; see also Bradley (n 22); and ET Swaine, 'Unsigning' (2003) 55 Stan L Rev 2061.
[26] VCLT, art 76.
[27] ibid art 76(2).
[28] The full list is in ibid art 77.
[29] See also art 102 of UN Charter.

Essential tasks of the depositary are receiving any signatures and instruments (ratifications, accessions, etc), and notifications and communications relating to the treaty. Central to its functions is the obligation to keep all parties and states entitled to become parties informed of every such signature, instrument, notification etc. This is particularly significant in the case of reservations and objections to reservations, as well as where a treaty is at the stage of coming into force. The depositary has no authority to interpret on behalf of the parties the information which it distributes or to control aspects of the operation of the treaty and its final clauses. Where there are differences among states over the interpretation and effects of the matter circulated by the depositary, it is for the states concerned, or any system established in the treaty, rather than the depositary to resolve the difficulty.

5 Consenting to Be Bound by a Treaty

(a) Decision to be bound

The Convention does not prescribe what measures must be fulfilled within a state for it to decide that it will become a party to a treaty. Two provisions, however, are particularly relevant. Article 26 provides that 'A party may not invoke the provisions of its internal law as justification for its failure to perform a treaty', while Article 46 provides:

> (1) A State may not invoke the fact that its consent to be bound by a treaty has been expressed in violation of a provision of its internal law regarding competence to conclude treaties as invalidating its consent unless that violation was manifest and concerned a rule of its internal law of fundamental importance.
> (2) A violation is manifest if it would be objectively evident to any State conducting itself in the matter in accordance with normal practice and in good faith.

Article 46 is largely self-explanatory and provides a test which it is very difficult for a state to meet.[30] Article 26 does not actually require a state to

---

[30] See *Land and Maritime Boundary between Cameroon and Nigeria (Cameroon v Nigeria: Equatorial Guinea intervening)* [2002] ICJ Rep 303, 429–31, where the Court rejected the assertion that Nigeria was not bound by a declaration constituting a treaty which entered into force on signature and which the Nigerian head of state had signed without ratification.

take measures to implement a treaty at the point at which it expresses its consent to be bound, but prudent conduct demands that a state checks that it will be able to meet its obligations as soon as the treaty enters into force for that state. This means that any necessary legislative or administrative measures are ready to be activated. Otherwise the state risks finding itself in breach of the treaty upon its entry into force.

(b) Signature as consent to be bound

Consenting to be bound is the subject of a general list of possibilities. Some are then the subject of particular attention in individual provisions. The general provision states: 'The consent of a State to be bound by a treaty may be expressed by signature, exchange of instruments constituting a treaty, ratification, acceptance, approval or accession, or by any other means if so agreed.'[31]

This provision, coupled with Article 12, which provides that signature is binding in three cases, offers instant confusion to the unwary. Having just established in Article 10 that signature is one of the means of showing completion of negotiations and that the text is authentic and definitive, here is the Convention's indication that signature can sometimes also be the definitive consent of a state to be bound by a treaty. The situations where it is definitive are where the treaty so provides, where there is other evidence showing that the negotiating states so agreed, or the intention of a state to give that effect to signature is in the representative's full powers or was expressed during the negotiation.[32]

From the confluence of the possibilities in Articles 11 and 12 arises the much encountered, but often mistaken, assumption that a 'signatory' state is a 'party' to a treaty. It may be, but more commonly it is not bound without having also lodged an instrument of ratification and the treaty having come into force for that state. The safe assumption is that 'signatories', unless shown otherwise, have only signed a treaty, while 'parties' are states bound by a treaty if it is in force. From the standpoint of the Vienna Convention, unless the treaty has come into force on signature, a state which signs a treaty become a 'contracting state' as defined in the

---

[31] VCLT, art 11.
[32] ibid art 12, which also acknowledges initialling constituting signature if so agreed and signature ad referendum becoming full signature if confirmed; on interpretation of 'contracting' see further ch 4, n 18 below.

Convention. 'Contracting' here indicates 'a State which has consented to be bound by the treaty, whether or not the treaty has entered into force'.[33]

This definition of 'contracting state' also covers states which have consented to be bound by the further means that are offered (ratification, acceptance, approval, accession etc), if the treaty is not yet in force when they give their consent to be bound or does not become binding for them until the lapse of a specified time. The same obligation applies to a contracting state as to a state which has signed subject to ratification, that is to refrain from acts which would defeat the object and purpose of the treaty. This is described in the case of a contracting state as an obligation continuing 'pending the entry into force of the treaty and provided that such entry into force is not unduly delayed'.[34] Unfortunately, in treaty drafting 'Contracting State', or sometimes 'High Contracting Party', is used to describe a party or prospective party, and the sensible VCLT definitions have failed to replace such usage with uniform, defined practice.

(c) Means of consent: ratification, accession etc.

The two-stage process of signature followed by ratification is now pretty much the norm for multilateral treaties. It has the advantage that it allows for orderly procedures leading to the treaty's entry into force and affords prospective parties time for consideration and implementation. However, signature subject to ratification is not the only option available for joining multilateral treaties. It has been long accepted that states which have not participated in negotiations, or which have not signed the treaty when it was open for signature, might become parties by lodging an instrument of 'accession'. This is a formal document, similar to an instrument of ratification in its undertaking of a commitment to be bound by the treaty and to perform fully the obligations which the treaty imposes.

The main point to note here is the definition in the Convention of 'ratification', 'acceptance', 'approval', and 'accession', which means, in each case, 'the international act so named whereby a State establishes on the international plane its consent to be bound by a treaty'.[35] Thus from the standpoint of international law, lodging an instrument of ratification with a depository or with the other party in the case of a bilateral treaty, is an act of purely international significance and is not to be confused (as it often is)

[33] ibid art 2(1)(f).
[34] ibid art 18(b).
[35] ibid art 2(1)(b).

with domestic measures to implement the treaty or to put the state in a constitutional position to become a party to it.

(d) Other forms of consent

International organizations become parties to treaties in essentially the same manner as states. There are, however, some circumstances in which states may become bound as members of an organization, such as the European Union. In principle, an international organization is an entity having legal personality distinct from its members. It is a matter of the internal competence of such an organization, of the substance of the treaty, and of the provisions in the final clauses of the particular treaty whether the member states of an organization need to become parties in their own right as well as the organization.

There is also the possibility of states becoming parties to treaties by succession where they have become independent from a state which had entered into treaties which the new state may wish to maintain. Some states have approached this matter on a treaty-by-treaty basis, by lodging a statement with the Secretary General of the United Nations indicating their approach to succession to treaties, or a combination of the two. The 1978 Vienna Convention on Succession of States in Respect of Treaties entered into force in 1996. However, it has a very small number of parties and it would be difficult to assert that it represents customary international law for the most part. It is controversial because of its differentiation between those states which have achieved independence from colonial rule and those which achieve independence by separation from a previous state.[36]

III Entry into Force

1 Mechanisms for Start Up

There is a range of possible procedures for entry into force. Bilateral treaties commonly enter into force upon signature, when the parties exchange instruments of ratification or when both sides have notified the other of completion of their domestic constitutional requirements. In the case of multilateral treaties, it was commonly the procedure that a treaty would

---

[36] 1496 UNTS 3, no 33356, it has twenty-three parties (as at 8 March 2023); and see A Sarvarian, 'Codifying the Law of State Succession: A Futile Endeavour?' (2016) 27 EJIL 789.

enter into force when all the negotiating states had consented to be bound, a procedure which is still the default position in the Vienna Convention if arrangements for entry into force are not set out in the treaty.[37] However, the more common arrangement now is for a treaty to indicate that it is to enter into force a specified number of days after the last of a stated number of instruments of ratification (or accession etc) has been deposited. Typically, such a treaty will then enter into force for any particular state which subsequently ratifies it, or accedes to it, a specified number of days after deposit of its instrument of ratification.

Such matters are very much in the hands of the negotiating states. Because ratification may take a long time, some treaties, or parts of treaties, are given provisional application. This means that the treaty is given temporary effect before general entry into force.[38] This can be specified in the treaty itself or by some other arrangement made by the negotiators, such as a resolution of the diplomatic conference at which a multilateral treaty is adopted. The Vienna Convention provides for termination of such provisional application (unless otherwise agreed) upon a state notifying others of its decision not to become a party to the treaty.[39] Provisional agreement can effectively achieve full force for the treaty. Thus, for example, the General Agreement on Tariffs and Trade (the predecessor of the regime applied by the World Trade Organization) never entered into force definitively but was applied provisionally for over forty years.[40]

2 Time Factors

Treaties do not have retroactive effect unless it is specified in the treaty that it is to so apply.[41] The Vienna Convention specifically applies only to treaties concluded by states parties to it after its entry into force, but this is stated to be without prejudice to the application of any rules to which a treaty would be subject under international law independently of the Convention.[42] This means that where the Convention states a rule of customary law its

---

[37] 1978 VCLT, art 24(2).
[38] ibid art 25; see also ILC Guide to Provisional Application of Treaties, with commentaries thereto, 2021 ILC Annual Report, ch V, UN Doc A/76/10.
[39] VCLT, art 25(2).
[40] Protocol of Provisional Application of the General Agreement on Tariffs and Trade 1947, 55 UNTS 308 no 814.
[41] VCLT, art 28.
[42] ibid art 4.

statement as a rule applicable in treaty relations does not alter its status as a rule of customary law. This can appear to produce a backdated rule. For example, the rules on treaty interpretation were not free from doubt as to their status as rules nor was there evidence of immediate acceptance of the formulation of their content at the time when the Convention was adopted. Yet they have since come to be accepted as statements of customary international law and thus have been applied to treaties concluded long before adoption of the Convention and before the later overt acceptance of the status of the rules.[43]

While the principle of non-retroactive application expressed in the Vienna Convention takes the point of conclusion of a treaty as the critical date, application of the provision does not appear to have raised the issue of the precise meaning of 'conclusion' considered above. Nevertheless, the term 'conclusion' has been avoided in the provision setting default rules on application of successive treaties relating to the same subject matter.[44] This refers to 'earlier' and 'later' treaties where a succession of treaties cover the same subject matter. The situation is not problematic where all parties to one multilateral treaty are parties to an earlier one or where rights and obligations can be implemented on an effectively bilateral basis. In the former case the later treaty applies, but leaving provisions of the earlier treaty applicable where compatible with the later one. In the second situation, treaty relations govern, so that the latest treaty in effect in the relations between any pair of states applies.[45] However, where the objective is a uniform regime and rules in one treaty are different in a later one applicable to the same facts, neither the Vienna Convention nor provisions in the later treaty can resolve the conflict. With the proliferation of treaties an increasing number of conflicting obligations may be expected to arise.[46]

---

[43] See eg *Arbitration regarding the Iron Rhine (IJzeren Rijn) Railway (Belgium/Netherlands)* (2005) XXVII RIAA 35 at 62, para 45 on application of the Vienna rules to nineteenth-century treaties.
[44] VCLT, art 30, but note also ibid art 40, which sets out default rules for states becoming parties to amending treaties.
[45] ibid art 30(4).
[46] For examples of attempts to deal with these difficulties see J Hill, *Aust's Modern Treaty Law and Practice* (4th edn, CUP 2023), chs 12, 15.

4
What the Treaty Means

> In most instances interpretation involves *giving* a meaning to a text.[1]

I Interpretation and Its Rules

Many, if not most, encounters with treaties (beyond routine applications) are concerned with some issue or difference over interpretation of a treaty's provisions. Even in routine applications it is necessary to give meaning to the provisions of the treaty before determining how they may apply to particular facts or issues. Professor Waldock, as Special Rapporteur of the International Law Commission (ILC) on the law of treaties, endorsed an earlier description of interpretation:

> The process of interpretation, rightly conceived, cannot be regarded as a mere mechanical one of drawing inevitable meanings from the words in a text, or of searching for and discovering some pre-existing specific intention of the parties with respect to every situation arising under a treaty ... In most instances interpretation involves *giving* a meaning to a text.[2]

'Giving' meaning is a better description than finding or discovering the meaning. This is because an interpreter has a role which necessarily goes beyond digging into the text to unearth a buried treasure. The 1969 Vienna

---

[1] Waldock, Third Report on the Law of Treaties [1964-II] Yearbook of the ILC 53, para 1, citing Pt III of the Harvard draft codification of international law in (1935) 29 AJIL Supp 653, 946 (original emphasis).
[2] ibid.

Convention provides some guidance to help the interpreter towards an interpretation. It indicates what is to be taken into account and, to a very much lesser extent, how this material is to be evaluated. However, the 'Vienna rules' are only a set of principles and guidance towards an interpretation. They do not complete the job. The interpreter therefore must use his or her own skill and judgement to reach an actual interpretation—to give meaning to the treaty.

Much of the process of developing the Vienna rules involved reducing draft articles generated in the ILC to a minimum and striking out difficult or contentious points. This has had two key consequences. First, the rules are so short that there is no point in trying to summarize them or paraphrase them (as some courts have unwisely attempted to do).[3] Second, the rules are somewhat elliptical and themselves need interpretation and explanation, sometimes best achieved by finding practical examples. Anyone interpreting a treaty needs first to familiarize themselves with the rules (including the headings of the articles). This section of the Vienna Convention has just three articles:

Section 3. Interpretation of Treaties

Article 31

General rule of interpretation

1. A treaty shall be interpreted in good faith in accordance with the ordinary meaning to be given to the terms of the treaty in their context and in the light of its object and purpose.
2. The context for the purpose of the interpretation of a treaty shall comprise, in addition to the text, including its preamble and annexes:
   (a) any agreement relating to the treaty which was made between all the parties in connection with the conclusion of the treaty;
   (b) any instrument which was made by one or more parties in connection with the conclusion of the treaty and accepted by the other parties as an instrument related to the treaty.

---

[3] For example, in *Ben Nevis (Holdings) Ltd v Revenue and Customs Commissioners* [2013] EWCA Civ 578, the English Court of Appeal did quote two of the three Vienna articles on interpretation, but the effect was somewhat outweighed by its much longer list of what it described as a 'summary of principles applicable to the interpretation of treaties'.

3. There shall be taken into account, together with the context:
   (a) any subsequent agreement between the parties regarding the interpretation of the treaty or the application of its provisions;
   (b) any subsequent practice in the application of the treaty which establishes the agreement of the parties regarding its interpretation;
   (c) any relevant rules of international law applicable in the relations between the parties.
4. A special meaning shall be given to a term if it is established that the parties so intended.

Article 32

Supplementary means of interpretation

Recourse may be had to supplementary means of interpretation, including the preparatory work of the treaty and the circumstances of its conclusion, in order to confirm the meaning resulting from the application of article 31, or to determine the meaning when the interpretation according to article 31:
(a) leaves the meaning ambiguous or obscure; or
(b) leads to a result which is manifestly absurd or unreasonable.

Article 33

Interpretation of treaties authenticated in two or more languages

1. When a treaty has been authenticated in two or more languages, the text is equally authoritative in each language, unless the treaty provides or the parties agree that, in case of divergence, a particular text shall prevail.
2. A version of the treaty in a language other than one of those in which the text was authenticated shall be considered an authentic text only if the treaty so provides or the parties so agree.
3. The terms of the treaty are presumed to have the same meaning in each authentic text.
4. Except where a particular text prevails in accordance with paragraph 1, when a comparison of the authentic texts discloses a difference of meaning which the application of articles 31 and 32 does not remove,

the meaning which best reconciles the texts, having regard to the object and purpose of the treaty, shall be adopted.[4]

Although the quoted texts are relatively brief, discussion of these principles risks being clouded by the language used in stating them. In particular, the word 'rule' may suggest some form of algorithmic or algebraic process that should lead to the correct meaning. As Waldock indicated (above), this is far from the case. What are commonly described as 'rules' for treaty interpretation in the 1969 Vienna Convention are principles or guidelines which mostly serve to provide help in finding a structure for a reasoned elucidation, after indicating a starting point for this. They give an indication of what is relevant material with some hints on how that material is to be used to formulate a properly reasoned interpretation. Waldock (again), in explaining the drafts that became the Vienna rules, wrote:

> The Commission was fully conscious ... of the undesirability—if not impossibility—of confining the process of interpretation within rigid rules, and the provisions of [the draft Articles] ... do not appear to constitute a code of rules incompatible with the required degree of flexibility ... any 'principles' found by the Commission to be 'rules' should, so far as seems advisable, be formulated as such. In a sense all 'rules' of interpretation have the character of 'guidelines' since their application in a particular case depends so much on the appreciation of the context and the circumstances of the point to be interpreted.[5]

The titles of the first two of the Vienna articles reveal significant features. First, for Article 31, 'rule' is in the singular in the title because the whole of the article, not just its first paragraph, constitutes the general rule for interpreting treaties. Second, 'supplementary' in the title of Article 32 means what it says. It does not mean 'subordinate' or 'subsidiary', except to the extent that one of the two uses of supplementary means is to 'confirm' a meaning reached by application of the general rule. The other use of supplementary means, which applies when the specified criteria are present (ambiguity, obscurity, manifest absurdity, or unreasonableness), is to

---

[4] Vienna Convention on the Law of Treaties, signed at Vienna, 23 May 1969: UN Doc A/Conf 39/28; UNTS 1155, 331; UKTS 58 (1980), Cmnd 7964; ATS 1974 No 2; (1969) 8 ILM 679; text here as in UN print of 2005 at https://legal.un.org/ilc/texts/instruments/english/conventions/1_1_1969.pdf.
[5] Sixth Report of Special Rapporteur (Waldock) [1966-II]) Yearbook of the ILC 94, para 1.

'determine' the meaning. In this latter case, providing the key element or elements to 'determine' the meaning is clearly neither subordinate nor subsidiary but, rather, definitive.

The use of the singular term 'rule' for a multiple set of precepts has its ancient or archaic analogy in what the *Oxford English Dictionary* describes as 'The code of discipline or body of regulations observed by a religious order' (eg the Rule of Saint Benedict, c 529 AD, consisting of over seventy chapters). The underlying idea, and the mode of use of a 'general rule' composed of several elements, was expressed in the ILC's Commentary on the then draft articles on interpretation:

> The Commission, by heading the article 'General rule of interpretation' in the singular and by underlining the connexion between paragraphs 1 and 2 and again between paragraph 3 and the two previous paragraphs, intended to indicate that the application of the means of interpretation in the article would be a single combined operation. All the various elements, as they were present in any given case, would be thrown into the crucible, and their interaction would give the legally relevant interpretation. Thus, Article 27 [now numbered article 31] is entitled 'General *rule* of interpretation' in the singular, not 'General *rules*' in the plural, because the Commission desired to emphasize that the process of interpretation is a unity and that the provisions of the article form a single, closely integrated rule.[6]

This 'crucible' approach was designed, as the Commission explained, to result in 'a single combined operation'.[7] An arbitral tribunal offered a slightly different description of how to apply the general rule, describing it as 'a process of progressive encirclement' which, by cycling through investigation of

---

[6] United Nations Conference on the Law of Treaties: Official Records: Documents of the Conference, A/CONF.39/11/Add.2, 39, para 8 and [1966-II] Yearbook of the ILC 219–20, para 8 (emphasis in original). The Commentary (ILC Commentary) accompanied the draft articles considered by the Vienna Conference in 1968–69 as the starting point for its preparation and adoption of the Vienna Convention. There are suggestions that para (1) alone of art 31 constitutes the general rule of interpretation in O Dörr and K Schmalenbach (eds), *Vienna Convention on the Law of Treaties: A Commentary* (Springer 2018) 561, 579–80. However, no substantiation for this is given, and the Commentary regards paras (2) and (3) as 'designed to incorporate the elements of interpretation set out therein into the general rule contained in para 1' (at 561), while para (4) provides an exception to para (1)), thus aligning the approach with the ILC's indication that the provisions of art 31 form a single rule.

[7] ILC Commentary (n 6) para 8.

the relevant elements, 'iteratively closes in upon the proper interpretation'.[8] The tribunal was examining the application of the first paragraph of Article 31, but the description may help understand how the whole general rule is to be applied. The interpretative elements set out in the general rule are not hierarchical, but they suggest a logical scheme for forming an interpretation.[9] Since the weight to be given to each particular element is dependent on the circumstances of the specific treaty and the issues that have arisen, the idea of iteratively closing in on the interpretation indicates the scope for going back through the elements as a judgement is progressively formed on their respective importance.

The opening words of the general rule of interpretation indicate that it is the *treaty* which is to be interpreted but that it is the *terms* of the treaty whose ordinary meaning is to be the starting point, their context moderating selection of that meaning, and the process being further illuminated by the treaty's object and purpose. While stressing that the general rule operates as a single combined process, for analytical purposes its elements must be separated. Hence each element is briefly noted here with examples of their application and the issues that arise.

II Elements of the General Rule

1 Good Faith: VCLT Article 31(1)

Much invoked, and accepted as a guiding factor in treaty interpretation (as well as in the law of treaties generally), good faith has a role as an adjunct to the process of interpretation rather than as an independent element.[10] One of the few examples of good faith functioning as an independent element was the *Venezuelan Preferential Claims* case.[11] Venezuela had agreed with certain states (referred to as the allied Powers) that 'all claims against

---

[8] *Aguas del Tunari v Bolivia* (ICSID ARB/02/03), Award of 21 October 2005, para 91.
[9] ILC Commentary (n 6) para 9: '[i]t was considerations of logic, not any obligatory legal hierarchy, which guided the Commission in arriving at the arrangement proposed in the article.'
[10] On good faith in international law generally see PJF O'Connor, *Good Faith in International Law* (Dartmouth 1991); R Kolb, *Good Faith in International Law* (Hart Publishing 2017); and Bin Cheng, *General Principles of Law as Applied by International Courts and Tribunals* (Stevens and Sons 1953) Pt II: 'The Principle of Good Faith' 105 ff; on good faith in the Vienna rules see R Gardiner, *Treaty Interpretation* (OUP 2015) 167–81.
[11] (1904) 1 HCR 55, esp 60–61; see also Cheng (n 10) 107–08.

Venezuela' should be the subject of special guarantees. The question then arose whether 'all claims' in the eventual Protocol meant that those of every creditor state should be given exactly the same guaranteed funding (including so-called neutral Powers), or whether the allied Powers which had negotiated the treaty should be paid off first. The arbitral tribunal invoked good faith as imposing a duty on the Government of Venezuela, when espousing the words 'all claims' in their negotiations with the allied Powers alone, such that the words could only mean the claims of these latter states.

The ICJ has not had occasion to place stress on good faith as a determining element in treaty interpretation. Judge Schwebel has, however, invoked good faith in a dissenting opinion to question whether an ICJ majority judgment had applied the Vienna rules properly when deciding whether Qatar and Bahrain had agreed that either state might refer their dispute to the ICJ. The majority had asserted that whatever may have been the motives of the parties, the Court would view the words used in certain minutes (which constituted an international agreement) as expressing their common intent, rather than looking to the preparatory work to elucidate their intent. Judge Schwebel saw the Court's approach as devaluing the actual intention of the parties and considered that it did not give sufficient or proper weight to the preparatory work to such an extent that it did not 'comport with a good faith interpretation of the treaty's terms'.[12]

Good faith has been taken to import a degree of reasonableness.[13] It was also regarded by the ILC as incorporating the principle of effectiveness in treaty interpretation. This principle has two manifestations. One is an established rule of legal construction—that a provision should be interpreted to give it some meaning rather than none (graced with the Latin formulation *ut res magis valeat quam pereat*). The more general application of the principle is that the interpreter should try to realize the object and purpose of the treaty, which is to say adopt a teleological approach so far as the terms allow. The ILC summed it up: 'When a treaty is open to two interpretations one of which does and the other does not enable the treaty to have

---

[12] *Maritime Delimitation and Territorial Questions between Qatar and Bahrain (Qatar v Bahrain)* (Jurisdiction and Admissibility) [1995] ICJ Rep 6, 35–37.
[13] See eg *Case Concerning the Auditing of Accounts Between the Kingdom of the Netherlands and the French Republic pursuant to the Additional Protocol of 25 September 1991 to the Convention on the Protection of the Rhine against Pollution by Chlorides of 3 December 1976 (Netherlands v France)*, Arbitral Award of 12 March 2004, 144 ILR 259, 290–300, paras 54–79; *United States—Import Prohibition of Certain Shrimp and Shrimp Products* WTO Report of Appellate Board AB-1998-4, WT/DS58/AB/R (12 October 1998) paras 158–59.

appropriate effects, good faith and the objects and purposes of the treaty demand that the former interpretation should be adopted.'[14]

2 Ordinary Meaning, Context, Object, and Purpose: VCLT Article 31(1)

While the ILC stressed that the whole of Article 31 constitutes the general rule of interpretation, it might of course be that in an actual instance of interpretation none of the elements beyond those mentioned in the first paragraph of Article 31 are present. This could explain why in many cases attention is given only to the article's first paragraph. It does not, however, explain why criticism of the Vienna rules suggests that they are overconcerned with textual and literal meaning of terms used. True, there was previously an established principle that it is not permissible to interpret that which has no need of interpretation, ie where the plain meaning is clear.[15] However, the Vienna rules effectively acknowledge that it is not as simple as that. The context, as well as the object and purpose of the treaty, must be taken into account in selecting which ordinary meaning is appropriate.

Professor McDougal was a prime instigator of the notion that that so-called textual interpretation would lead to literal interpretation. He directed his criticism at what he saw in the Vienna rules as an 'insistent emphasis upon an impossible, conformity-imposing textuality'. The effect was to suggest that there is undue attention paid to the ordinary meaning of terms used in a treaty.[16] This chimes in with a fairly common tendency to mistake the first paragraph of Article 31 as the whole of the general rule of interpretation and even to truncate that to ordinary meaning. Yet the ILC, and the text of Article 31, make it very clear that the *starting point* is the ordinary meaning of the terms used *in their context and in the light of the object and purpose of the treaty*.[17]

---

[14] Commentary on draft articles [1966-II] Yearbook of the ILC 219, para 6; and see use of object and purpose by the ICJ to hold that its order of provisional measures was mandatory in effect: *LaGrand (Germany v USA)* [2001] ICJ Rep 466, 502–06, paras 101–09.

[15] Emmerich Vattel, *Vattel's The Law of Nations*, Book II, Ch XVII, *The Interpretation on Treaties* (1758 edition, trans by C G Fenwick) (Washington DC: Carnegie Institution, 1916), § 263; and see further Gardiner (n 10) ch 2, section 3.

[16] MS McDougal, 'The International Law Commission's Draft Articles upon Interpretation: Textuality *Redivivus*' (1967) 61 AJIL 992.

[17] See Official Records of the United Nations Conference on the Law of Treaties, vol 3 (Documents of the Conference), ILC Commentary on Draft Articles, 40, para (9).

This is not a mandate for literal interpretation. It is the context which establishes (or confirms), for example, that the term 'Contracting States' imports a relationship between each state and a treaty, rather than that the states are getting smaller![18] Further, the multiplicity of meanings offered by dictionaries for most words rebuts any criticism of the Vienna rules for their alleged over-reliance on the 'ordinary meaning'. It makes selection of ordinary meaning from a range of meanings inevitable. Recourse must be had to context and the other aids prescribed by the rules for selection of the appropriate ordinary meaning. This was well demonstrated by Judge Anderson at the International Tribunal for the Law of the Sea when considering whether the word 'bond' included the possibility of conditions which are non-financial in nature. He found twelve different meanings in *Webster's Dictionary* and fourteen in the *Oxford English Dictionary* (including, he noted, the name of the type of special paper used for the originals of the judgment in the case which the Court was deciding). He narrowed the choice down to the two meanings having a financial and a legal connotation as these were the ones directly bearing on the issues in the case. He homed in on the latter because the use of a bond to enable release of an arrested vessel is clearly part of a legal process rather than a purely financial transaction.[19]

Context in the Vienna rules means not just the provisions immediately surrounding a key word or phrase under interpretation, but also the whole treaty and associated instruments in a broader sense as identified in Article 31(2). However, the idea of 'context' in connection with a treaty risks being understood to include the circumstances surrounding the negotiation and motivations which gave rise to the treaty. In the Vienna rules the circumstances surrounding conclusion of a treaty are specifically mentioned as supplementary means (Article 32). They are not an element in the general rule. It also needs to be noted that the object and purpose mentioned in the general rule is the object and purpose of the treaty. Giving effect to this inevitably means taking account in many instances of a plurality of objects and purposes. However, in giving effect to the immediate context in which

---

[18] The Court of Appeal in the United Kingdom considered the meaning of a 'contracting country' as contrasted with 'contracting States' in the context of a treaty on carriage of goods by road, but it did not consider shrinkage: *Chloride Industrial Batteries v F & W Freight* [1989] 1 WLR 823; and see R Gardiner, 'Air Law's Fog' (1990) 43 CLP 159, 167–70.

[19] Judge Anderson (dissenting) in *The 'Volga' (Russian Federation v Australia) (2002)* (2003) 42 ILM 159, 188–90 and 192.

a controversial term or phrase is located, the object and purpose of those provisions is relevant. That is an inherent part of the notion of context.

How a court may deal with an argument based on a literal meaning by taking account of the context is vividly shown by *Witold Litwa v Poland*, a case before the European Court of Human Rights.[20] The claimant asserted that his detention for a few hours at a sobering up centre after being assessed by a doctor as 'moderately intoxicated' was not in accordance with the European Convention on Human Rights. Article 5(1)(e) of that treaty allows 'the lawful detention ... of persons of unsound mind, alcoholics or drug addicts or vagrants'.

The claimant's argument was that an 'alcoholic' is someone addicted, not someone who is merely drunk. The Court recognized that common usage of the term 'alcoholics' denotes addiction, but the immediate context included other categories of people detained in order to be given medical treatment, or because of considerations dictated by social policy, or on both these grounds. Taking the main reasons why the Convention allowed detention as being not only danger to public safety but also the detainee's own interests as necessitating detention, the Court saw the object and purpose of the treaty provision as not directed specifically to detention of persons in a clinical state of alcoholism. The risk of public disorder or harm to the intoxicated person themselves arose whether or not they were addicted to alcohol.

Thus a broader meaning was to be given to 'alcoholics' than the dictionary definition. This interpretation was confirmed by looking at the history of the formulation of the provision, which showed a desire to meet the concerns of those states which wanted to preserve the legality of their measures to control abuse of alcohol, the term 'alcoholics' being included in the English text in an attempt to align it with the French language of the draft provision.[21]

If this shows liberal use of the immediate context in helping to identify the appropriate ordinary meaning of a term, using a treaty's object and purpose to shed light on the meaning is not an opportunity to subordinate the terms of the treaty to its general purpose. 'Object and purpose' is a phrase used in practice as a composite term without any attempt at an arcane distinction between the words 'object' and 'purpose'. That a treaty may have more than one object and purpose is so obvious that questioning

---

[20] ECtHR App no 26629/95, Judgment of 4 April 2000.
[21] ibid, esp at paras 34, 36–39, and 60–62.

the permissibility of investigating several different objectives has not been a feature of case law.

A good example of practical use of object and purpose is the *Whaling* case at the ICJ. In that case, Australia and Japan each argued that one object and purpose should be dominant, that is conservation and sustainable exploitation, respectively.[22] The Court examined the paragraphs of the preamble to the Convention to identify its object and purpose, noting that its objectives were further indicated in the final paragraph of the preamble, which states that the contracting parties 'decided to conclude a convention to provide for the proper conservation of whale stocks and thus make possible the orderly development of the whaling industry'. Taking into account the preamble and other relevant provisions of the Convention, the ICJ therefore declined to take the object and purpose of the Convention as providing a general basis for a restrictive or an expansive interpretation of a provision for taking whales for scientific purposes.[23]

3 Attribution of Meaning by the Parties

Three elements of the general rule of interpretation are based on the meaning attributed to a treaty by agreement of the parties to it. These are: (i) agreements at the time of conclusion of a treaty; (ii) subsequent agreements; and (iii) agreements deduced from the practice of the parties in applying the treaty.[24] There is growing recognition of the importance of these elements of the general rule through the work of the ILC.[25] It is only relatively recently that a growing number of treaties have been open to the possibility of interpretation by a court, tribunal or other international body. This has meant that in the case of older treaties, and any modern ones that lack provision for third party adjudication, differences over interpretation could only be effectively resolved by negotiation and agreement between the parties. The Permanent Court of International Justice stated that 'the right of giving an authoritative interpretation of a legal rule belongs solely to the

---

[22] *Whaling in the Antarctic (Australia v Japan: New Zealand intervening)* (Judgment) [2014] ICJ Rep 226, 251–52 [56]—[58].
[23] ibid para 58.
[24] VCLT, arts 31(2)(a) and 31(3)(a) and (b), respectively.
[25] See ILC 'Draft conclusions on subsequent agreements and subsequent practice in relation to the interpretation of treaties, with commentaries', Chapter IV of Annual Report A/73/10 (2018) https://legal.un.org/ilc/texts/instruments/english/commentaries/1_11_2018.pdf endorsed by the UN General Assembly in Resolution 73/202 of 20 December 2018.

person or body who has power to modify or suppress it'.[26] Thus, the underlying reason why agreements on interpretation have such strong potential significance for interpretation is because a treaty is essentially 'owned' by the parties.[27] Other states generally have no legitimate say as to how the treaty is to be interpreted unless it be as states which have been involved in its negotiation and they have a right to become parties to it.

Where there is a clear agreement among all parties to a treaty as to its interpretation that is an element which offers the greatest weight in application of the general rule. However, uncertainty over the extent of agreement, lack of clarity in its terms, and limits on its duration may reduce the effectiveness of this element as a determinant of meaning. Distinct from these three forms of interpretative agreement, the Vienna Convention has a further element which lies towards the outer limit of weight as something to be taken into account. This is described as 'any instrument made by one or more parties in connection with the conclusion of the treaty and accepted by the other parties as an instrument related to the treaty' (Article 31(2)(b)). The 'instruments' are typically those, such as instruments of ratification, which may include interpretative declarations. Unilateral in character, and therefore clearly not agreements, their acceptance as being related to the treaty justifies their place in the general rule; but the unilateral character of an interpretative declaration means it cannot by itself be dispositive as an interpretation.

Both agreements as to interpretation and instruments accepted as related to a treaty warrant further attention. There is, however one common issue in the case of agreements in connection with conclusion of a treaty and instruments made in connection with conclusion of a treaty. This is the problem of identifying when a treaty is concluded.[28] In the general rule, agreements on interpretation in connection with conclusion of a treaty are distinguished from 'subsequent' agreements which suggests conclusion must be a specific point in time. This points to the moment at which a treaty is 'done' or signed. In the case of instruments connected with conclusion of a treaty, interpretative statements may be made at the time of signing and when instruments of ratification are deposited. Hence in this case the

---

[26] *Delimitation of the Polish-Czechoslovakian Frontier (Question of Jaworzina)* (Advisory Opinion) (1923) PCIJ Series B no 8, 37.
[27] J Crawford, 'Subsequent Agreements and Practice from a Consensualist Perspective', ch 3 in G Nolte (ed), *Treaties and Subsequent Practice* (OUP 2013), 31.
[28] See ch 3, section II.2 above.

'process' meaning of 'conclusion' is more appropriate to embrace the range of possible times.

(a) Agreements in connection with conclusion of a treaty: VCLT Article 31(2)(a)

Agreements between the parties as to interpretation recorded at the time it is concluded may be specific and formal, such as those in a separate Protocol. Alternatively, they may be recorded in a Final Act, or in an explanatory report adopted alongside the opening of the treaty for states' participation.[29]

An example of a very specific and formal agreement is the 'Protocol on the Interpretation of Article 69 of the European Patent Convention'.[30] The Protocol sought to establish a balance between the approaches to interpretation used in different legal systems by indicating an interpretative direction avoiding an unduly narrow and literal construction of a patent's claims on the one hand and, on the other, an excessively general approach resulting from viewing the claims as merely an aid to finding the essence of the invention and protecting that.

(b) Other instruments connected with conclusion: VCLT Article 31(2)(b)

While agreements among the parties to a treaty about the meaning of its provisions provide very strong indications of its proper interpretation, unilateral indications by one or more parties as to how they consider it should be interpreted have a more variable significance. The Vienna Convention does not offer a definition of an interpretative declaration, but the ILC Guide to Reservations has one: ' "Interpretative declaration" means a unilateral statement, however phrased or named, made by a State or an international organization, whereby that State or that organization purports

---

[29] See eg Final Act of the United Nations Conference on the Law of Treaties A/CONF.39/26, Official Records, Documents, 381 https://legal.un.org/diplomaticconferences/1968_lot/docs/english/conf_docs/a_conf39_26.pdf and Report of the Executive Directors of the International Bank for Reconstruction and Development on the Convention on the Settlement of Investment Disputes between States and Nationals of Other States (March 1965) http://icsidfiles.worldbank.org/icsid/ICSID/StaticFiles/basicdoc/partB.htm.

[30] Convention on the Grant of European Patents (European Patent Convention) 1973 and Protocol on the Interpretation of Article 69 of the Convention 1973.

to specify or clarify the meaning or scope of a treaty or of certain of its provisions.'[31]

As noted above, the most common opportunities for such statements are on signature of a treaty or in, or lodged with, a state's instrument of ratification. An example of practice is the number of declarations were made on signature and ratification of the Treaty for the Renunciation of War 1928 (the Pact of Paris or the Kellogg–Briand Pact). Some declarations concerned the possibility of sanctions being imposed by the League of Nations, while others stated rights of self-defence.[32] The true effect of the declarations was not resolved, although it appears that most other states and writers regarded them as interpretative declarations rather than reservations.[33]

The effect of an interpretative declaration can be challenged both as to whether it is actually a reservation in disguise or where the substance is not accepted. An example is the list of declarations and reservations accompanying the instrument of accession to the Vienna Convention deposited by Syria, where the fourth item (D) stated:

> The Government of the Syrian Arab Republic interprets the provisions in article 52 as follows:
> The expression 'the threat or use of force' used in this article extends also to the employment of economic, political, military and psychological coercion and to all types of coercion constraining a State to conclude a treaty against its wishes or its interests.[34]

The United Kingdom rejected the interpretation and drew attention to what it saw as the more authoritative treatment of the point:

> The United Kingdom does not accept that the interpretation of Article 52 put forward by the Government of Syria correctly reflects the conclusions reached at the Conference of Vienna on the subject of coercion;

---

[31] ILC, 'Guide to Practice on Reservations to Treaties', Guideline 1.2. Addendum to Report of the International Law Commission, Sixty-third session (2011), UN General Assembly Official Records, Sixty-sixth Session, Supplement No 10, A/66/10/Add.1.
[32] See Frank Horn, *Reservations and Interpretative Declarations to Multilateral Treaties* (North Holland 1988)274 ff.
[33] ibid 275.
[34] *Status of Multilateral Treaties Deposited with the Secretary-General of the United Nations*, UN document ST/LEG/SER.E/24 (2005) Syrian declaration D https://treaties.un.org/pages/Treaties.aspx?id=23&subid=A&clang=_en.

the Conference dealt with this matter by adopting a Declaration on this subject which forms part of the Final Act...[35]

States sometimes find other occasions than conclusion of treaties to make interpretative declarations relating to provisions of treaties. The legal effect of one such declaration was considered by the ICJ in its Advisory Opinion on the *International Status of South West Africa* (1950):

> Interpretations placed upon legal instruments by the parties to them, though not conclusive as to their meaning, have considerable probative value when they contain recognition by a party of its own obligations under an instrument. In this case the declarations of the Union of South Africa support the conclusions already reached by the Court.

The Court was considering official statements made by the Government of South Africa indicating that it would continue to administer South-West Africa in the spirit of the mandate it had been given under the Covenant of the League of Nations which was no longer in force. The Court found that the declarations supported the interpretation which it had established on other grounds. Although this was not an interpretative declaration connected with the conclusion of a treaty, the ILC accepted this as evidence that a declaration which was so connected could have a role in confirming an interpretation achieved by application of other elements of the general rule.[36]

(c) Subsequent agreements: VCLT Article 31(3)(a)

Agreements on interpretation made during the 'life' of a treaty did not attract much attention as a separate element of the general rule until, some thirty years after the Vienna Convention entered into force, the ILC undertook a detailed study under the description 'Subsequent agreements and subsequent practice in relation to interpretation of treaties'.[37] The UN General Assembly endorsed the ILC's work, annexing the text of the Commission's conclusions and commentaries to a resolution to bring them to the attention of all member states.[38]

---

[35] ibid, UK statement on ratification.
[36] See 'Guide to Practice on Reservations to Treaties' [2011-II(3)] Yearbook of the ILC 23, 322, Guideline 4.7.1, commentary paras (25)–(26).
[37] The Analytical Guide to the Work of the International Law Commission lists the relevant documents from 2012 to 2018, following the transition from the previous description of the topic as 'Treaties over time': https://legal.un.org/ilc/guide/1_11.shtml.
[38] UNGA Resolution 73/202 of 20 December 2018.

Because subsequent agreements on interpretation are most likely to be reached in order to address some issue over the treaty that has arisen since its conclusion, provided the agreement is clear and acceptable to all parties, there is likely to be little occasion for controversy over it. There are, however, some points to be noted. First, an agreement which is claimed to be interpretative of an earlier treaty must be clearly related to that earlier agreement. A subsequent treaty between the same parties as an earlier one does not constitute an interpretative agreement unless some relationship can be shown between the two.[39] Second, it is the fact of agreement on an interpretation rather than the form of agreement which is what makes the agreement admissible as an interpretative element. On this point the ILC concluded: 'An agreement under article 31, paragraph 3 (a) and (b), requires a common understanding regarding the interpretation of a treaty which the parties are aware of and accept. Such an agreement may, but need not, be legally binding for it to be taken into account.'[40]

Third, even a less formal agreement may become merged with the next element of the general rule through consistent practice confirming the agreement.

(d) Subsequent practice: VCLT Article 31(3)(b)

This is one of the elements of the general rule which shows that interpretation is not simply 'textual', that is exegesis or argument derived from focus only on the text of the treaty. Nevertheless, in most cases subsequent practice will involve examining some form of written records of what has been done in application of the treaty. The evidence that practice is in implementation of a particular treaty may include diplomatic exchanges, policy statements by parties, press releases, the opinions of government legal advisers, official guidance on legal questions, executive decisions, and international and national judicial decisions.

Thus prominent types of national practice are executive, legislative, and judicial acts. However, the key test is whether the practice of sufficient parties is such as to demonstrate agreement on the treaty's meaning.

---

[39] See *Case concerning Maritime Delimitation in the Area between Greenland and Jan Mayen (Denmark v Norway)* [1993] ICJ Rep 38, 51, para 28.

[40] ILC Draft conclusions on subsequent agreements and subsequent practice in relation to the interpretation of treaties, with commentaries, Conclusion 10 (ILC 2018 Report A/73/10, ch IV) https://legal.un.org/ilc/texts/instruments/english/commentaries/1_11_2018.pdf. Following this endorsement by the UNGA (n 338), the 'draft conclusions' are cited as 'conclusions' in text and notes below.

II Elements of the General Rule   87

Subsequent conduct by individual parties may provide supplementary support for an interpretation but to constitute a subsequent agreement shown by practice a substantial degree of uniformity of conduct with no evidence of difference is required or, if the conduct is unilateral, that the agreement of the other party or parties is manifest. It is the agreement, not practice, of all parties that must be shown, though formal agreement is not required in the examples where this element has been considered. In 1999 the ICJ emphasized the role of subsequent practice in treaty interpretation, endorsing the ILC's commentary on what at the time of the commentary were draft provisions of the VCLT:

> The importance of such subsequent practice in the application of the treaty, as an element of interpretation, is obvious; for it constitutes objective evidence of the understanding of the parties as to the meaning of the treaty. Recourse to it as a means of interpretation is well-established in the jurisprudence of international tribunals.[41]

More recently, the ILC has provided numerous examples of consideration of subsequent practice in the commentaries to its conclusions on subsequent agreements and subsequent practice, and in assessing the weight to be given to subsequent practice.[42] There are, however, some distinctions to be drawn in use of subsequent practice. Practice may resolve deliberate or unintentional ambiguity, or it may act as a means of developing the operational value of a treaty. Some treaties, however, are designed to allow for more progressive development than can be attributed to resolving uncertainties over existing terms. This has given rise to the notion of 'evolutionary' or 'evolutive' interpretation.[43] These are analytical terms that have

---

[41] *Kasikili/Sedudu Island (Botswana/Namibia)* [1999] ICJ Rep 1045, 1076, para 49, quoting from [1966-II] Yearbook of the ILC 221, para 15. The Court listed examples of its own examination of subsequent practice of the parties in the application of a treaty: *Corfu Channel* (Merits, Judgment) [1949] ICJ Rep 25; *Arbitral Award Made by the King of Spain on 23 December 1906* (Judgment) [1960] ICJ Rep 206–07; *Temple of Preah Vihear* (Merits, Judgment) [1962] ICJ Rep 33–35; *Certain Expenses of the United Nations (Article 17, paragraph 2, of the Charter)* (Advisory Opinion) [1962] ICJ Rep 157, 160–61, 172–75; *Military and Paramilitary Activities in and against Nicaragua (Nicaragua v United States of America)* (Jurisdiction and Admissibility, Judgment) [1984] ICJ Rep 392, 408–13, paras 36–47; *Territorial Dispute (Libyan Arab Jamahiriya/Chad)* (Judgment) [1994] ICJ Rep 34–37, paras 66–71; *Legality of the Use by a State of Nuclear Weapons in Armed Conflict* (Advisory Opinion) [1996–I] ICJ Rep 75, para 19.

[42] See the ILC Conclusions (n 40) and for assessing the weight to given to this element see Conclusion 7: ibid 51–63.

[43] As to how subsequent agreements and subsequent practice may provide evidence for determining whether a proper interpretation of a treaty envisages evolutionary interpretation see ILC Conclusions (n 40) Conclusion 8.

been ascribed to account for changes within a treaty regime that was designed with such an expectation or inherent in its long-term or other indicative characteristics.

These analytical terms have not permeated greatly into case law, but in a case before the European Court of Human Rights in 1986 about whether an entitlement to a statutory sickness allowance was a civil right within the meaning of article 6 of the human rights convention, a group of dissenting judges found that state practice had not developed to the point where the parties could be said to be agreed on the 'civil' or other character of an entitlement to such health benefits and found that an evolutive interpretation of article 6(1) led to no different conclusion:

> An evolutive interpretation allows variable and changing concepts already contained in the Convention to be construed in the light of modern-day conditions ... but it does not allow entirely new concepts or spheres of application to be introduced into the Convention: that is a legislative function that belongs to the Member States of the Council of Europe. The desirability of affording proper safeguards for the adjudication of claims in the ever-increasing field of social security is evident. There are, however, limits to evolutive interpretation and the facts of the present case go beyond those limits as far as Article 6 (1) para. 1 (art. 6–1) is concerned.[44]

This seems a helpful description of how evolutionary interpretation differs from an interpretation based on subsequent practice evidencing agreement on interpretation and shows the probable limits of evolutionary interpretation. There is, however, the loosely related issue of how subsequent practice and amendment are to be differentiated. If the parties have established a practice sufficient to meet the requirements of Article 31(3)(b) VCLT but which is at variance with the meaning to be attributed to the treaty by applying the other elements of the general rule, does the practice showing agreement of the parties trump (for example) the ordinary meaning? This may seem theoretical since if all parties are agreed on an interpretation, who would have standing to contest their interpretation?

---

[44] *Feldbrugge v Netherlands*, ECtHR Case no 8/1984/80/127 (Judgment of 23 April 1986), joint dissenting opinion of Judges Ryssdal, Bindschedler-Robert, Lagergren, Matscher, Sir Vincent Evans, Bernhardt, and Gersing, paras 23–24.

The issue is, nevertheless, a real one now that third party adjudication offers private parties access to determination of their rights under treaties on matters such as human rights, investments, or consular access. What weight are courts and tribunals to give to 'interpretations' by parties that go beyond the limits described in the quotation above?

The ILC has addressed this in its conclusions on subsequent agreements and subsequent practice by stating:

> It is presumed that the parties to a treaty, by an agreement or a practice in the application of the treaty, intend to interpret the treaty, not to amend or to modify it. The possibility of amending or modifying a treaty by subsequent practice of the parties has not been generally recognized. The present draft conclusion is without prejudice to the rules on the amendment or modification of treaties under the 1969 Vienna Convention and under customary international law.[45]

The ILC's detailed examination of case law in its commentaries on this conclusion shows the reluctance of courts and other tribunals to accept anything more than a theoretical possibility of amendment by interpretation (if that), but that this remains a grey area.

A final point on subsequent practice is whether practice in or of international organizations is relevant to treaty interpretation. The main issue which this raises is well illustrated by the practice in the UN relating to the Charter provision (Article 27(3)) requiring that decisions of the Security Council on all matters other than procedural ones are made by an 'affirmative' vote of nine members including 'concurring' votes of the permanent members. 'Affirmative' and 'concurring' very strongly suggest that all the permanent members must vote in favour of a resolution for such a decision to be made. Yet from early days of the UN, 'concurring' members was interpreted as fulfilled by abstention or absence, rather than requiring a vote in favour. This converted the obvious ordinary meaning of 'concurring' votes to permanent members not casting a negative vote (ie a 'veto'). The ICJ has endorsed this interpretation.[46]

---

[45] See ILC Conclusions (n 40) Conclusion 7(3).
[46] See *Legal Consequence for States of the Continued Presence of South Africa in Namibia (South West Africa)* [1971] ICJ Rep 16, 22, para 22.

Here the firmly established practice of an organ of the UN, an organ which consists of only a small number of member states, has been taken as a compelling interpretation of a treaty. Given that the UN Charter has a great many parties, this perhaps parallels the position regarding treaties which are not constitutions of international organizations. Sufficient practice by relevant parties to a treaty coupled with evidence of concurrence by all other parties gives great weight to practice as an indicator of meaning.

This example is one of interpretation of an organization's own constitutive treaty where accepted practice within the organization is viewed as demonstrating the corporate understanding of the parties as to the internal functioning of the organization. In a different category are treaties which fall within the remit of the organization but, rather than regulating its internal working, affect activities outside it. The *Whaling case* provides an example.[47] Under the relevant convention, the International Whaling Commission is empowered to make recommendations to the parties to the treaty on matters relating to whales or whaling. The ICJ observed that: 'These recommendations, which take the form of resolutions, are not binding. However, when they are adopted by consensus or by a unanimous vote, they may be relevant for the interpretation of the Convention or its Schedule.'[48]

The ILC has given guidance on several aspects of practice arising in the work of international organizations, including those concerning decisions adopted within the framework of a 'Conference of States Parties', constituent instruments of international organizations, and pronouncements of expert treaty bodies. The ILC's conclusions envisage relevant subsequent practice being admissible in so far as it expresses agreement in substance between the parties on interpretation, regardless of the form and the procedure by which the decision was adopted. This includes adoption by consensus. However, in relation to pronouncements by expert treaty bodies, the ILC's conclusion indicates that silence by a party is not be presumed to constitute subsequent practice accepting an interpretation of a treaty in the pronouncement.[49]

---

[47] *Whaling in the Antarctic* (n 22).
[48] ibid 248, para 46.
[49] ILC Conclusions (n 40) Conclusions 11, 13.

4 Relevant Rules of International Law: VCLT Article 31(3)(c)

The requirement to take into account relevant rules of international law is the element of the general rule of interpretation which underwent the most extreme distillation when drawn up by the ILC. Its origin, invisible in the eventual text, was an attempt to incorporate into the rules of interpretation a reflection of the so-called 'intertemporal law'. The intertemporal rule, as commonly expressed in the form stated in the arbitral award in the *Island of Palmas* case, has two limbs: first, that '[a] juridical fact must be appreciated in the light of the law contemporary with it, and not the law in force at the time when a dispute in regard to it arises or falls to be settled' and, second, that the principle which subjects creation of a right to the law in force at the time the right arises 'demands that the existence of the right, in other words its continued manifestation, shall follow the conditions required by the evolution of law'.[50]

Applicability of those propositions of general international law to interpretation of treaties was a reflection of statements of the ICJ in the 1971 *Namibia* case.[51] The case concerned the legal consequences of continued assertion by South Africa of control over what was then Southwest Africa pursuant a mandate under the defunct Covenant of the League of Nations. In issue was whether the original concept of a 'sacred trust of civilisation' embodied in the mandates under the supervision of the League, and the subsequent development of international law, made the principle of self-determination applicable to all non-self-governing territories under the Charter of the United Nations. The Court stated the general proposition that '[a]n international instrument has to be interpreted and applied within the framework of the entire legal system prevailing at the time of the interpretation'.[52] It also stated:

> Mindful as it is of the primary necessity of interpreting an instrument in accordance with the intentions of the parties at the time of its conclusion, the Court is bound to take into account the fact that the concepts embodied in Article 22 of the Covenant—'the strenuous conditions of

---

[50] (1928) 2 RIAA 829, 845.
[51] *Legal consequences for States of the continued presence of South Africa in Namibia (South West Africa), notwithstanding Security Council Resolution 276 (1970)* (Advisory Opinion) [1971] ICJ Rep 16.
[52] ibid 31, para 53.

the modern world' and 'the well-being and development' of the peoples concerned—were not static, but were by definition evolutionary, as also, therefore, was the concept of the 'sacred trust'. The parties to the Covenant must consequently be deemed to have accepted them as such.[53]

In making those propositions, which closely resemble the two limbs of the intertemporal rule, the ICJ did not refer to the Article 31(3)(c) VCLT. However, in developing that provision just a few years before the ICJ's Opinion, the ILC's first suggestion was that 'interpretation' of a treaty should follow the first part of the rule and 'application' the second part. That, however, proved both unworkable and an inappropriate measure of how time factors play out in treaty interpretation. The concise wording of the ultimate text left the provision little used in early years of the VCLT, but it is now recognized as requiring the interpreter to take account of two factors which, in analysis of case law, have come to be known as 'systemic integration' and the 'evolutionary interpretation' mentioned above.[54]

The idea of systemic integration is that a treaty is to be interpreted with attention to the rules and obligations of the complete system of international law in so far as they are relevant and apply to the parties.[55] Systemic integration includes consideration of any rights and obligations arising from other treaties pertinent to the subject matter of the treaty which is being interpreted. Evolutionary interpretation (briefly explained above) is the aspect of systemic integration which has a focus of the second part of the intertemporal law—the evolution of the relevant law and circumstances of its application.

An arbitral award in the *Iron Rhine* case provides a demonstration of both these aspects of this element of the general rule (as well as an excellent example of treaty interpretation applying the Vienna rules).[56] Treaties of 1839 and 1873 between Belgium and the Netherlands opened the way for a railway from Belgium to Germany across the Netherlands. While

---

[53] ibid.
[54] Professor Sands identified the emerging role for the provision and opportunities to make the rule 'operational': P Sands, 'Treaty, Custom and the Cross-fertilization of International Law' (1998) 1 Yale Human Rights & Dev LJ 85.
[55] C McLachlan, 'The Principle of Systemic Integration and Article 31(3)(c) of the Vienna Convention' (2005) 54 ICLQ 279 and P Merkouris, *Article 31(3)(C) VCLT and the Principle of Systemic Integration: Normative Shadows in Plato's Cave* (Brill 2015).
[56] *Arbitration regarding the Iron Rhine (IJzeren Rijn) Railway (Belgium/Netherlands)* (2005) XXVII RIAA 35.

some provisions apt to cover maintenance, extension, and upgrading were included, the parties could not have foreseen the advances in electrification, track design, freight stock, etc, developments which needed to be considered when the mostly disused line was being considered for reactivation.

The arbitral tribunal identified the intertemporal rule as being of the type envisaged by Article 31(3)(c) VCLT and noted that it has long been established that the understanding of conceptual or generic terms in a treaty may be seen as an essentially relative question depending on the development of international relations. The tribunal nevertheless considered that this was not a case of conceptual or generic terms in the treaty in issue, but rather of new technical developments to be taken into account. The tribunal decided that 'an evolutive interpretation, which would ensure an application of the treaty that would be effective in terms of its object and purpose [would] be preferred to a strict application of the intertemporal rule'.[57]

In line with the object and purpose of the treaty and the fact that the treaty was of no fixed duration, the tribunal saw it as open to a 'dynamic and evolutive' approach to interpretation and that it was therefore necessary 'to read into' the relevant treaty provisions 'the provisions of international law as they apply today'.[58] These provisions included the emergent environmental norms which the tribunal linked with the application of Article 31(3)(c) and which would have to be taken into account where the railway was being re-established in areas of special protection or conservation.[59]

While this arbitral award and other applications of the principles of systemic integration and evolutionary interpretation attest to the important potential of relevant rules of international law as an element of interpretation, there are some associated difficulties. The main one arises from the reference to relevant rules being those 'applicable in the relations between the parties', particularly in the case where the relevant rules are those in a treaty other than the one being interpreted. Who are 'the parties'? Does this require: (i) that all parties to the treaty being interpreted must be parties to any other treaty being invoked; (ii) that all parties to the dispute over interpretation must be parties to any other treaty being invoked; (iii) that a rule being invoked from any other treaty must be shown to be a customary rule; or (iv) that a rule being invoked in another treaty must have been implicitly accepted or tolerated by all parties to the treaty under interpretation?

[57] ibid para 80.
[58] ibid paras 81–84.
[59] ibid paras 58–60.

There has not been sufficient uniform practice to provide a single selection from these options. The ILC did touch on the issue in considering fragmentation of international law, but its conclusion suggests that in consideration of rules in another treaty, the weight to be given to relevant material is relative to the extent to which it reveals a common understanding of the aggregated provisions:

> *Application of other treaty rules.* Article 31(3)(c) also requires the interpreter to consider other treaty-based rules so as to arrive at a consistent meaning. Such other rules are of particular relevance where parties to the treaty under interpretation are also parties to the other treaty, where the treaty rule has passed into or expresses customary international law or where they provide evidence of the common understanding of the parties as to the object and purpose of the treaty under interpretation or as to the meaning of a particular term.[60]

Article 31(3)(c) might also be thought to provide an umbrella for guidance in interpretation from sources which do not appear to fall strictly within its terms. There are numerous treaties which follow common forms, sometimes derived from an international model, from work within an international organization, or from common practice, but with variations in some detail. Examples of these are bilateral investment treaties (BITs), agreements for avoidance of double taxation, air transport agreements, consular agreements, and extradition treaties. Similarly, there may be occasions for reference to interpretation of the term used in treaties between other parties. In practice international tribunals do make such reference, though without indication of which element of the general rule of interpretation is being deployed. A better justification of this practice than a loose interpretation of Article 31(3)(c) may be that in identifying an ordinary meaning of terms used in a specialist subject it is reasonable to identify what meaning is ordinarily given by the collective of specialists rather than a general or dictionary meaning. There is also the lawyers' general inclination to consider precedent even if not in any way binding.

This element's field of application is only gradually appearing. One case which has been a prominent, if an uncertain harbinger of what is permissible, is the *Oil Platforms* case at the ICJ.[61] The USA had destroyed some

---

[60] ILC Annual Report [2006-II(2)] Yearbook of the ILC 180, para 21.
[61] *Oil Platforms (Islamic Republic of Iran v United States of America)* (Merits) [2003] ICJ Rep 161.

Iranian oil platforms when defending shipping in the Gulf during a war between Iran and Iraq. In issue was whether the USA had violated a provision assuring 'freedom of commerce' (Article X) in its 1955 treaty with Iran. The treaty also stated that its provisions did not 'preclude the application of measures ... necessary to fulfil the obligations of a High Contracting Party for the maintenance or restoration of international peace and security, or necessary to protect its essential security interests' (Article XX). The majority judgment of the ICJ judgment took the general international law of self-defence as the starting point, referring to Article 31(3)(c) of the Vienna Convention in support of this approach. The Court found that the USA could not justify its actions by reference to the international law of self-defence but that there was no breach of the treaty because Article X did not extend to cover the matter in dispute. While the international law of self-defence might be relevant if the wording of Article XX made this appropriate, the approach of the majority was the object of powerful criticism by two ICJ judges in their separate opinions (although concurring in the overall result that the USA had not violated a treaty obligation)). On the majority's approach to interpretation, Judge Higgins wrote:

> The Court has, however, not interpreted Article XX, paragraph 1(d), by reference to the rules on treaty interpretation. It has rather invoked the concept of treaty interpretation to displace the applicable law. It has replaced the terms of Article XX, paragraph 1(d), with those of international law on the use of force and all sight of the text of Article XX, paragraph 1(d), is lost.[62]

In similar vein, Judge Kooijmans took the view that the question was not whether the USA had acted in self-defence under general international law but whether it had violated a treaty. If it had been necessary for the Court to interpret Article XX(1)(d), '[t]he proper approach ... would have been to scrutinize the meaning of the words "necessary to protect the essential security interests" in Article XX, paragraph 1(d)'.[63]

---

[62] [2003] ICJ Rep 225, 238, Separate Opinion at para 49.
[63] [2003] ICJ Rep at 259, Separate Opinion, paras 42–43.

5 Special Meanings: VCLT Article 31(4)

Even without the extreme approach of the majority in the *Oil Platforms* case, taking account of relevant rules of international law offers considerable scope for widening the range of elements to include in the crucible of interpretation. The provision on special meaning is quite the opposite. It envisages narrowing down the identification of meaning where evidence shows this to have been intended by the parties.

There are two main types of special meaning. The first is where the terms have a meaning associated with some particular area of activity. The second is where there is evidence favouring a meaning at odds with what would ordinarily be viewed as the meaning. The first is really just an emphatic application of the requirement of the first element of the general rule to use the context in finding the ordinary meaning. The second is most readily fulfilled by a definitions provision in a treaty which can provide the clearest evidence of a required meaning which is not necessarily the obvious one.

There is little case law investigating what evidence is required to establish a special meaning and most assertions have failed to show one. One instance where this was investigated concerned Article 33 of the UN Convention on Refugees which provides: 'No contracting state shall expel or return ("refouler") a refugee ...'[64] The French text has: '*n'expulsera ou ne refoulera*', with no insertion after '*refoulera*'.[65] Both languages are equally authentic, so it is therefore clear that the English term 'return' was to align with the established French meaning of '*refoulment*'. '*Refoulment*' is described in a leading work on refugee law as 'summary reconduction to the frontier of those discovered to have entered illegally and summary refusal of admission ... [and] thus to be distinguished from expulsion or deportation'.[66]

---

[64] 189 UNTS, 139, 176; and see *R v Immigration Officer at Prague Airport ex parte European Roma Rights Centre* [2004] UKHL 55, [2005] 2 AC 1, 31; and *Sale v Haitian Centers Council* 509 US 155 (1993).

[65] 189 UNTS, 139, 177.

[66] GS Goodwin-Gill and J McAdam, *The Refugee in International Law* (4th edn, OUP 2007) 241.

III Supplementary Means of Interpretation: VCLT Article 32

1 Preparatory Work and Circumstances of Conclusion

Two supplementary means of interpretation are specifically mentioned in Article 32, but this is not an exclusive list. The identified supplementary means are preparatory work (commonly known as *travaux préparatoires* or just 'the *travaux*') and 'the circumstances of conclusion' of a treaty. Most of the attention given to this article in case law and literature has been on preparatory work. The significance of the circumstances of conclusion of a treaty has not been extensively recognized. This is perhaps unfortunate as confusion was sown at the time of the negotiation of the Vienna convention by those who used the term 'context' to refer to both the circumstances surrounding conclusion of the treaty and the rest of the text accompanying the terms being interpreted. This leads to a significant misunderstanding of the distinction made in the rules of interpretation where context is often of key significance in selecting the appropriate ordinary meaning, while circumstances of conclusion come into play as supplementary means.

It is however understandable that a major focus has been on preparatory work because this is commonly claimed to assist in interpretation. However, the text of the article is not very clear. 'Supplementary', 'recourse', and 'confirm' do not point the interpreter in a clear direction. Further, the layout of the article on page or screen may mislead the reader towards viewing the paragraphs (a) and (b) as governing all the preceding text when closer reading shows that it is only when 'determining' the meaning by reference to preparatory work that the requirements in those paragraphs apply. Thus, somewhat paradoxically, examination of the preparatory work of this article is necessary to understand its purport.

Preparatory work has no established definition but most frequently is taken to refer to records of negotiations and includes documents used by, or available to, the negotiators. The UN General Assembly resolution convening the Vienna Conference specified the ILC's draft articles as the basic proposal on which the conference was to work, and requested the UN Secretary General to present to the conference all relevant documentation.[67]

---

[67] UNGA Resolution 2166 (XXI) (5 December 1966).

The Final Act of the Vienna Conference noted that the conference had had before it the relevant records of the ILC relating to the law of treaties and recorded the participation by Sir Humphrey Waldock as expert consultant having been the ILC's special rapporteur. Although preparatory work was one of the aspects of the draft rules on which there was debate, the outcome did not involve substantial departure from the ILC drafts. Hence courts, tribunals, and commentators have not shown hesitation in referring to the work of the ILC as significant preparatory work for the 1969 Convention.

The opening phrase of Article 32 offers the interpreter the option of 'recourse' to supplementary means of interpretation. For preparatory work, the important distinction is between studying or referring to preparatory work, and relying on it. Waldock reported to the Vienna conference on the ILC's approach: 'There had certainly been no intention of discouraging automatic recourse to preparatory work for the general understanding of a treaty.'[68] In an earlier explanation he had written:

> There is, however, a difference between examining and basing a finding upon *travaux préparatoires*, and the Court [PCIJ and ICJ] itself has more than once referred to them as confirming an interpretation otherwise arrived at from a study of the text. Moreover, it is the constant practice of States and tribunals to examine any relevant *travaux préparatoires* for such light as they may throw upon the treaty. It would therefore be unrealistic to suggest, even by implication, that there is any actual bar upon mere reference to *travaux préparatoires* whenever the meaning of the terms is clear.[69]

This centres on the first of the two uses of supplementary means envisaged by Article 32, that is *confirming* a meaning ascertained by applying the general rule. In this sense 'confirming' has a very general meaning. It would be of very limited value to confirm a meaning which was clear by application of the general rule. Yet if the meaning were not clear, use of the preparatory work to buttress an emerging meaning would go beyond the strict notion of confirming something. However, this latter approach is very much accepted practice. In *Witold Litwa v Poland*, the strict meaning of 'alcoholics' strongly imported an element of addiction.[70] It is difficult,

---

[68] UN Conference on the Law of Treaties, Summary Records of First Session (26 March–24 May 1968) UN Doc A/Conf.39/11, p 184, para 69.
[69] 'Third Report on the Law of Treaties' [1964-II] Yearbook of the ILC 58, para 20.
[70] Note 20 above.

III Supplementary Means of Interpretation: VCLT Article 32

therefore, to escape the assumption that the preparatory work, which so clearly indicated that the term 'alcoholics' was included with the common understanding that this would allow measures to combat drunkenness, must have influenced the adoption of that meaning, even if the preparatory work was only accorded a confirmatory role in the formal presentation of the interpretative argument.

Thus there is something of a sliding scale between the weight of the elements in the general rule and the strength or clarity of what is revealed by preparatory work. Waldock (again) affirms this:

> Recourse to *travaux préparatoires* as a subsidiary means of interpreting the text, as already indicated, is frequent both in State practice and in cases before international tribunals. Today, it is generally recognized that some caution is needed in the use of *travaux préparatoires* as a means of interpretation. They are not ... an authentic means of interpretation. They are simply evidence to be weighed against any other relevant evidence of the intentions of the parties, and their cogency depends on the extent to which they furnish proof of the *common* understanding of the parties as to the meaning attached to the terms of the treaty.[71]

Quite different is the position where a definite meaning cannot be reached by application of the general rule and it is the preparatory work which provides the interpretation. Because this raises the preparatory work to pole position in *determining* the meaning, prerequisites are set. Use to determine meaning is only permitted when the interpretation according to Article 31 leaves the meaning ambiguous or obscure, or leads to a result which is manifestly absurd or unreasonable.

The judgment in *Witold Litwa v Poland* illustrates what appears to be a reluctance to resort to use of supplementary means to determine meaning and a preference to relegate preparatory work to a supporting role. It is difficult to find explicit findings of a failure in application of the general rule sufficient to allow preparatory work to determine the meaning. In *US— Measures Affecting Gambling*, however, when investigating whether the term 'sporting' included gambling, the Appellate Body of the WTO concluded that:

---

[71] [1964-II] Yearbook of the ILC 58, para 21 (footnotes omitted, emphasis in original).

[a]pplication of the general rule of interpretation set out in Article 31 of the *Vienna Convention* leaves the meaning of 'other recreational services (except sporting)' ambiguous ... Accordingly, we are required, in this case, to turn to the supplementary means of interpretation provided for in Article 32 of the *Vienna Convention*.[72]

The thorough investigation of preparatory work in that case showed how difficult it can be to achieve a clear outcome from this source, a situation which becomes more complex where the propriety of relying on preparatory work comes to be weighed up against what the records show. This may explain the controversial case of *Qatar v Bahrain*.[73] The question was whether an Arabic verb in a dual form meant that the two disputant states could only submit a case to the ICJ jointly or whether either of the two could separately submit it. An earlier version drawn up in the course of negotiations included an explicit indication that either of the two parties could submit the case, but this became transformed to the controversial wording. Observing that the records were fragmentary, the majority concluded:

> The Court is unable to see why the abandonment of a form of words corresponding to the interpretation given by Qatar to the Doha Minutes should imply that they must be interpreted in accordance with Bahrain's thesis. As a result, it does not consider that the *travaux préparatoires*, in the form in which they have been submitted to it—i.e., limited to the various drafts mentioned above—can provide it with conclusive supplementary elements for the interpretation of the text adopted; whatever may have been the motives of each of the Parties, the Court can only confine itself to the actual terms of the Minutes as the expression of their common intention, and to the interpretation of them which it has already given.[74]

It is difficult, however, to resist the strong implication apparent from the change in wording that the indication of a requirement for joint submission

---

[72] *United States—Measures Affecting the Cross-Border Supply of Gambling and Betting Services* WTO Appellate Body Report of 7 April 2005, WT/DS285/AB/R, para 195.
[73] *Maritime Delimitation and Territorial Questions between Qatar and Bahrain (Qatar v Bahrain)* (Jurisdiction and Admissibility) [1995] ICJ Rep 6.
[74] [1995] ICJ Rep 6, 22, para 41.

of the case had been removed during the negotiating process. This was the focus of the dissent by Judge Schwebel:

> If the object of the Parties—if their common intention—was to make clear that 'both Qatar and Bahrain had the right to make a unilateral application to the Court', the provision that 'either of the two parties may submit the matter' would have been left unchanged. That wording achieved that object clearly, simply, and precisely. As it was, that unchanged phraseology authorized either of the two Parties to make unilateral application to the Court. To suggest that the change of that phraseology to 'the two parties' rather imports that each of the Parties—because of that change—is entitled to make a unilateral application to the Court is unintelligible.[75]

Analysis suggests that the majority of the Court considered that a reasonably clear interpretation by application of the general rule should not be displaced by inferences from fragmentary preparatory work showing no clear common understanding. In contrast, the Schwebel dissent found the deductions which could be made from the preparatory work were much stronger evidence than the uncertainties of the meaning in the text.[76] Whatever view one takes of the respective merits, this case shows that the value of the Vienna rules lies more in providing the structure and elements for interpretative argument, while the skill and judgement of the interpreter is the further essential criterion for reaching a sound interpretation.

2 Other Supplementary Means

In addition to the circumstances of conclusion mentioned above, two other types of supplementary means warrant mention. Explanatory reports and studies by experts may be difficult to classify. Such a report may be contemporaneous with conclusion of a treaty, part of the preparatory work, may amount to a subsequent agreement, constitute interpretation by agreed common practice, or simply be official or academic analysis. Whether such material falls into one of the categories in the general rule or is simply

---

[75] [1995] ICJ Rep 6, 34–35.
[76] The interpretative arguments were much more extensive than those highlighted here: see further Gardiner (n 10) 366–73.

supplementary material, the principle is clear that if it shows that the parties are agreed on the meaning of a treaty, that is a useful factor in its interpretation. Thus, for example, the Explanatory Report on the 1980 Hague Child Abduction Convention was drawn up after the conference at which the Convention was concluded.[77] Although based on preparatory work and records of the adopting conference, it does not claim to record specific agreements on interpretation. Nevertheless, the Report has been taken by several national courts as highly authoritative, though it is unclear whether this is as a contemporaneous set of agreements, subsequent agreements by acceptance of the Report in practice, or simply as supplementary means of interpretation under Article 32 VCLT.

Also difficult to locate precisely within the Vienna rules are the maxims or canons of interpretation. These are commonly denoted by their Latin tags. Examples are: '*ut res magis valeat quam pereat, contra proferentem, eiusdem generis, expressio unius est exclusio alterius, generalia specialibus non derogant*'.[78] These were viewed by the ILC as of potential practical assistance but not as rules of interpretation.[79] Thus the maxims or canons may be part of the apparatus for identifying the ordinary meaning of terms or may be classified as supplementary means.

IV Languages: VCLT Article 33

Much less attention has been given to this provision than the two preceding articles on treaty interpretation for the obvious reason that issues of linguistic comparison do not arise in all, or many, cases. However, as it is common practice to use languages of both parties in the case of bilateral treaties and several languages in the case of multilateral ones, there is scope for divergence despite best efforts to align meanings. Discussion of the language provisions in the ILC tried to preserve a notion of unity of a treaty in however many languages it had been authenticated.[80] However,

---

[77] 'Explanatory Report on the 1980 Hague Child Abduction Convention', prepared by Elisa Pérez-Vera, Hague Conference on Private International Law Actes et documents de la Quatorzième session, p. 428.

[78] See J Klingler, Y Parkhomenko, and C Salonidis (eds), *Between the Lines of the Vienna Convention?: Canons and Other Principles of Interpretation in Public International Law* (Kluwer 2019), where each maxim is given chapter-length analysis with reference to illustrative cases.

[79] See Humphrey Waldock, 'Third Report on the Law of Treaties' [1964-II] Yearbook of the ILC 54 [5]–[6].

[80] See ch 3, section II.4(b) above.

problems have arisen particularly where states have used languages other than their own in negotiations and their 'official' translations have introduced variances.[81]

Unfortunately, the tendency to use an increasing number of authentic languages has not been matched by retention of the earlier practice of indicating that in the case of divergence or difference over meaning a particular language is to prevail. Where present, such an indicated priority is preserved by the Vienna rules.[82] Otherwise, the text is equally authoritative in each language and the terms of the treaty are presumed to have the same meaning in each authentic text. Inevitably, legal concepts and terms may be difficult to reproduce in languages where legal terms may attract their own nuances.

A major problem is that the linguistic competence of judges and arbitrators is unlikely to be sufficient to resolve difficulties where experts in the relevant languages disagree. The tendency is to focus on the languages of the court or tribunal that correspond to those of the treaty, or translations into the languages of court or tribunal.[83] The article was the only one of the three on interpretation to be significantly changed at the Vienna conference from the draft offered by the ILC. This was to add the indication that 'a meaning shall be adopted which is most consonant with the object and purpose of the treaty' where differences between languages could not otherwise be reconciled by reference to the Vienna rules.[84]

V Conclusion

Interpreting a treaty involves examining its text, gaining an understanding by exploring all the relevant materials, and evaluating the various elements indicated in the rules of interpretation. The Vienna rules provide indications of what is to be taken into account in giving meaning to a treaty, but

---

[81] cf *Kiliç v Turkmenistan* ICSID Case No ARB/10/1, Decision of 7 May 2012; and *Muhammet Çap v Turkmenistan* ICSID Case No ARB/12/6 (13 February 2015).
[82] VCLT, art 33(1).
[83] See eg the approach of the ICJ in *LaGrand Case (Germany v USA)* [2001] ICJ Rep 466.
[84] For the limited value of this in resolving language difficulties see contrasting outcomes in cases cited in n 81, but see also the use of art 33 in *LaGrand* above.

they only provide limited pointers to the value to be attached to the elements present in any particular case. Thus application of these rules does not lead to a single inevitable result in each instance. The interpreter's skill and judgement are essential added factors. However, the rules do provide guidance for a properly argued attribution of meaning.

5
Bringing Treaties Home

> It would be sufficient to recall the fundamental principle of international law that international law prevails over domestic law. This principle was endorsed by judicial decision as long ago as the arbitral award of 14 September 1872 in the *Alabama* case between Great Britain and the United States, and has frequently been recalled since, for example in the case concerning the *Greco-Bulgarian 'Communities'* in which the Permanent Court of International Justice laid it down that
>
> 'it is a generally accepted principle of international law that in the relations between Powers who are contracting Parties to a treaty, the provisions of municipal law cannot prevail over those of the treaty' (PCIJ, Series B, No 17, 32).[1]

I Introduction

1 General Considerations

The central question of this chapter is whether an individual or company can rely on a treaty when entering into transactions governed by domestic law or when involved in proceedings in the courts of a country? The answer may be best understood by examining the way in which international law and national legal systems relate to one another.[2] With the proliferation of

---

[1] Advisory Opinion of the International Court of Justice on *Applicability of the Obligation of the Arbitrate under section 21 of the United Nations Headquarters Agreement of 26 June 1947* ('PLO Observer Mission' case) [1988] ICJ Rep 12, para 57 https://www.icj-cij.org/public/files/case-related/77/077-19880426-ADV-01-00-EN.pdf. This chapter is based in part on revised material from ch 4 of R Gardiner, *International Law* (Longman 2003). For more detailed accounts see D Sloss, 'Domestic Application of Treaties', ch 15 in D Hollis (ed), *The Oxford Guide to Treaties* (2nd edn, OUP 2020).

[2] The terms 'domestic', 'municipal', and 'national' law are used in this chapter interchangeably to denote law which is not public international law.

treaties having provisions which directly impact the lives and work of individuals and companies, national legal systems provide the arena in which treaties will very commonly be encountered, even if concealed behind a veil of domestic legislation in many instances. After stating some general considerations, the first stage in examining these matters is identifying which treaties require implementation in national law, or which provisions of a particular treaty so require.

2 Treaties Require Good Faith Performance

The extract from the International Court's Advisory Opinion set out above puts treaties under the spotlight of the general proposition that international obligations prevail over domestic law. Thus every state has an obligation to give full effect to every commitment established by the terms of every treaty to which it is a party. This is clear not only from the proposition in Article 26 of the Vienna Convention ('Every treaty in force is binding upon the parties to it and must be performed by them in good faith'), but also from the prohibition in Article 27: 'A party may not invoke the provisions of its internal law as justification for its failure to perform a treaty...'[3]

Some modern constitutions have detailed provisions on treaties aimed at ensuring proper consideration and implementation of their obligations. For example, the Polish constitution of 1997, in addition to a general provision on respect for international law (Article 9), has a requirement of prior consent by statute for ratification of an international agreement on listed subjects: peace, alliances, political or military treaties; constitutional freedoms, rights or obligations of citizens; membership of an international organization; those raising substantial financial responsibilities; and those otherwise regulated by statute and where the constitution requires a statute (Article 89). Other international agreements must be notified to parliament, and principles and procedures for conclusion and termination are to be specified by statute (Article 89). Once ratified and promulgated in the

---

[3] Article 27 qualifies this by stating: 'This rule is without prejudice to Article 46.' Article 46, however, is not a true exception to the principle. It identifies circumstances in which a state can in effect deny that it is a party, rather than whether a state can reject a substantive provision because of a conflicting provision of internal law. It renders invalid apparent participation in a treaty by a state which has ostensibly become a party but in violation of a rule of its internal law of fundamental importance, such violation being manifest (that is objectively evident to any state conducting itself in the matter in accordance with normal practice and in good faith). In these circumstances it is clear to every other state that the particular state is not a party.

Polish official journal, an international agreement constitutes part of the domestic legal order and is to be applied directly, unless its application depends on the enactment of a statute.[4]

3 National Legal Systems: 'Monism' and 'Dualism'

Analysis of the relationship of international law with law created within states tends to be in terms of 'monism' and 'dualism'. The former approach is based on the idea that law is a single system of which international and municipal law are component parts. Dualism holds that international and municipal law operate in two independent spheres with appropriate bridges between them. While this may have analytical attraction, the practicalities of treaty application are actually obscured by assumptions of how classification into monism or dualism applies to individual states, particularly when considering implementation of treaties. The best that can be said is that each national legal system may show an approach whose predominant features suggest one or other type of relationship, but neither category offers a complete description of how treaties are actually implemented in particular states. This can be amply demonstrated by examples, but it is first necessary to establish how to identify which obligations need implementation within national legal systems.

II International Law's Requirements

1 International and Municipal Consequences of Treaties Distinguished

Whether a treaty's obligations require application of its provisions within a party's municipal system depends on the substance of the provisions. Some

---

[4] See the Polish Parliament (*Sejm*) website (giving Polish and English text): https://www.sejm.gov.pl/prawo/konst/angielski/kon1.htm. There are further provisions on procedural requirements and for treaties on giving competence to international organizations, laws established by such organizations being applied directly and having precedence in the event of a conflict of laws (articles 90 and 91)), and see L Kulaga, 'The Implementation of International Agreements in the Polish Legal System. The Selected Aspects of Practice in Recent Two Decades' (2020) 9 Polish Rev Intl & Eur L 125. cf the French constitution considered in section III.5 of this chapter.

may only affect international relations of states and therefore have no effect on the internal legal order. To give an example, a treaty of alliance may place an obligation on states to go to one another's assistance militarily if specified circumstances arise. Such a treaty creates obligations which affect only the international relations of the states parties to it. No change is required to the law applying within such a state.

Ostensibly similar in legal effect, a peace treaty may simply establish that two states are no longer at war. As such, the legal position established by the treaty may take effect just between the two states parties to it. Peace replaces war. There may be no legal effect beyond a reset of relations in international law, though further possibilities are indicated below.[5] In contrast, a treaty which creates a defined criminal offence and requires states to make the offence punishable in their own legal systems necessarily has to take effect within domestic law because that is the arena in which the criminal law is envisaged as applying. Thus in this case there are provisions which take effect both on the international plane, in the sense of the mutual commitment to fulfil the treaty, and within municipal law in the practical application of criminal law.

However, the division of treaty provisions into the categories of those taking effect solely internationally and those having effect on and in domestic law is not always so simple. A peace treaty can also produce consequences within the domestic law of the states concerned. Individuals may be affected if, for example, national laws have attributed consequences to being an enemy alien present within the territory. Being an enemy alien may have led to internment and to sequestration of property. Commercial transactions with nationals of an enemy state may have been abrogated or prohibited for the duration of the war, as may travel to and from there, or any activity likely to advance the enemy's cause.

Hence, a treaty of peace may significantly change the status of individuals and corporations, the legitimacy of their activities and their legal relations, even though these are matters directly regulated by domestic law. The treaty itself may be silent on such matters. If the legal consequences within each state of the outbreak of hostilities have only been prescribed by their respective domestic laws, reversal of such measures is in principle for the domestic law. Equally, however, a peace treaty may lay down requirements

---

[5] cf P Rowe and M Meyer, 'The Geneva Conventions (Amendment) Act 1995: a Generally Minimalist Approach' (1996) 45 ICLQ 476, 478.

to be implemented within each state.[6] In this latter case, the choice is either to use the relevant terms of the treaty as the text of the domestic law or to pass bespoke laws to reflect each of the treaty obligations. This choice is not usually the concern of international law. The state must simply comply with its international obligations in full and in good faith. Constitutional arrangements within the state will dictate what are the necessary and appropriate processes.

Although not a peace treaty in the sense of an instrument relating to the cessation of war, the Treaty for the Renunciation of War as an Instrument of National Policy 1928 (known variously, and more simply, as 'the Pact of Paris' or 'the Kellogg–Briand Pact') was drawn up for maintenance of peace by renunciation of war.[7] It provides a good illustration of terms of the first kind described above, that is terms effective on the international plane. Its operative provisions are very brief:

Article I
The High Contracting Parties solemnly declare in the names of their respective peoples that they condemn recourse to war for the solution of international controversies, and renounce it, as an instrument of national policy in their relations with one another.

Article II
The High Contracting Parties agree that the settlement or solution of all disputes or conflicts of whatever nature or of whatever origin they may be, which may arise among them, shall never be sought except by pacific means.

It is easy to see that the primary role of such provisions is as a compact between states in their relations with one another. Although there is a self-declared representative role in the words 'in the names of their respective peoples', it is somewhat far-fetched to imagine that were the text of the treaty made part of the internal law of a party to it, an effective action would lie in the courts on the application of a citizen to restrain a dictator bent on violating the treaty's requirements. The real test, however, for determining a treaty's effect on the internal legal order is whether, on their

---

[6] See eg Annex II to the Treaty of peace between Israel and Jordan 1994, 2042 UNTS 351, No 35325, setting out the amounts of water the parties may extract from rivers in their territories.
[7] General Treaty for Renunciation of War as an Instrument of National Policy, Paris, 1928, 94 LNTS 57.

correct interpretation, the provisions of the treaty require implementation in domestic law. This is not the place to evaluate the failure of the Pact of Paris in its immediate ends (though one of its legal consequences was to provide part of the basis for the indictment of war criminals at the end of the Second World War and their trials at Nuremberg and Tokyo). The point to note is that legal consequences of the Pact depended on its status as an instrument of international law to be invoked before an international tribunal (if any had jurisdiction), rather than as a statement of legal requirements to be implemented in municipal law. The Pact could take its effect without municipal implementation.

The UN Charter, in contrasting length to the Pact of Paris, has over 100 articles. Yet most of these provisions concern the constitution, function, and powers of the various organs which form the UN. Even those which establish obligations for states do not, for the most part, directly affect the law within Member States. One which does have this capacity is the power of the Security Council to impose 'mandatory' sanctions by resolutions under Article 41 of the UN Charter. These resolutions may require a whole range of domestic measures to achieve 'complete or partial interruption of economic relations and of rail, sea, air, postal, telegraphic, radio, and other means of communication'. Obvious consequences for private parties include preventing performance of contracts and cessation of normal banking and financial transactions. Hence, in the United Kingdom, for example, implementation of Charter is effected by the United Nations Act 1946, which is extremely short as it only provides the powers necessary to implement resolutions under Article 41.

The United Kingdom's assessment of the UN Charter can be taken as an example of a dualist approach to treaties. What is necessary to comply with obligations is recognized by legislation. Yet that is not the complete picture. Article 94 of the Charter provides that 'Each Member of the United Nations undertakes to comply with the decision of the International Court of Justice in any case to which it is a party'. The United Kingdom's legislation does not provide powers to achieve an effect equivalent to those for a Security Council mandatory resolution. There has not yet been an issue over this for the UK, but there has in the USA. The approach of the US constitution to treaties can be viewed as monist: Article VI provides that 'all treaties made, or which shall be made, under the authority of the United States, shall be the supreme law of the land'. Yet the US Supreme Court did not consider that this required Texas to comply with a judgment of the ICJ on failure to accord Mexican nationals the benefit of provisions in the Vienna Convention on Consular Relations 1963 because the Court did not consider the treaty to indicate explicitly that it was to take direct effect and there had been no congressional legislation to achieve this either.[8]

2 A Treaty May Require Provisions in Municipal Law

An example of a treaty which has provisions patently requiring implementation by law within the national legal systems of parties to it is the aviation sabotage treaty which stipulates:

> THE STATES PARTIES TO THIS CONVENTION
> …
> HAVE AGREED AS FOLLOWS:
> *Article 1*
> (1) Any person commits an offence if he unlawfully and intentionally:
>   (a) performs an act of violence against a person on board an aircraft in flight if that act is likely to endanger the safety of that aircraft; or
>   (b) destroys an aircraft in service or causes damage to such aircraft which renders it incapable of flight or which is likely to endanger its safety in flight; …
>
> *Article 3*
> Each Contracting State undertakes to make the offences mentioned in Article 1 punishable by severe penalties.[9]

These two articles provide a standard definition of offences which the treaty requires each party to make punishable by severe penalties. Proper implementation necessarily gives a role to the criminal law of each such state. How, then, must this be achieved? The answer is that each state must use its appropriate constitutional means. If this requires an addition to the criminal code, new legislation, promulgation of an edict, allocation to

---

[8] *Medellín v Texas* 552 US 491 (2008); and see DL Sloss, 'Taming Madison's Monster: How to Fix Self-Execution Doctrine' (2015) 6 BYU L Rev 1691.
[9] Convention for the Suppression of Unlawful Acts against the Safety of Civil Aviation, Montreal, 1971, 974 UNTS 177, no 14118; crimes now included in expanded list in the treaty revised at Beijing, 2010: https://www.icao.int/secretariat/legal/Docs/beijing_convention_multi.pdf.

courts of a particular level of jurisdiction, special sentencing powers for judges, or whatever, the state must establish the offence, exactly as defined, and use the appropriate means to make it capable of resulting in severe penalties for perpetrators.

3 Monist and Dualist Approaches to Implementation

This example from criminal law relating to protection of aviation is helpful for examining the advantages and disadvantages of some of the differing methods used by states in their constitutions to give effect to treaties. The main distinction is between those states whose constitutions use processes that result in the whole of a treaty automatically having the status of an authoritative legal text within the domestic legal system, and those which assess what obligations arise from the treaty and adjust their domestic law in whatever way is necessary to comply with those obligations.

Consider the effect of the first of these approaches (monist). Article 1 of the Montreal/Beijing Convention (quoted above) defines offences. If the treaty text itself becomes part of the internal law of a state, there is no obvious difficulty in the definitions of the offences becoming part of that law and being applied in their treaty form. Article 3, however, is rather different. It is couched in terms of an obligation on a state party to do something ('to make the offences mentioned in Article 1 punishable by severe penalties'). Would the obligation be met by a constitutional process which simply made this text part of domestic law? A court applying Article 3 might be able to achieve a result consistent with the state's obligations by applying some general legal principle which gives preference to compliance with international obligations. In other words, assuming constitutional authorization, the court might achieve the correct result simply by adopting an appropriate interpretation of 'severe penalties' and imposing such penalties on the guilty.

Yet there could still be difficulties. A literal reading of the text could lead a court to look in the criminal code to see whether the defined offences had been included in any category for which 'severe penalties' are specified, and to find them absent if no additional legislation had been enacted. Equally, these treaty provisions give no details of procedure. Which court within a state could try these offences? If a case came before a court lacking the power to impose a severe penalty, simply bringing the treaty text into the domestic legal order would not have fulfilled the obligations of the state if the legal procedure had not been recalibrated to enable the case to reach an appropriate court.

4 More than Monism May Be Required

Thus, while legal systems whose constitutions automatically incorporate treaties in domestic law could appear to offer complete effect being given to a treaty, there may be a greater prospect of actual compliance through a constitutional procedure which requires examination of the treaty to identify every obligation which arises and to make consequent legislative provision. This, in the above example, should succeed in establishing appropriate criminal offences reflecting the definitions in Article 1, in ascribing jurisdiction to an appropriate court, and in requiring penalties to be imposed within an appropriately severe range.[10]

Another type of provision which shows some of the potential consequences of the two main differences in approach is the 'empowering' provision. Such a provision does not have an effect unless a state party to the treaty does something. For example, the UN Convention on the Law of the Sea provides that: 'Every State has the right to establish the breadth of its territorial sea up to a limit not exceeding 12 nautical miles.'[11] This provision recognizes the right of each state to determine the breadth of its territorial sea up to the specified limit. Simply making the text of the treaty part of domestic law achieves little obvious effect for the provision. It would give no indication of the actual limit which the state has fixed. Something further is

---

[10] cf art 1 of the OECD Convention on Combating Bribery of Foreign Public Officials in International Business Transactions 1997, 2802 UNTS 225 no 49274, which requires parties to 'take such measures as may be necessary to establish that it is a criminal offence under its law for any person intentionally to offer, promise or give any undue pecuniary or other advantage, whether directly or through intermediaries, to a foreign public official'. Thus parties must check their domestic legislation and bring it into line with the Convention's obligations. Merely making the Convention part of domestic law is not sufficient. That this is recognised to be the case is demonstrated by the fact that even states considered to be of a monist disposition have passed implementing legislation (see individual country reports at https://www.oecd.org/daf/anti-bribery/countryreportsontheimplementationoftheoecdanti-briberyconvention.htm).

[11] See art 3. One hundred and thirty-seven parties to the Convention set a 12-nautical mile territorial sea, while some ten states claimed a territorial sea of less than 12 nautical miles; twenty-four former claimants to more than 12 nautical miles have reduced the breadth to 12 nautical miles: http://iilss.net/legal-status-of-the-territorial-sea-international-law-of-the-sea-losc-cases/ (visited 21 June 2023). On implementing the UN Convention see D H Anderson, 'British Accession to the UN Convention on the Law of the Sea' (1997) 46 ICLQ 761.

clearly required, whether by law, decree, proclamation, or whatever process the relevant constitution provides, to state what the breadth actually is.[12] This, however, is an optional act, there being no treaty obligation except to keep any claim to a maximum of 12 nautical miles.

5 'Self-executing' Provisions and 'Direct Applicability'

The circumstances just described are sometimes said to raise the issue of whether a treaty is capable of being 'self-executing' or 'directly applicable'. This has slightly different meanings in different legal systems. The idea is, however, that some treaty provisions are of a sufficiently precise character and contain appropriate formulations for them to be able to take effect within a national legal system without further elaboration or clarification.

A classic example of treaties establishing a code of rules capable of direct application is the collection of treaties on carriage by air. To enable passengers, cargo, and mail to be carried by air internationally without subjection to differing, and possibly conflicting, national legal regimes, the 1929 Warsaw Convention (its successive amendments, and the revised Convention of Montreal 1999) have established a set of rules on contract and tort or delict which standardize documents of carriage, the regime for liability and compensation for death, injury, loss of luggage and cargo, and for delay. The treaties also indicate which parties' courts have jurisdiction over claims for these occurrences.[13] These rules are mandatory and exclusive, the treaties giving them supremacy over any contractual provisions seeking to oust them or diminish their effect.[14] Courts around the world have, therefore, made numerous judgments (not always consistent) interpreting the rules as they are expressed in the treaties' own terms.

---

[12] Another practical illustration of the need to go further than simply making a treaty part of domestic law is art 2 of the Convention on the Taking of Evidence Abroad in Civil or Commercial Matters, The Hague, 1970, 847 UNTS 240 no 12140, which provides that each state party 'shall designate a Central Authority which will undertake to receive Letters of Request coming from a judicial authority of another Contracting State'. Simply making such a provision domestic law would not constitute compliance with the treaty as no Central Authority would have been designated.
[13] Convention for the Unification of Certain Rules relating to International Carriage by Air, Warsaw, 1929, amending Protocols of The Hague 1955, Guatemala City 1971, Montreal Additional Protocols 1 to 3 and Protocol 4 1975, and Convention for the Unification of Certain Rules for International Carriage by Air, Montreal, 1999.
[14] See eg arts 26, 29, and 49 of the Montreal Convention, 1999.

Nevertheless, even a set of such readily applicable provisions does not necessarily provide completely satisfactory implementation of the treaties. The differing regimes in successive amendments to the carriage by air treaties, and the possibility of states becoming parties to any one (or more) of these treaties after their entry into force, may require some domestic trigger for national implementation to take effect. The earlier treaties also have provisions for gold clauses as measures of compensation with provisions for their conversion into national currencies in a manner to be determined by each state party, while the later ones use Special Drawing Rights of the IMF, the method of conversion determining the value in national currencies of Member States. National courts may simply admit evidence from the depositories (Poland and the International Civil Aviation Organization) as to which states are parties to which treaties, although some domestic form of certification of parties may provide greater clarity for the courts.[15] Likewise, although a market price of gold might be the means by which courts could give direct effect to the relevant treaty provisions, the complexities of the former system of official gold prices and the uncertainties arising from the abandonment of fixed parities has led to some states specifying equivalents in their currencies by national measures.

6 Further Analysis of Treaty Obligations

Another analysis, in further explanation of the examples given above and useful in helping to predict which treaty provisions are likely to receive attention in courts of states parties to them, is that given by Professor Sloss:

> States conclude treaties to regulate three different types of relationships: *horizontal* relations between and among States, *vertical* relations between States and private actors (including natural persons and corporations), and *transnational* relations between private actors who interact across national boundaries.[16]

While the provisions regulating horizontal relations—those purely inter-state—are unlikely to be amenable to proceedings in national courts,

---

[15] The United Kingdom uses statutory instruments described as 'Parties to Conventions Orders' where legislative provision is not made by (or continued from) the European Union.
[16] Sloss (n 1) 364, text to n 107 (emphasis in original).

those dealing with transnational relations are particularly likely to be implemented nationally and potentially the subject of adjudication and enforcement in national courts. In the case of vertical relations, there may be some treaties which provide for international adjudication on rights of private actors—such as human rights treaties or bilateral investment treaties—but these may also cover matters which can come before national courts.

Points to note in this analysis are that treaties may not deal with relations exclusively in one of these categories and that treaties regulating vertical and transnational relations do so by virtue of the horizontal relationship between states parties to them even if reliance on that relationship may not be a prominent feature of the regime such treaties institute. Thus, for example, bilateral investment treaties typically provide for an investor to take a host state to international arbitration (vertical relations), but also commonly provide for arbitration between the states parties to the treaty for ultimate differences over its application or interpretation (horizontal relations), and for enforcement of arbitral awards in national courts.

A further point to note is that controversial legal issues in the application of treaties within national jurisdictions are those which feature in law reports and writings about law. However, it must be emphasized that application of treaties occurs constantly without courts or tribunals being involved at all. Entry into a country of people and goods of foreign origin maybe a treaty entitlement administered by immigration and customs officials. Classification of products for levying taxes or other duties, description of medicines, recognition of diplomas and professional qualifications, and exemptions from double taxation are examples of routine application of treaties by officials and those having any administrative, employment or other functions.[17]

---

[17] In the UK, for example, the Court of Appeal (England and Wales) noted that articles in the Convention on Jurisdiction, Applicable Law, Recognition, Enforcement and Co-operation in Respect of Parental Responsibility and Measures for the Protection of Children, The Hague, 1996 refer to 'administrative' as well as judicial authorities, and there is nothing in the Convention to suggest that only a court can determine whether the application of the ordinary choice of law rule would be 'manifestly contrary to public policy': *Home Secretary v GA and others* [2021] EWCA Civ 1131.

III National Requirements and Procedures

1 Forms of Constitutional Implementation

The intricacies of the variations in methods of implementation of treaties within different states give scope for extensive and detailed accounts. There have been studies of a number of states for those needing that depth of detail.[18] What is attempted here is an identification and overview of issues which may present themselves to those encountering treaties within national legal systems.

Against the background of the differing types of treaty obligations to which national systems must give effect, the various constitutional arrangements can be enumerated. First, there are those constitutions which simply make any treaty to which the state is party internal law without any further action beyond any necessary authorization of the person who is to give definitive consent to be bound whether by ratification, accession, signature, or whatever method the treaty requires ('automatic' or 'constitutional' incorporation). Second, and more common, is a combination of this first technique and further domestic actions, such as decrees or forms of subordinate legislation taking up any elements of the treaty which require this, or specifying the date of entry into force, listing parties and so on ('textual incorporation with legislative details'). These two means of implementation fit under the monist label, rather loosely in the second case.

A third method of implementation is for a legislative act to incorporate the text of the treaty wholesale into domestic law ('legislative textual incorporation'). This could be by a law setting out the treaty and making, or giving authority to make, any further necessary measures of the kind indicated as an adjunct to the second method. Finally, the fourth way of giving effect to a treaty is to transform its requirements by legislation into provisions of domestic law, or those of its provisions which necessitate adjustment of existing domestic law. The third and fourth methods could be labelled dualist, although the third differs little in effect from the second.

---

[18] See eg D Hollis, M Blakeslee, and B Ederington (eds), *National Treaty Law and Practice* (Martinus Nijhoff 2005); FG Jacobs and S Roberts (eds), *The Effect of Treaties in Domestic Law* (Sweet and Maxwell 1987); R Gaebler and AA Shea (eds), *Sources of State Practice in International Law* (Brill-Nijhoff 2014); and CA Bradley (ed), *The Oxford Handbook of Comparative Foreign Relations Law* (OUP 2019).

2 Distinguish Prior Authorization for Participation from Implementation

There are three phases in the involvement of the organs of a state with treaties. First, before a treaty is negotiated there may be procedures for establishing a negotiating position. Second, once negotiations are complete, domestic procedures may be necessary before the state can become a party. Third, and separately or in parallel with the second phase, there may be legislative procedures for implementing the treaty's terms. Thus, deciding whether to become a party to a treaty is distinct from implementing it, although domestic procedures for authorizing the relevant organ of the state to ratify a treaty may in monist states also have an implementing effect.

Although there are many examples of commissions and bodies of specialist interest within states which advise on, or prepare, a state's approach to the terms of a potential treaty, any legislative commitment to specific terms in a negotiating mandate risks unduly fettering the scope of manoeuvre in negotiation of a treaty. The first of these phases is therefore generally not formally legislative. The second and third phases, however, are neither sequential nor readily examined without attention to the constitutional features of each state. There are, nevertheless, some features which can be identified by reference to the analysis in terms of monism and dualism.

This has been made explicit in the United Kingdom, for example, where the government exercises the Crown's prerogative powers in relation to treaties. As it has been put judicially, '[t]he Government may negotiate, conclude, construe, observe, breach, repudiate or terminate a treaty'.[19] 'Subject to any restrictions imposed by primary legislation, the general rule is that the power to make or unmake treaties is exercisable without legislative authority ... This principle rests on the so-called dualist theory, which is based on the proposition that international law and domestic law operate in independent spheres.'[20]

---

[19] *JH Rayner (Mincing Lane) Ltd v Department of Trade and Industry* [1990] 2 AC 418, 476 (Lord Templeman).
[20] See *R (on the application of Miller and Another) v Secretary of State for Exiting the European Union* [2017] UKSC 5, para 55; and see *Heathrow Airport Limited, and Ors v Her Majesty's Treasury* [2021] EWCA Civ 783, paras 140 ff.

3 Domestic Approval

After a treaty has been negotiated, and if it is subject to ratification, the opportunity is usually afforded to differing organs within a state to participate in the decision whether to become bound by a treaty. In the approach described as monism this process is bound up with the state's constitutional procedure, commonly but misleadingly described as 'ratification'. What is in fact being considered here is the domestic process by which the relevant organs of the state assent to the state being bound by the treaty and making it part of the law of the state. At risk of over-generalizing, the prevailing practice appears to be that governments are responsible for the negotiation and conclusion of treaty texts, while legislatures play a part in assenting to the treaty and controlling its implementation, thus to that extent determining whether the state can become a party to a treaty:

> Generally speaking, states demonstrate remarkable uniformity in distributing their treaty-making authority internally. In every case, the states surveyed assign the power to negotiate and conclude treaties to the executive.
>
> The fact that states empower only their executives to make treaties binding on the state does not mean that they exercise such power unencumbered. In fact, all of the states surveyed reported limitations on the exercise of this power ... These restrictions primarily apply to the executive's ability to actually consent to a treaty on behalf of the state. However, limitations on the executive's capacity may also operate more generally.[21]

As suggested above, an important factor in analysis of the different domestic approaches lies in the two different uses of the term 'ratification'—the inaccurate but colloquial for domestic processes and the international usage in the law of treaties.[22] The domestic processes differ from state to state, but typically may involve approval by a legislative body, such approval giving the government authorization to carry out the international step of ratification and, or alternatively, giving the treaty provisions effect in domestic law such that international ratification may take place without risk of domestic law being inadequate to comply with the treaty's obligations.

---

[21] Hollis (n 18) 19, 23.
[22] See ch 3 above.

Where the domestic process both authorizes deposit of an instrument of ratification and has the internal effect of making the entire treaty part of the state's domestic law there may, nevertheless, need to be further measures of a legislative nature to make the treaty effective, as shown above. Further, it is sometimes possible for the constitutional process necessary to prepare for ratification to affect the terms of the treaty. For example, in the USA the constitution provides for advice and consent of the Senate as a prerequisite to the President ratifying a treaty. If the Senate makes its consent conditional the President may have to arrange for further negotiations to adjust the treaty or decide to withhold ratification. An example is the 1794 Jay treaty between the USA and Great Britain. The Senate rejected a provision restricting trade between the USA and British possessions in the West Indies. Great Britain did not object to removal of this provision and the treaty was duly ratified.[23]

It was, however, because of a condition proposed by the Senate that the USA did not become a party to the Vienna Convention. The Senate required that on ratification a special understanding or interpretative statement be lodged regarding Article 46 of the VCLT. Article 46 provides that a state may not claim its consent to a treaty is invalid because a domestic irregularity meant that consent to the treaty was given in breach of its internal law, unless that violation was 'manifest and concerned a rule of its internal law of fundamental importance'. The Senate's proposed understanding or statement was to the effect that it is a rule of the internal law of the USA of fundamental importance that no treaty is valid for the USA, nor is the giving of consent for the USA to be bound by a treaty permissible, unless the Senate has given its advice and consent to that treaty, or the treaty's terms have been approved by law. Such an interpretative statement could have cast doubt on treaties classed in the USA as 'executive agreements', that is treaties which, by established practice in the USA, have long been concluded by the executive, alone or with legislative support but without advice and consent of the Senate. Failure by the executive and Senate to agree on this issue precluded ratification of the Vienna Convention.[24]

---

[23] See C Bradley, *International Law in the U.S. Legal System* (OUP 2015) 35–39, where it is also noted that in an 1803 boundary treaty between the same parties an amendment proposed by the Senate was not accepted by Great Britain and the treaty was never ratified, but that Senate reservations, understandings, and declarations have become a generally accepted practice of the USA.

[24] See E Criddle, 'The Vienna Convention on the Law of Treaties in U.S. Treaty Interpretation' (2003–2004) 44 Va J Intl L 431, 442–43.

Historically, those Commonwealth countries which follow the British dualist tradition have had fewer written indications of constitutional arrangements for treaty participation and implementation. The matter has been largely left to the executive and its need to bring forward legislative proposals where this is necessary to comply with the prospective obligations. In the United Kingdom, the domestic procedure before ratification has been put on a statutory basis. Part 2 of the Constitutional Reform and Governance Act 2010 provides, under the heading 'Ratification of Treaties', that as a general rule a treaty may not to be ratified unless laid before Parliament for twenty-one sitting days and neither House has resolved that the treaty should not be ratified.[25] This practice was formerly known as 'the Ponsonby rule' and was implemented by the treaty being laid as published in the 'Miscellaneous' series of 'Command Papers'. Unless vetoed by resolution, the treaty could thereafter be ratified and would then be published in the UK Treaty Series. The Act uses a definition of 'treaty' close to that in the Vienna Convention but substitutes the phrase 'binding under international law' for 'governed by international law', to allow exclusion of those non-binding instruments which may have legal consequences under international law without constituting agreements binding as treaties.

The American system provides the choice for implementing treaties indicated above. The president may ratify after completion of the constitutional process or conclude it as an 'executive agreement' relying, as necessary, on legislative provisions enacted by Congress in the ordinary way. This ostensibly simple distinction—between treaties which on their own terms are capable of having effect within domestic law without further elaboration and those which need supplementary legislation—is complicated by distinctions that have been introduced into the application of the constitutional arrangements to treaties. 'Direct applicability' (as an alternative to 'self-executing') is the term sometimes used to describe the character of treaty provisions as 'statute-like' domestic law to be applied by the courts.[26]

Numerous factors are taken into account to decide whether a treaty has direct applicability and is self-executing.[27] While this has the advantage that

---

[25] For analysis and further details see J Barrett, 'The United Kingdom and Parliamentary Scrutiny of Treaties: Recent Reforms' (2011) 60 ICLQ 225.
[26] JH Jackson, 'United States' in FG Jacobs and S Roberts (eds), *The Effect of Treaties in Domestic Law* (Sweet and Maxwell 1987) 144; see further RE Dalton, 'The United States, ch 20 in D Hollis, M Blakeslee, and B Ederington (eds), *National Treaty Law and Practice* (Martinus Nijhoff 2005).
[27] See Jackson (n 18) 152–53.

the courts must become very familiar with all aspects of a treaty which they are having to consider, the approach is complex and may produce divergent results and has been criticized in the USA itself.[28] A system in which a parliamentary process determines the substance of what provisions of a treaty the courts are to apply, and provides any necessary supplementary law, generally allows for the government to present the issues to the legislature following consideration and advice by specialists who are familiar with international law and conversion of treaties into domestic form.

4 Implementing Treaties in a Dualist System

(a) The United Kingdom as a paradigm

The constitutional arrangements in all the countries which can be classified as having a predominantly dualist approach are too variegated in their details for examination here. However, as many of these have practices derived from the United Kingdom's approach, this is taken as a rough paradigm. Where a treaty's provisions require a change in municipal law, the constitutional arrangements of the United Kingdom envisage legislation. Such legislation is often described as 'incorporating' the treaty. The term has no standard definition and describes no uniform practice, although it is commonly used in judgments. 'Incorporating' a treaty here means legislative action to enable compliance, whether the treaty text itself is set out in the legislation or not.[29] It is clearer, therefore, to describe such legislation as 'implementing' the treaty, but courts still tend to use the terms 'incorporation' and 'incorporated'.[30]

---

[28] ibid 148–49.
[29] The terminology can be confusing because where the relationship between general international law and the law in the United Kingdom is being described, judges use 'incorporation' to describe automatic reception of an international rule into the domestic law, which is to say, reception without the intervention of Parliament: see eg *Trendtex Trading Corporation v Central Bank of Nigeria* [1977] 1 QB 529, 553 (Lord Denning), and see Lord Hoffmann in text to n 163 below; and see S Fatima, 'The Domestic Application of International Law in British Courts', ch 27 in CA Bradley (ed), *The Oxford Handbook of Comparative Foreign Relations Law* (OUP 2019).
[30] See eg *Re G (A Child)* [2021] UKSC 9, para 1, where the Supreme Court refers to a treaty as 'incorporated' by legislation, which set out detailed implementing provisions but scheduled only some of the articles of two treaties: Child Abduction and Custody Act 1985 (long title: 'An Act to enable the United Kingdom to ratify two international Conventions relating respectively to the civil aspects of international child abduction and to the recognition and enforcement of custody decisions').

III National Requirements and Procedures

The power of the executive in the UK to enter into treaty relations derives from the historic power of the sovereign and is therefore described as a 'royal prerogative' power. That such powers are not subject to judicial review ('non-justiciable') is a principle which has been considerably whittled away, though to a limited extent for treaties. The two principles on the legal status of international treaties in domestic courts remain as stated in *Rayner v Department for Trade and Industry* and which can be summarized:

(a) Municipal courts have no competence to rule on or enforce rights arising out of transactions between states; and
(b) the royal prerogative gives the government power to make treaties but does not extend to altering the law or affecting rights of individuals without the intervention of Parliament.[31]

However, it was also made clear in *Rayner* that this did not mean that the courts are never entitled to construe a treaty—far from it. Several examples were given in that case of where this is permissible, including most prominently where the treaty is directly incorporated into English law by an act of Parliament or is relevant to interpreting an Act.[32]

'Construing' a treaty amounts to interpreting it—a different matter from deciding whether a right or obligation in a treaty may be invoked. Interpretation in national courts is considered below. However, the idea that treaty provisions are only known within a 'dualist' system if they are the subject of legislation is mitigated to some extent. Ways by which treaties may come to be considered by UK courts other than by express statutory implementation include:

(1) review of ministerial action following use of prerogative powers:
(2) the presumption than an interpretation of law in the UK should wherever possible accord with the UK's international obligations;
(3) application of rules of international law expressed in treaties; and
(4) (with much doubt) application of a doctrine of legitimate expectation.

---

[31] *JH Rayner (Mincing Lane) Limited v Department for Trade and Industry* (n 19) 499–500.
[32] The list of examples is digested in *R (KTT) v Secretary of State for the Home Department* [2021] EWHC 2722 (Admin) para 16.

An example of item (1) (review of action following use of prerogative powers) is the UK's implementation of the 1951 UN Refugees Convention.[33] In the 1950s, control of entry into the UK by those not nationals of the UK was within the prerogative powers exercised by the Home Office at UK borders. The Convention could therefore be ratified by the UK and then respected by administrative action. Aspects of entry gradually took on statutory elements, but the detailed reflection of the Convention has been in the Home Office's Immigration Rules in successive documents laid before Parliament. Nevertheless, with the introduction of opportunities for appeals to courts and tribunals, judicial examination and interpretation of the Convention and Protocol has been extensive.

As regards item (2) (presumption of conformity with international obligations), the courts have indicated:

> [I]f the terms of the legislation are not clear but are reasonably capable of more than one meaning, the treaty itself becomes relevant, for there is a prima facie presumption that Parliament does not intend to act in breach of international law, including therein specific treaty obligations; and if one of the meanings which can reasonably be ascribed to the legislation is consonant with the treaty obligations and another or others are not, the meaning which is consonant is to be preferred.[34]

Of item (3) (accepting customary international law rules expressed in treaties), a good example is provisions of the VCLT treated as reflecting international customary law. Those to which most common reference is made are the rules of interpretation in Articles 31–33, but several others are also treated as readily available statements of international law without express incorporation by legislation.[35]

---

[33] Primary legislation eventually defined the treaty as 'the Convention relating to the Status of Refugees done at Geneva on 28 July 1951 and the Protocol to the Convention' and provided that 'Nothing in the immigration rules (within the meaning of the 1971 [Immigration] Act) shall lay down any practice which would be contrary to the Convention': Asylum and Immigration Appeals Act 1993, ss 1 and 2.

[34] *Salomon v Commissioners of Customs* [1967] 2QB 116, 143 (Lord Diplock); and see Fatima (n 29) 494–95.

[35] See eg *Reyes v Al-Malki* [2017] UKSC 61; and *Belhaj v Straw* [2017] UKSC 3, considering art 53 VCLT (peremptory norms); *Routier v Revenue and Customs Commissioners* [2019] UKSC 43; and *R (Bashir) v Secretary of State for the Home Department* [2018] UKSC 45, considering art 29 VCLT (territorial scope of treaties); and *R (Al-Jedda) v Secretary of State for Defence* [2006] EWCA Civ 327, considering art 30 VCLT (successive treaties).

As to item (4) (legitimate expectation), the spark of a challenge to the dualist notion that legislation is necessary for obligations under a treaty to be enforceable in national courts came in the *Teoh* case in the Australian courts, but this has not taken the firm hold which some observers initially thought it might.[36] Teoh, a foreign national, challenged a deportation decision on grounds that the relevant official had not made the best interests of his Australian children 'a primary consideration' as required by the 1989 UN Convention on the Rights of the Child.[37] Australia had ratified the Convention but had not implemented it by legislation.[38] The successful challenge to deportation was based on the ground that ratification created a 'legitimate expectation' that the official decision makers would apply the broad principles of the Convention in so far as consonant with the national interest and not contrary to statutory provisions to do so. However, this case does not give carte blanche for courts to treat unimplemented treaties as a source of law. *Teoh* can be regarded as authority for the more limited administrative law requirement of fairness, namely that a claimant should be given an opportunity to be heard before the adjudicator decides to put aside a particular factor which might reasonably be regarded as relevant.[39] Courts in the UK have adopted mixed views on *Teoh* (not generally favourable), but there may be scope for a more generous application of the principle of legitimate expectation in relation to treaties concerning human rights.[40]

(b) Reflecting obligations and reproducing provisions

The techniques by which Parliament implements treaty obligations fall into two main groups. The first uses legislative language (usually supplied by parliamentary draftsmen) to reflect the obligations in the treaty. The second reproduces the actual text of the treaty provisions (or selected substantive ones). Such reproduction is most commonly in a schedule to an Act, though in some cases—notably extradition treaties and those for avoidance of double taxation—the provisions are sufficiently uniform among the

---

[36] *Minister of State for Immigration and Ethnic Affairs v Teoh* [1995] HCA 20.
[37] See art 3.
[38] The Attorney-General had, however, declared the Convention to be an international instrument relating to human rights and freedoms pursuant to the Australian Human Rights and Equal Opportunity Commission Act 1986.
[39] See A Edgar and R Thwaites, 'Implementing Treaties in Domestic Law: Translation, Enforcement and Administrative Law' (2018) 19 Melb J Intl L 24, 43–44.
[40] See analysis of case law by Lord Kerr in *R (SG and Others) v Secretary of State for Work and Pensions* [2015] UKSC 16, paras 235–46 and on human rights, paras 247–57.

numerous treaties (though by no means identical) for Parliament to have given powers for the treaty provisions to be made law by being set out in subordinate legislation (usually in an Order in Council).

(c) Transforming treaty terms

The first, and older, way in which legislation has been used to implement treaty obligations that are to bind the United Kingdom produces a transfer or conversion of the provisions of the treaty into the accepted form and terminology of Acts of Parliament. This approach has been (confusingly) described as 'direct' enactment, although it could better be thought of as 'transforming' the obligations in the treaty into UK statutory language.[41] An example of this technique is Part III of the Arbitration Act 1996 which implements the New York Arbitration Convention.[42]

Such a method has the advantage that those applying the treaty within the domestic legal system deal with wording and mechanisms that fit the idiom and order of the rest of the law and legal system in the United Kingdom. However, this method bears the risk of inadvertently departing from the requirements of the treaty, or giving the judiciary scope to do so. It disguises the actual language of the treaty, and it may contribute to the risk of use of inappropriate English methods of construction and interpretation when judges are addressing provisions derived from a treaty.

(d) Legislating the treaty's text

As has been shown above, using legislation to ascribe legal force to treaty provisions reproduced in their authentic words is not necessarily the best way to proceed. The main advantages should be accessibility of the actual text of the treaty and an enhanced possibility that the international regime which the treaty establishes will be followed more readily. These advantages have frequently been somewhat negated at the legislative stage, however, by Parliament's not including the whole of the treaty's text in the legislation. Only selected provisions are given the force of law.[43] The basis for the

---

[41] See F Bennion, *Statutory Interpretation* (2nd edn, Butterworths 1992) 459: 'an Act may embody, whether or not in the same words, provisions having the effect of the treaty (in this Code referred to as direct enactment of the treaty)'.

[42] The Convention on the Recognition and Enforcement of Foreign Arbitral Awards 1958 was previously implemented in the UK by the Arbitration Act 1975 (now repealed).

[43] See eg Consular Relations Act 1968, which provides that certain provisions of the Vienna Convention on Consular Relations 1963 set out in a schedule to the Act are to have the force of law, but art 36 which gives foreign nationals who are arrested a right to be informed that they may request that their national state's consul be informed and for the consul to visit and to assist them unless the prisoner expressly opposes action on their behalf; art 36 is implemented

selection has been demonstrated above.[44] On a strict view, only provisions which create obligations that are to be applicable and interpreted in domestic law need be included.

The weakness of this is twofold. First, interpretation of particular provisions of a legal instrument may be hampered if they are approached in isolation from the rest. The formulation of treaties and the principles for their interpretation differ from the structure of English statutes and how they are interpreted.[45] Second, treaties do not contain only substantive provisions, that is provisions of a quasi-legislative character or quasi-contractual nature. The regime created by a treaty is a complete product of treaty relations which may require dispositive action as well as a statement of rules. These relations are established pursuant to the final clauses of each treaty.[46] The final clauses, which are often omitted from legislation, may include provisions on reservations and other important modifiers of the substantive legal obligations that are created. They may also regulate the relationship of one treaty with other treaties, as well as setting out all the modalities of participation by states (signature, ratification, requirements for entry into force, etc.). Absence of these provisions has contributed to judicial misunderstanding of the application of treaties.[47]

(e) Consequence of differing legislative approaches

Issues which the choice of method may raise can be seen in the statement of Lord Oliver, when he said:

> Where, for instance, a treaty is directly incorporated into English law by Act of the legislature, its terms become subject to the interpretative jurisdiction of the court in the same way as any other Act of the legislature.[48]

Aside from the uncertainty as to what Lord Oliver meant by 'directly incorporated',[49] his statement leaves three matters unclear: first, the circumstances

---

in the UK by instructions to the police, currently s 7 of Code C under the Police and Criminal Evidence Act 1984.

[44] See examples in text to nn 7–11 above.
[45] See ch 4 above.
[46] See ch 1, section I.3 above.
[47] See RK Gardiner, 'Air Law's Fog: The Application of International and English Law' (1990) 43 CLP 159.
[48] See *JH Rayner (Mincing Lane) v Dept of Trade* (n 19) 500, citing *Fothergill v Monarch Airlines Ltd* [1981] 2 AC 251.
[49] In *Fothergill v Monarch Airlines Ltd* (n 48), on which Lord Oliver was basing his remark, the relevant statute (the Carriage by Air Act 1961) set out the text of the Convention in English and French in a schedule (with some of the final clauses omitted).

in which a court is to construe a treaty; second, how it is to perform that task; and, third, whether there are any considerations to be taken into account that are different from those applying in other situations of statutory construction.

On the first point, it is clear that terms of a treaty which have been made part of an Act verbatim fall to be interpreted by the courts, but this is not the only situation where the interpretative jurisdiction arises in the context of treaties. Courts in the United Kingdom have had regard to the meaning of relevant treaty provisions where an Act does not 'directly incorporate' a treaty. This has been so even where the Act made no explicit reference to the treaty at all.[50]

The second way in which Lord Oliver's statement is disappointingly unclear is in its assertion that the 'interpretative jurisdiction' is the same for Acts containing treaty provisions as for any other Act. This does not acknowledge the international dimension of implementing a treaty. The third point is really a variant of the second. For example, the established approach to interpreting statutes containing material of domestic origin allows only a very limited role for preparatory work and materials external to the Act.[51] In contrast, use of preparatory materials of treaties and regard for the circumstances that led to their conclusion, are a regulated part of the proper means for interpreting treaty provisions together with the major role accorded to the practice of states in a treaty's implementation.

(f) Considering treaties as aid to statute

There is the principle of statutory interpretation that where there is legislative ambiguity or uncertainty over a point which could bear on the United Kingdom's international obligations, such ambiguity or uncertainty should be resolved in a manner consistent with those obligations rather than in violation of them.[52] However, it is not clear that a court in the UK must first find ambiguity in a statutory provision if it is to follow a lead to a treaty. One view is that only where the words of the statutory provision are 'reasonably

---

[50] See *Salomon v Commissioners of Customs & Excise* [1967] 2 QB 116, where the Court of Appeal accepted that even where an Act makes no mention of a treaty, cogent extrinsic evidence to connect the treaty with the Act would permit the Court to look at the treaty to elucidate the Act.
[51] See *Pepper v Hart* [1993] AC 593.
[52] Limitations on the extent of this presumption were examined in *R v Secretary of State ex parte Brind* [1991] 1 AC 696.

capable of more than one meaning' is the treaty relevant.[53] As to this, the Law Commission long ago noted:

> This does not seem to deal with the situation where the words of a provision, in the context of the national instrument alone, appear reasonably to have only one meaning, although in the context of a treaty they might offer a choice of meanings.[54]

This problem comes into even sharper focus when the English rules of statutory interpretation point to a clear meaning, while application of a treaty would result in a different outcome.[55] For example, the English courts had held that legislation which provided for a surviving spouse to become a statutory tenant by succession even if unmarried but living with a deceased tenant 'as his or her wife or husband' did not apply to couples of the same sex (in the days before civil partnerships). However, later application of a treaty—the European Convention on Human Rights—required that this provision be read as including same sex couples.[56]

Further, it may not always be clear whether it is unexpressed implementation of a treaty provision or application of the principle of seeking to conform to international obligations which is to guide the judicial approach in a particular case. In *Mandla v Dowell Lee*, the House of Lords had to consider the meaning of 'racial' group and 'ethnic origins' in the Race Relations Act 1976.[57] Lord Fraser noted that although the 1976 Act (which followed earlier comparable legislation) did not refer to the 1969 International Convention on the Elimination of All Forms of Racial Discrimination, the United Kingdom had ratified it in 1969, before the Act came into force. States parties undertook to prohibit discrimination in all its forms, and the words of the Convention were very close to the words in the Act and therefore consistent with the United Kingdom legislation having been passed in implementation of the obligation imposed by the Convention.[58]

---

[53] *Salomon v Commissioners of Customs & Excise* (n 34) 143.
[54] Report of the Law Commission on *The Interpretation of Statutes* (Law Com Rep No 21, 1969) 10, para 14.
[55] See *Hiscox v Outhwaite* [1992] 1 AC 562 and n 135 below.
[56] *Ghaidan v Godin-Mendoza* [2004] UKHL 30.
[57] [1983] 2 AC 548.
[58] ibid 564–65.

(g) Combined role of courts and Parliament

The above shows that where legislation actually gives effect to treaty obligations without specifically referring to the treaty, the courts may view the international obligations of the United Kingdom as a relevant element in applying the law, but without assuming responsibility to implement the treaty. That responsibility rests with Parliament, a role which it can fulfil by legislating when there is an issue of treaty interpretation on which the courts may require guidance.[59] Equally, Parliament may set up some continuing process for implementation.[60]

An example of the latter can be seen in the Asylum and Immigration Appeals Act 1993. Section 2 provides: 'Nothing in the immigration rules (within the meaning of the 1971 [Immigration] Act) shall lay down any practice which would be contrary to the Convention.'[61] Since Immigration Rules are subject to parliamentary approval, this means that Parliament has a measure of control in ensuring that the Refugee Convention's obligations are observed. However, the question of whether a practice under the rules is contrary to the Convention may come before the courts in proceedings for judicial review, and thus require a court to consider the proper interpretation of the Convention itself.[62]

(h) Function of courts in the United Kingdom

How will a court in the United Kingdom come to consider a treaty? The attention of a court will generally be drawn to a potentially relevant treaty either by implementing legislation which directly or indirectly leads to a treaty, or because the treaty forms part of the background to the dispute or of the body of law in a general sense pertinent to the dispute.[63] Obviously

---

[59] See eg the Carriage by Air and Road Act 1979, s 2, which gave a legislative interpretation of the same provisions which had been in issue in *Fothergill v Monarch Airlines Ltd* (n 48). Courts may also have to decide how the present state of international law interacts with treaty obligations but legislative resolution remains with Parliament: *Benkharbouche v Embassy of the Republic of Sudan* [2017] UKSC 62 and draft State Immunity Act 1978 (Remedial) Order 2022.

[60] See ss 8 and 9 of the International Transport Conventions Act 1983, which provide for amended versions of transport conventions to be given effect by Order in Council.

[61] Section 1 of the 1993 Act provides: '"The Convention" means the Convention relating to the Status of Refugees done at Geneva on 28th July 1951 and the Protocol to that Convention.' For the incorporating effect of the 1993 Act see *Secretary of State for the Home Department v JS (Uganda)* [2019] EWCA Civ 1670, para 43.

[62] See *Mandla v Dowell Lee* (n 57).

[63] See *Salomon v Commissioners of Customs & Excise* (n 50); see also *R v G* [2003] UKHL 50 (Lord Steyn) para 53 referring to the 1989 UN Convention on the Rights of the Child as supporting a change in the test of recklessness to take account, particularly in the case of a child, of a person's awareness of risk and whether it was unreasonable to take that risk.

the terms of the treaty itself may give an indication of whether it purports to cover the matter in hand. To that extent, at the very least, when a court make its initial decision to investigate whether a treaty is to be taken into account it may be necessary for the court to interpret the treaty.

There are, however, situations where courts will not look at a treaty, or will look at it only as background but reject it as part of the applicable law. This distinction can be seen by comparing the cases of *In Re Westinghouse*[64] and *British Airways v Laker Airways*.[65] The former case concerned the Evidence (Proceedings in Other Jurisdictions) Act 1975. One question was whether a request from a foreign court for evidence to be taken in the United Kingdom should be granted where grounds were advanced for refusing this under a treaty. Although the 1975 Act made no reference to the relevant Hague Convention, the House of Lords accepted that the Act was passed, at least in part, to give effect in English law to the Convention. That implicit tie to the Convention entitled the court to consider whether the particular request for evidence was inconsistent with the provisions of the Act in the light of the Convention provisions which the Act implemented.[66]

In contrast, in *British Airways v Laker Airways* the House of Lords was invited to consider whether a British airline's assertions (that other British airlines had violated the law by setting fares which damaged its business) should be tried under English law or American law. Procedures for setting fares and regulation of agreements between airlines on fares were the subject of provisions in a treaty, a bilateral air services agreement between the United Kingdom and the USA. Nevertheless, the Court held that as the air services agreement was not part of English law, even implicitly in the sense of the Hague Convention described above, the House of Lords did not take into account (still less interpret) the provisions of the treaty.

Similarly, in *JH Rayner (Mincing Lane) v Dept of Trade and Industry*,[67] the treaty establishing the International Tin Council (ITC), the Sixth International Tin Agreement, had not been made part of English law even though it was mentioned in an Order in Council[68] concerning privileges

---

[64] [1978] AC 547.
[65] [1985] 1 AC 58.
[66] The Convention on the Taking of Evidence Abroad in Civil or Commercial Matters 1970, 847 UNTS 231; art 23 of the Convention allowed certain evidence to be excluded from compliance with letters of request. Article 12(b) allowed the court to have regard to possible prejudice to the sovereignty of the United Kingdom. See *In Re Westinghouse* (n 64) 608, 616 (Lord Wilberforce).
[67] [1990] 2 AC 418.
[68] The International Tin Council (Immunities and Privileges) Order 1972, SI 1972/120, art 2.

and immunities under the International Organisations Act 1968, an order which also conferred on the ITC the legal capacities of a body corporate. The issue in the litigation concerned aspects of the personality of the ITC as an international legal person. Although the House of Lords considered the International Tin Agreement as a relevant background fact, the effect of the agreement as the constitution of the ITC was not before the House of Lords. It was not a matter governed by English law.

(i) The court is not resolving an international dispute

When a court within a state interprets and applies a treaty, it is unlikely that it will be exercising a power to make a ruling on a dispute between states parties to a treaty. In the light of this it is necessary to approach the notion of 'interpretation of a treaty' with some caution. Such a process of interpretation by domestic courts does not mean adjudicating on the treaty as between the parties bound by it. Equally, it does not mean ruling on the effect of the treaty as an instrument of international law but rather as an element of law relevant to a matter or dispute governed by municipal law.

This distinction between a treaty as an instrument binding two or more states as a matter of international law and the role of a treaty within the municipal law sphere in a dispute involving private entities (which are not parties to the treaty) is reflected in the reluctance of British courts to pronounce on treaties which have not been brought into domestic law by legislation. Yet it is difficult to see what objection there could be to English courts taking a view on the meaning of any relevant treaty. In the Supreme Court in the United Kingdom Lord Sumption has stated: 'If it is necessary to decide a point of international law in order to resolve a justiciable issue and there is an ascertainable answer, then the court is bound to supply that answer.'[69]

5 Implementing Treaties in a Civil Law System

(a) France as a paradigm

Taking the French constitution as a prime example of how a civil law system accommodates treaties, one might expect to find a clear set of rules indicating how the state is to become a party to a treaty and how its

---

[69] *Benkharbouche v Embassy of the Republic of Sudan* [2017] UKSC 62, para 35.

implementation is to be effected. This is substantially the case, but the adoption of successive constitutions, and adjustments made to the latest one by amendments and by the institutions of the French state in their application of it, have shown some issues which can arise even in a system essentially governed by written rules.

While successive French constitutions have had a nationalist emphasis, as regards international law 'most French legal scholars, and perhaps more importantly key participants in the judicial process, regard the [1958] Constitution as fundamentally monist'.[70] It has been asserted, however, that before the preceding (1946) Constitution, France's approach to treaties could be characterized as more akin to dualist since a separate decree of promulgation was required to give a treaty domestic effect.[71] However, publication remains a key stage in the process of implementation of treaties in France. So it is probably best to conclude that, as between monism and dualism in respect of treaties, through the current Constitution as affected by decisions of French institutions 'France offers a rather hybrid picture'.[72] This is largely because the Constitution provides that treaties or international agreements touching on any subject from a substantial list of matters do require a law to be passed by Parliament before ratification; but as soon as the proper formalities have been completed and promulgation has taken place, the treaty is authoritatively incorporated into French law which points to a strong component of monism.

(b) The French constitution

Before exploring the 1958 Constitution's provisions on treaties it is necessary, in the light of more recent developments considered below, to note the reference in the Constitution's brief preamble to the 1789 Declaration of the Rights of Man and to the principles of national sovereignty as being 'confirmed and complemented by the Preamble to the Constitution of 1946'.[73] The 1946 Constitution included as recital 14: 'The French Republic, faithful to its traditions, shall respect the rules of public international law'

---

[70] MA Rogoff, 'Application of Treaties and Decisions of International Tribunals in the United States and France: Reflections on Recent Practice' (2006) 58 Maine LR 405, 435.
[71] GL Neuman, 'The Brakes that Failed: Constitutional Restriction of International Agreements in France' (2013) 45 Cornell ILJ 257, 263.
[72] J Bell and others, *Principles of French Law* (2nd edn, OUP 2008) 18–19.
[73] All translations of the Constitution and extracts here from cases of the *Conseil Constitutionnel* are those offered by the *Conseil Constitutionnel* (subject to the stern caveat that these are for reference only and that the French text is solely authoritative) www.conseil-constitutionnel.fr.

and as recital 15: 'Subject to reciprocity, France shall consent to the limitations upon its sovereignty necessary to the organisation and preservation of peace'.[74]

Title VI of the 1958 French Constitution, headed *Des Traités et Accords Internationaux*, provides in Article 52 for the President to negotiate and ratify treaties and to be informed of any negotiations for the conclusion of an international agreement not subject to ratification. It also provides that:

> Article 53
> 'Peace treaties, trade agreements, treaties or agreements relating to international organization, those committing the finances of the State, those modifying provisions which are the preserve of statute law, those relating to the status of persons, and those involving the ceding, exchanging or acquiring of territory, may be ratified or approved only by an Act of Parliament [*une loi*].
> They shall not take effect until such ratification or approval has been secured.
> No ceding, exchanging or acquiring of territory shall be valid without the consent of the population concerned.
>
> Article 54
> If the Constitutional Council, on a referral from the President of the Republic, from the Prime Minister, from the President of one or the other Houses, or from sixty Members of the National Assembly or sixty Senators, has held that an international undertaking (*engagement international*) contains a clause contrary to the Constitution, authorization to ratify or approve the international undertaking involved may be given only after amending the Constitution.
>
> Article 55
> Treaties or agreements duly ratified or approved shall, upon publication, prevail over Acts of Parliament, subject, with respect to each agreement or treaty, to its application by the other party.'[75]

Although the preamble to the 1958 Constitution takes in by reference the preamble of the 1946 one, and thus the reference to the various rights

---

[74] ibid.
[75] Texts of Constitution (as amended but omitting arts 53–1 and 53–2) from https://www.conseil-constitutionnel.fr/en; also relevant is art 61, which is considered below in the context of the role of the *Conseil Constitutionnel*.

of man and to respecting international law, the substance of the articles on treaties has provided scope for differing views on several issues. The range of treaty classes listed in Article 53 is extensive, but precisely what is included is not always clear. While respect for the rules of public international law and the primacy of treaties seem unambiguous in principle, Article 55 does not specify the relationship of treaties with the Constitution except to the extent that Article 54 requires an amendment before ratification of a treaty, that is where an international commitment (*engagement international*) has been found to include a provision contrary to the Constitution. This involves evaluating the treaty whose ratification is being proposed as against the Constitution, but *not* whether any implementing Act (*loi*) gives full effect to the treaty's obligations. Further, the article indicates that the treaties prevail over Acts of Parliament but it does not suggest they prevail over the Constitution.

While treaties in the categories listed in Article 53 require a *loi*, no indication is given of the manner of implementation of other treaties and international agreements, although they nevertheless prevail as indicated once approved and published. Further, the roles of the different organs of the French state in relation to treaties, other than that of the President and of the *Conseil Constitutionnel*, are not fully elaborated, nor it specified who is to determine whether a treaty is being duly applied by another relevant party or how this is to be assessed.

Title VI of the 1958 Constitution refers to treaties and international agreements. In connection with the latter, Article 52 uses the phrase *la conclusion d'un accord international non soumis à ratification*, suggesting a simple binary distinction between treaties which require ratification and those which do not. However, a circular of 30 May 1997 by the French Prime Minister on drawing up and concluding international agreements equated international agreements not subject to ratification with agreements in simplified form and those which become binding by signature only.[76] While the Minister of Foreign Affairs signs international agreements in simplified form and those taking effect on signature, those treaties nevertheless require the prescribed parliamentary process if they come within the list in Article 53 of the Constitution. For those which do not come within the list there is, however, a requirement of approval which is met by a presidential decree and publication of the agreement in the *Official Journal*.[77]

---

[76] P Gaïa, 'Le Conseil constitutionnel, le Conseil d'État et les normes internationales: duel ou duo?' (2021) 125 Revue française de droit constitutionnel 3, 7–8.
[77] ibid 8.

The French manner of differentiating between treaties and international agreements (in the sense of their treatment in the French Constitution) draws together the differentiation in international processes for treaties which require ratification—mainly those in solemn form, and those by which a state becomes bound by, or upon, signature—which includes those in simplified form. The French approach has similarities to the US distinction between treaties and executive agreements. Another similarity is as regards the consequences of a treaty becoming part of the internal legal order, if that description can be applied to what is widely regarded as a monist relationship. The constitutional applicability of treaties and international agreements means that in France where the substantive provisions are sufficiently elaborated and appropriately formulated to constitute rules of law they can be applied so as to have direct effect. Those provisions which are targeted at action to be taken by states parties to treaties or which require further elaboration for their application cannot be directly invoked domestically.

A note of caution must be sounded as regards legal measures flowing from French membership of the European Union. Although treaty-based, and in some instances giving effect to treaties to which the EU is a party, law derived from EU sources is of a *sui generis* character. The EU treaties make their own provisions for direct effect of regulations and provide requirements for implementation of directives. In a somewhat similar fashion treaties concerning human rights have a distinctive effect within the French legal system. Successive treaties relating to the constitution of the EU have led to amendments to the French Constitution to accommodate them.

The Constitution's provision on reciprocity (treaties and agreements prevail subject to their 'application by the other party') is not applied to law derived from EU sources nor in the case of human rights treaties.[78] Where it does apply, there has been some uncertainty over how this provision is to be understood and given effect. An earlier approach of requesting advice from the Ministry of Foreign Affairs and treating its views as conclusive has been adjusted towards understanding the requirement as allowing an assumption of implementation by the other party unless measures have been taken on the international plane to suspend the treaty, or parts of it, or to take measures in response to breaches of it.[79] This adjustment, however, has

---

[78] Rogoff (n 70) 459, n 317.
[79] On suspension of treaties in response to breach see ch 6, section IV.2 below.

not been by amendment of the Constitution but by decisions of the *Conseil d'État*, the extent of which is considered below.

(c) The *Conseil Constitutionnel*

A significant role regarding treaties is given to the *Conseil Constitutionnel*, an innovation of the 1958 Constitution and consisting of nine members nominated by the Presidents of the Republic, the National Assembly, and the Senate—three each. Aside from those institutional acts which are to be submitted to a referendum, the *Conseil* may receive referrals of Acts of Parliament or of a treaty to rule on their conformity with the Constitution. Until recent constitutional amendments such referrals could only be made before ratification, approval or an Act took effect. Further, referral could only be made by the Presidents of the Republic, National Assembly, and the Senate respectively, by the Prime Minister, sixty members of the National Assembly or sixty senators.[80] This, with the requirement of a ruling within one month from referral (or even sooner if the period is abridged) meant that before the recent amendment there were very circumscribed possibilities for a law or a treaty to be assessed for compatibility with the Constitution. A substantive limitation was (and is) that such compatibility of the treaty with the Constitution was the only field of review, and most emphatically not whether the law fully implemented the obligations of the treaty.

If the *Conseil Constitutionnel* declares a provision unconstitutional the proposed law is to be neither promulgated nor implemented.[81] In such circumstances the Constitution may be amended. This has happened on a few occasions, for the most part in connections with successive treaties concerning the European Union and the European bodies which preceded it.[82] More generally, however, there have been amendments to allow for France to participate in international agreements, such as on grant of asylum to refugees, and to become a party to the Rome Statute of the International Criminal Court.[83]

---

[80] See Constitution, art 61, the addition of members of the Assembly and senators being by an amendment of 1974.
[81] ibid art 62.
[82] M-C Cadilhac and C Rapoport, ' "In Between Seats": The Conseil constitutionnel and the CETA' (2018) 3(2) J L and Integration 811, 813–14.
[83] See Constitution, arts 53–1 and 53–2, respectively.

The classic understanding of the Constitution before the most recent amendments was stated by the *Conseil Constitutionnel* in its grounds for its decision in a 1975 reference on a proposed law on abortion:

> 4. Decisions made under Article 61 of the Constitution are unconditional and final, as is clear from Article 62, which prohibits the promulgation or implementation of any provision declared unconstitutional; on the other hand, the prevalence of treaties over statutes, stated as a general rule by Article 55, is both relative and contingent, being restricted to the ambit of the treaty and subject to reciprocity, which itself depends on the behaviour of the signatory state or states and on the time at which it is to be assessed;
> 5. A statute that is inconsistent with a treaty is not ipso facto unconstitutional;
> 6. Review of the rule stated in Article 55 cannot be effected as part of a review pursuant to Article 61, because the two reviews are different in kind;
> 7. It is therefore not for the Constitutional Council, when a referral is made to it under Article 61 of the Constitution, to consider the consistency of a statute with the provisions of a treaty or an international agreement.[84]

The effectiveness of such review of the constitutionality of proposed Acts of Parliament as for the proposed ratification or approval of treaties, was somewhat precarious. It depended on reference being made by those from a limited number of persons with authority to make a reference, and review could only be before promulgation of the Act, after which implementation of the treaty as French law could not be impugned. This was radically altered by constitutional amendments which took effect in 2010. These provide that in proceedings before a court of law, if it is claimed that a statutory provision infringes the rights and freedoms guaranteed by the Constitution, the matter may be referred by the *Conseil d'État* or by the *Cour de Cassation* to the *Conseil Constitutionnel*.[85] If the *Conseil Constitutionnel* declares the provision to be unconstitutional it is repealed as from publication of

---

[84] Decision No 74–54 DC of 5 January 1975, *Loi relative à l'interruption volontaire de la grossesse*.
[85] See Constitution, art 61–1.

decision of the *Conseil Constitutionnel* or a later date if so specified in the decision. Such decisions of the *Conseil Constitutionnel* are supreme.[86]

This new procedure for reference of a *Question Prioritaire de Constitutionalité* is notable for enabling a tribunal—the *Conseil Constitutionnel*—to strike down Acts of Parliament already promulgated and in force, something which the 1958 Constitution had avoided by only allowing review at a preliminary stage when it could stop or redirect the legislative process. The threefold purpose of the new provisions was summarized as:

'1) to eradicate unconstitutional norms;
2) to enable citizens to invoke individual constitutional rights; and
3) to ensure the pre-eminence of the Constitution in the hierarchy of norms.'[87]

Professor Hunter-Henin points out that the French courts could already give priority to a treaty over and Act of Parliament (Article 55, French Constitution), such as one on human rights as applicable in a particular case, but without striking down the legislation.[88] Although the amendments appear to add to this the possibility of review of constitutionality, Hunter-Henin also points out conditions which must be met for the lower courts to refer matters upwards for the *Cour de cassation* or the *Conseil d'Etat* to then act as filters of what goes to the *Conseil Constitutionnel*.[89]

Exercise by the *Conseil Constitutionnel* of its review powers can be illustrated by two recent cases. The first is its ruling on the Comprehensive Economic and Trade Agreement (CETA)—a treaty with Canada which on the European side was with both the European Union and its Member States (a 'mixed' agreement). The *Conseil* ruled that it did not contain unconstitutional clauses.[90] For present purposes, the ruling is of particular assistance for its general guidance on the relationship of treaties with the French Constitution. In explaining France's membership of the Union, the *Conseil Constitutionnel* asserted the position of the French Constitution as supreme law within France:

---

[86] ibid art 62 (as amended).
[87] M Hunter-Henin, 'Constitutional Developments and Human Rights in France: One Step Forward, Two Steps Back' (2011) 60 ICLQ 67, 168.
[88] ibid 168.
[89] ibid 173–76.
[90] Decision no 2017–749 DC of 31 July 2017.

9. The French Republic participates in the European Union under the conditions set forth in Title XV of the Constitution. Pursuant to Article 88-1 of the Constitution: "The Republic shall participate in the European Union, constituted by States which have freely chosen to exercise some of their powers in common, by virtue of the treaties of the European Union and the Functioning of the European Union, as derived from the Treaty signed in Lisbon on 13 December 2007". It is also dedicated to the existence of a legal order of the European Union integrated within the national legal order and distinct from the international legal order.

10. In confirming the place of the Constitution at the pinnacle of the national legal order, these constitutional provisions enable France to participate in the creation and development of a permanent European organisation vested with legal personality and endowed with decision-making powers as a result of the transfer of competence consented to by the Member States.

11. However, when the commitments signed to this effect or those which are closely related to this goal contain a clause that is unconstitutional, call into question the rights and freedoms guaranteed by the Constitution or run contrary to the essential conditions for the exercise of national sovereignty, authorisation to ratify them may only be granted after amending the Constitution.

For these purposes, the *Conseil Constitutionnel* evaluates the compatibility of international agreements with the '*bloc de constitutionnalité*'. The '*bloc*' is a collection of norms given that description in French scholarship and consisting of 'the 1789 Declaration of the Rights of Man and of the Citizen, the preamble of the 1946 Constitution of the Fourth Republic, the Environmental Charter of 2004 (*Charte de l'environnement*), fundamental principles recognized by the laws of the Republic (*les principes fondamentaux reconnus par les lois de la République*), constitutional objectives (*objectifs de valeur constitutionnelle*), and a number of other general principles'.[91]

It has been noted that the CETA decision was only the fourteenth time the *Conseil Constitutionnel* has been asked to review an international agreement prior to proposed ratification and that before its 1992 decision on

---

[91] J Larik, 'Prêt-à-ratifier: The CETA Decision of the French Conseil constitutionnel of 31 July 2017' (2017) 13 European Constitutional LR 759, 763; see also Cadilhac and Rapoport (n 82) 813–14.

the Maastricht Treaty it had not held any international agreement to conflict with the Constitution.[92] Of these fourteen cases only five involved treaty commitments outside the EU framework.[93] Thus, Article 54 of the Constitution has not been greatly invoked. Even when assessed in conjunction with the other avenue for review of constitutionality via Articles 61 and 61-1 of the Constitution, the total of referrals has been low and a number of major treaties with ostensible potential for constitutional implications have escaped referral.[94]

Article 61-1 of the Constitution, one of the provisions which took effect in 2010, was the basis for consideration of the second case summarized here. In *Geoffrey F. and others* (concerning conditions of custody of detained persons), the *Conseil Constitutionnel* gave a ruling on applications for a priority preliminary ruling on the issue of constitutionality raised by the *Cour de Cassation* (Criminal Division).[95] The *Conseil Constitutionnel* decided that provisions of the Code of Criminal Procedure, as in force in 2000, were unconstitutional by reason of absence of recourse to a judicial authority in seeking an end to a violation of a person's dignity resulting from their conditions of pre-trial detention.

Although the *Conseil Constitutionnel* relied mainly on elements of the *bloc de constitutionnalité* as grounds for its decision, it also cited the European Convention on Human Rights and stated that it 'must rule on the disputed provisions independently of the interpretation made by the Cour de Cassation in its aforementioned rulings, nos 1399 and 1400 of 8 July 2020, in order to make them compatible with the requirements arising from the European Convention for the Protection of Human Rights and Fundamental Freedoms'.[96] The ruling was made in October 2020 but repeal of the offending provisions was postponed to 1 March 2021 because of the 'excessive consequences' immediate implementation would impose.[97]

While this decision suggests that in the area of human rights the *Conseil Constitutionnel* has some role in treaty implementation in conjunction with the Constitution, the main conclusion is that the principal function of the *Conseil* in connection with treaties is to uphold the Constitution, with

---

[92] Larik (n 91) 769–70.
[93] Cadilhac and Rapoport (n 82), noting that a Constitutional amendment was indicated as a requirement for treaty participation in seven cases and was completed in six of them.
[94] See Neuman (n 71) 275–76, who lists several of these, with statistics showing referral to be few in relation to the number of treaties entered into by France.
[95] Decision no 2020–858/859 QPC of 2 October 2020.
[96] ibid 'Grounds' (*fonds*) para 11.
[97] ibid para 19 and Decision, art 2.

suggestions for amendment where required. Thus the role of the *Conseil* is more one of ensuring that a treaty is constitutionally compatible rather than that it is actually implemented.

(d) The *Conseil d'État* and the *Cour de Cassation*

While in treaty matters the *Conseil Constitutionnel* has a remit limited to evaluating treaties for compliance with the French Constitution, and ensuring the Constitution's supremacy, the *Conseil d'État* and the *Cour de Cassation* have more extensive roles in application of treaties. This is primarily because of the provision in Article 55 of the Constitution that treaties prevail over Acts (*lois*) (subject to the reciprocity requirement described above). Although quite different in other respects, the *Conseil d'État* and the *Cour de Cassation* can be examined together in considering treaties in French law because of the parallel track on which Article 55 of the Constitution sets them. This parallelism is shown by decisions on the application of that article. In its judgment in *Jacques Vabre*, the *Cour de Cassation* held that by virtue of Article 55 a treaty has authority superior even to a later Act and that in the instant case the relevant treaty, the 1957 Treaty of Rome establishing the European Economic Community, should be applied to defeat the application of a French domestic tax law.[98]

Although this decision could have been attributable to the particular interplay between the European Community treaty regime and that of Member States, the principle of superiority of a treaty provision over domestic law has been applied to treaties generally.[99] The conclusion of the *Conseil d'État* in the case of *Nicolo* (1989) has been taken as indicating the same approach as that taken by the *Cour de Cassation*. However, the short finding in *Nicolo* that the regime for treatment of electors from French overseas territories in elections to the European Parliament was not inconsistent with the Treaty of Rome did not produce such an explicit enunciation, but it did note Article 55 as the relevant constitutional provision.[100]

The *Conseil d'État* and the *Cour de Cassation* are the venues to which issues concerning the application and interpretation of treaties ultimately go up from lower courts and tribunals. In principle, treaty provisions are applicable in French courts and tribunals after duly undergoing the

---

[98] *Administration des Douanes v Société Cafés Jacques Vabre* Cour de Cassation, Chambre Mixte, du 24 mai 1975, 93 International Law Reports 240–67.
[99] See Hunter-Henin (n 87) 171; see also Gaïa (n 76) 53–54.
[100] *Arrêt Nicolo*, Conseil d'Etat, Assemblée, du 20 octobre 1989, 108243, publié au recueil Lebon; see also Hunter-Henin (n 87) 170–71.

constitutional processes described above and having been published. In practice, however, leaving aside treaties which produce obligations taking effect solely in international relations, for those that are to be applied in French courts and tribunals there is the further requirement that the relevant provisions have direct effect.[101] The tests for this are similar to those for whether a treaty is self-executing in the law of the USA. Key among these is the requirement that relevant provisions are sufficiently precise and complete so as to be capable of direct application. As is the case in legal systems described as dualist, this requires examination of the content of a treaty to see whether it requires further legislative or administrative action to enable compliance and application.[102]

A feature of the French Constitution which takes into French law an aspect of treaties which is, at least in origin, a matter of treaty relations, is the subjection of the primacy of a treaty over other French law to it being applied reciprocally by the relevant other party. Clearly this can really only apply where the treaty is one which imposes reciprocal obligations of a concordant nature, described in civil law (and sometimes in relation to treaties) as 'synallagmatic'. This has been observed by a French *Rapporteur Public* who also noted that lack of reciprocity cannot therefore be invoked with regard to 'humanitarian treaties'.[103] This was so held by the *Conseil Constitutionnel* in relation to the Rome Statute of the International Criminal Court, and it had been implicitly admitted by the *Conseil d'État* and the *Cour de Cassation* in applying the European Convention on Human Rights to nationals of states not parties to it.[104]

In accepting that the reciprocity requirement does not apply to the law of the European Union derived from the treaties forming the basis of that organization, the *Cour de Cassation* and the *Conseil d'État* have put this on the basis that EU law, in place of international law remedies for non-compliance with EU treaties, substitutes those obtainable from the European Court of Justice (now the Court of Justice of the European Union).[105] The *Conseil Constitutionnel* endorsed this approach in its ruling on consistency of a European Community Directive on voting rights with the French Constitution.[106] That decision related specifically to Article

---

[101] Rogoff (n 70) 450–51.
[102] ibid.
[103] *Cheriet-Benseghir*, Conseil d'État 09/07/2010, No 317747, Conclusions de Mme Gaëlle Dumortier.
[104] ibid.
[105] Neuman (n 71) 354–55.
[106] Décision no 98–400 DC du 20 mai 1998.

88–3 of the French Constitution which contained a requirement of reciprocity which, the *Conseil Constitutionnel* considered, was met upon the deposit of the last instrument of ratification to be lodged by a Member State.[107] That was, however, linked with the possibility of a remedy for any breach being available at the ECJ. Hence who is to decide whether the other relevant party is implementing and performing obligations under the treaty has remained problematic in the ordinary run of treaties to which Article 55 applies.

Reciprocity was a central issue in *Chevrol* where the claimant had sought recognition in France of a medical qualification obtained in Algeria.[108] Article 5 of the Declaration of Principles concerning Cultural Co-operation in the 1962 Evian Accords between France and Algeria provided: 'The degrees and diplomas granted in Algeria and in France under the same conditions with respect to curricula, duration of studies and examinations shall automatically be valid in both countries.'[109]

The French Ministry of Foreign Affairs tersely advised the *Conseil d'Etat* that Article 5 of the declaration could not be regarded as having been in force on the relevant date since the condition of reciprocity laid down in Article 55 of the Constitution was not met. As regards interpretation of treaties the *Conseil d'Etat* in 1990 ceased to treat the advice of the Ministry of Foreign Affairs as conclusive.[110] However, this change had not been transposed to apply to the Constitution's reciprocity requirement. The established practice was to defer to the Ministry. Recognition of the qualification was therefore refused.

Mme Chevrol took the case to the European Court of Human Rights.[111] Her principal submission was that she had been denied her right to a 'tribunal' hearing within the meaning of Article 6(1) of the European Convention on Human Rights. In the French proceedings she had

---

[107] ibid Consideration 5.
[108] *Mme Yamina Chevrol*, Conseil d'Etat, Assemblée, du 9 avril 1999, 180277, Lebon; and see Rogoff (n 70) 436–41.
[109] 507 UNTS 25, no 7395, 75: the 'Evian Accords' were agreements between France and the Provisional Government of the then future independent state of Algeria which were recognized as a treaty by France in an 'Exchange of letters and declarations adopted on 19 March 1962 at the close of the Evian talks, constituting an agreement between France and Algeria', Paris and Rocher Noir (3 July 1962); that their publication in France was effective as a treaty is confirmed by the specific reference to art 55 of the French Constitution in the recitals (the '*vu*' section) of the judgment in *Chevrol* and earlier case law.
[110] *GISTI* case, Conseil d'Etat, Assemblée, du 29 juin 1990, 78519, publié au recueil Lebon, considered further in Pt IV, 3(d) on interpretation in civil jurisdictions, below.
[111] *Chevrol v France* (App no 49636/99), Judgment of 13 May 2003.

attempted to produce evidence to show that the Evian Accords had been applied by the Algerian government recognizing equivalence of qualifications.[112] However, that evidence had not been taken into account. The European Court's conclusion was that 'the applicant cannot be considered to have had access to a tribunal which had, or had accepted, sufficient jurisdiction to examine all the factual and legal issues relevant to the determination of the dispute.'[113] Even after this judgment, however, the *Conseil d'État* declined to overturn its previous decision. This may have been influenced by having heard the *Commissaire du Gouvernement* argue that a change to implement a decision of the European Court of Human Rights in a civil case should be by legislation, to bring these civil matters into line with the French Criminal Code which expressly authorized re-examination of cases after a judgment of the European Court of Human Rights.[114]

Despite the refusal to change the position immediately after Chevrol, the approach was nevertheless modified some ten years later. In its considerations (*motifs*) in Cheriet-Benseghir, the *Conseil d'État* ruled that when the issue of reciprocity is raised, it is up to the judge to investigate the matter and, after receiving the observations of the Minister for Foreign Affairs and, where appropriate, those of the state in question, to submit these observations to adversarial debate (*au débat contradictoire*) in order to assess whether legal and factual elements establish that the condition relating to the application of the treaty by the other party is, or not, fulfilled.[115]

It has been noted that in the application of treaties the *Conseil d'État* and the *Cour de Cassation* do not always march exactly in step. An example is the assessment of the possible direct effect of the UN Convention on the Rights of the Child. The *Cour de Cassation* is reported as having denied direct effect of any provisions of the Convention on the basis that Article 4 of the Convention requires parties to take 'all appropriate legislative, administrative, and other measures for the implementation of the rights recognized in the present Convention'.[116] The *Conseil d'État* in different cases examined different provisions of the Convention, finding that one did produce direct effects in French law while others only established obligations in relations between states.[117]

---

[112] ibid para 60.
[113] ibid para 80.
[114] Rogoff (n 70) 439–40.
[115] *Cheriet-Benseghir* (n 103).
[116] 1577 UNTS 3, no 27531. See also Rogoff (n 70) 451–53, where further case law is indicated as showing a rebuttable presumption of direct effect.
[117] Rogoff (n 70).

The *Conseil d'État*'s article by article assessment of whether a treaty has direct effect can be seen as a reflection of the same differentiation made in the legal system deployed in the United Kingdom. The main difference is that in that system the potential for effects within the national legal order is determined in advance of the United Kingdom becoming a party to a treaty by the requirement for legislative action with regard to those elements of a treaty which are to have effect in domestic law, while in the French and American systems an assessment has to be made by the courts after the treaty has become domestic law, unless legislation has in fact already made the matter clear.

6 The European Union and Its Predecessors

Inclusion of an international organization may at first seem out of place in a chapter dealing with the implementation of treaties within national legal systems. However, there is scope for debate whether the European Union is only an international organization or is a 'superstate'.[118] Certainly, it has characteristics which distinguish it from other international organizations and is set up in a way which enables both its own constitutive treaties and other treaties to which it becomes a party to have effects within the national legal systems of its Member States. There are therefore two main areas of interest in the context of treaties as elements of international law. First is the question whether, as constitutive instruments of a European Union, the treaties establishing the Union and governing its function are of a different nature from other multilateral treaties? Second, and perhaps more directly germane to implementation of treaties in national legal systems, is how these treaties and others entered into by the European Union and its predecessor institutions have effect with its Member States.

(a) Implementing the treaties establishing the European Union

The short answer to the question whether the treaties establishing the Union and governing its function (and the predecessor treaties) are of a different nature from other multilateral treaties is that in form and ostensible legal basis they are not different. However, the European Court of Justice early

---

[118] See eg KK Patel and M Dale, *Project Europe: A History* (CUP 2020), ch 6: 'Superstate or Tool of Nations?' The terms 'European Union' and 'EU' are used in this section without differentiation between the Union and its predecessors except where specifically indicated.

on sought to make a distinction: 'By contrast with ordinary international treaties, the EEC Treaty has created its own legal system which, on the entry into force of the Treaty, became an integral part of the legal systems of the Member States and which their courts are bound to apply.'[119]

'Ordinary international treaties' is not a category widely acknowledged elsewhere; but integrationist developments have produced a regime of European law which results in distinctive effects even if the originating treaties are not essentially different from any governed by international law. Extensive revision of the constitutional arrangements of the European Economic Community and the related Communities eventually led to the institution being grounded on two treaties signed in Lisbon in 2007: the Treaty on European Union (TEU) and the Treaty on the Functioning of the European Union (TFEU).[120] The former simply provides in its Article 47 that 'The Union shall have legal personality'. This serves to provide an international legal personality (without explicitly stating it) for purposes of acts in international relations, as is evidenced by the acceptance by non-Member States of the EU (and its appropriate predecessor bodies) as a treaty party; but the provision does not clarify the legal nature of the body comprising the organization and its Member States.

There is considerable scope for discussion about analogies with compacts establishing federations or confederations or whether the European Union is something which functions in the conjoint realms of international and internal law. In the realm of international law previous use of the term 'union' has occurred in identification through the political act resulting in the name of a state—the USSR or 'Soviet Union', or has been in the specialist areas of intellectual property, such as the Paris Union (industrial property), the Berne Union (copyright), the Budapest Union (deposit of microorganisms) etc.

For the purpose of effectiveness of the treaties constituting the European Union it is fortunately not necessary to resolve the precise label which it is appropriate to apply to the institution. However, the distinctive legal order established by its constitutive treaties warrants attention. An early claim as to the legal effect of the constitutive treaties was made in the *Van Gend en Loos* case by the European Court of Justice:

---

[119] *Costa v Ente Nazionale per l'Energia Elettrica (ENEL)* [1964] ECR 585, 593. The term European Court in this section refers to the European Court of Justice (ECJ) and the same court as later renamed the Court of Justice of the European Union (CJEU).

[120] Consolidated versions are in *Official Journal of the European Union* (7 June 2016) C202/13 and C202/47, respectively.

> [t]he Community constitutes a new legal order in international law, for whose benefit the States have limited their sovereign rights, albeit within limited fields, and the subjects of which comprise not only the member-States but also their nationals. Community law, therefore, apart from legislation by the member-States, not only imposes obligations on individuals but also confers on them legal rights. The latter arise not only when an explicit grant is made by the Treaty, but also through obligations imposed, in a clearly defined manner, by the Treaty on individuals as well as on member-States and the Community institutions.[121]

This was further elaborated by the Court in *Costa v ENEL*, stating:

> The pre-eminence of Community law is confirmed by Article 189 which prescribes that Community regulations have an 'obligatory' value and are 'directly applicable within each member-State' ... It follows from all these observations that the rights created by the Treaty, by virtue of their specific original nature, cannot be judicially contradicted by an internal law, whatever it might be, without losing their Community character and without undermining the legal basis of the Community.[122]

Supremacy of a treaty and its direct applicability were not innovations of the European Court of Justice, nor was the concept of direct effect.[123] However, they are prominent features of the law of the European Communities and Union. Direct applicability and direct effect are broadly comparable to a treaty becoming part of the domestic legal order and to its provisions being open to invocation in the courts under the constitutions of the USA and France described above. The *Van Gend en Loos* extract quoted above demonstrates the monist nature of the European institutional law. The essential test for direct effect is also similar to those of the two constitutions just mentioned. The essence is whether a treaty provision is capable of being directly implemented.

The position is more nuanced when it comes to subordinate legislation of the EU. This is shown by the difference between Regulations and Directives. Article 288 TFEU provides:

---

[121] *NV Algemene Transport- en Expeditie Onderneming Van Gend en Loos v Neder-Landse Tariefcommissie* [1963] CMLR 105, 129. See also R Schütze, *European Union Law* (3rd edn, OUP 2021) 152–54.
[122] *Costa v Ente Nazionale per l'Energia Elettrica (ENEL)* [1964] CMLR 425, 456.
[123] E Denza, *The Intergovernmental Pillars of the European Union* (OUP 2002) 14–15.

A regulation shall have general application. It shall be binding in its entirety and directly applicable in all Member States.

A directive shall be binding, as to the result to be achieved, upon each Member State to which it is addressed, but shall leave to the national authorities the choice of form and methods.

This, again, offers some parallels with treaties in the sense that regulations are like those treaties that have direct effects while directives are like treaty provisions which require domestic implementation through some form of legislative action. However, there are two important distinctions in that, first, no domestic action at all is required by a Member State to become bound by a regulation and, second, directives can have some direct effects in that:

> [a] member-State which has not adopted the implementing measures required by the directive in the prescribed periods may not rely, as against individuals, on its own failure to perform the obligations which the directive entails.... Therefore ... [the] member-State may not apply its internal law—even if it is provided with penal sanctions ... , to a person who has complied with the requirements of the directive.[124]

(b) Implementing treaties entered into by the European Union and its Member States

While the primacy of European law over that of Member States became clear in the manner described above, as regards other treaties of the organization and its members the position is more complex. First, Article 216 TFEU provides for the EU to conclude international agreements where it is a matter in which it has competence under its own 'constitutional' law (summarizing the position in a general way).[125] The same article provides that 'Agreements concluded by the Union are binding upon the institutions of the Union and on its Member States'. This has established a position broadly comparable to that in the USA where after the due procedures a treaty becomes the supreme law of the land. A treaty duly concluded in accordance

---

[124] *Pubblico Ministero v Tullio Ratti* [1980] 1 CMLR 96, 110, paras 22 and 24; and Schütze (n 121) 171.
[125] For procedures by which the EU becomes a party to treaties see P Craig and G de Búrca, *EU Law* (7th edn, OUP 2020) 398–402.

with its internal procedures becomes binding, in principle, throughout the legal system of the EU and within its members' national legal systems. If, however, the substance of a treaty requires acts of a legislative character, spelling out how the treaty is to be implemented, these measures are drawn up in the form of regulations or directives (as described above) so that the particularities take effect in all Member States.

Thus it can be seen that there arises in EU law the same differentiation with regard to treaties which it makes with non-Member States between the treaty being binding and applicable throughout its institutions and membership, but not necessarily having direct effect—that is to say not necessarily being invocable in its treaty form in national courts. This has been a major concern of the European Court. It has to decide whether any treaty arising in a case before it is one which can have direct effect within Member States or is one which is solely effective through EU regulations or directives.

A prominent example is the case of the World Trade Organization's regime and the previous General Agreement on Tariffs and Trade. Put in general terms, the Court has concluded that because of the modalities of reciprocity, the role of negotiation, and the system of dispute settlement (among other factors), the relevant treaties are not ones which can simply be applied by the Court itself and by direct effect in Member States—too much depends on the bodies within the EU that are equivalent to the executive and legislature within a state interacting with other parties to trade treaties and implementing the outcomes.[126] In the case of other treaties dealing with trade matters, such as its Association Agreements with states aspiring to membership, the European Court has looked to particular provisions to assess potential for direct effect, with extensive and detailed case law on this aspect of implementing its treaty relations within its institutions and Member State.[127]

The main further complexities arise in three situations. One is where Member States of the EU have treaty relations with each other or with non-Member States established before their membership. Second, Member States may have treaty relations with each other or with non-Member States in matters which were not within the competence of the EU when treaty relations were established. Third, there may be treaties whose provisions are

---

[126] ibid 408–22.
[127] ibid.

partly within areas of the competence of the EU but partly remaining with that of Member States ('mixed agreements').

On the first matter, as regards existing treaties between Member States, the normal rules of international law on successive treaties relating to the same subject matter would mean that the relevant obligations of the EU treaty (and more in point its predecessor treaties) would apply to allow the later provisions to take effect. As regards treaties between Member States and non-members dating from before the founding Treaty of Rome came into force at the start of 1958, or before their accession in the case of states which joined later, rights and obligations are not affected by the provisions of the European treaties.[128] However, to the extent that such earlier treaties conflict with the EU constitutive treaties, Member States are required to take all appropriate steps to eliminate incompatibilities.[129]

An example of this is provided by *Commission v Portugal* before the European Court. Portugal had a bilateral agreement with Yugoslavia on maritime matters dating from before it became a member of the EU and which included cargo-sharing provisions which ran foul of the European treaties' competition rules. Portugal did not manage to negotiate an appropriate change in the treaty as required by an EEC Regulation. The Court held that:

> [b]y failing either to denounce or to adjust the contested agreement so as to provide for fair, free and non-discriminatory access by all Community nationals to the cargo-shares due to the Portuguese Republic, as provided for in Council Regulation ... the Portuguese Republic has failed to fulfil its obligations under Articles 3 and 4(1) of that regulation.[130]

As regards the second set of issues (later treaty relations of Member States with non-Member States), one of the features of the development of the European Union and its predecessor institutions has been the considerable increase in its areas of competence. Such expansion has meant its increasing assumption of control of international matters. Hence, treaties of Member States with members or non-Member States which fell within those areas of increased competence, or which included provisions relating

---

[128] TFEU, art 351.
[129] ibid.
[130] Case C-84/98 *Commission of the European Communities v Portuguese Republic* (judgment of 4 July 2000) [2000] ECR 1-5219, 5238-39.

to those areas, came to be matters for the Union's bodies to handle in international relations generally and treaty relations in particular. However, for the EU or its predecessors to become a party to a treaty required that the treaty already opened up that possibility or was one whose parties were prepared amend the final clauses to accept the EU as a party. If the EU was not a party but had acquired internal competence, Member States would have to bring their treaty relations in line with the EU's requirements.

An example of this is international civil aviation. After the Second World War, rights to operate air services on international routes were negotiated bilaterally resulting in a large network of bilateral treaties. These regulated access by airlines to routes in a manner inconsistent with the EEC/EU competition rules. One feature of the bilateral agreements was that the rights of airlines were anchored to each bilateral by a provision requiring that an airline be substantially owned and effectively controlled by the state, or nationals of the state, whose right it was to exercise. With liberalization of aviation competition, particularly between the USA and several members of the EU, the European Commission brought cases before the European Court against eight Member States arguing that features of the agreements regulating fares, computer reservations, and other matters infringed the competition rules in the EU which had acquired competence over aviation matters by completion of a single market for aviation within the EU.[131] The Court's judgments in favour of the Commission led to the defendant Member States being required to negotiate amendments to their bilateral agreements or the EU being mandated to negotiate with third states to achieve a collective modification of the nationality provision, for example.

The determination of which areas fall within the competence of the EU, which are retained by Member States, and which are matters of shared competence raises extremely complex issues of internal EU law, but with external consequences. Third party states cannot be expected to make determinations on these matters but have to decide whether to accept the EU, its Member States individually or collectively, or both the EU and its members together as prospects for treaty relations. What can be noted here is that the rule of *pacta sunt servanda* binds both the organization and the Member States if they are together as parties to a treaty (as it does to the Member States or the EU if individually parties to treaties). This means that it is an internal matter for the EU and its members to decide how to

---

[131] Case C-466/98 *Commission of the European Communities v United Kingdom of Great Britain and Northern Ireland* (Open Skies Agreements) ECLI:EU:C:2002:624.

approach negotiation and implementation of treaties. This applies where the product is a mixed agreement—where both the EU and Member States are parties to a treaty. Any legislative action required to fulfil the treaty's obligations must be taken by both the EU and its Member States.

Where individual Member States take it upon themselves individually or collectively to negotiate a treaty with a non-Member State or within an international organization on a matter in which the EU may have an interest or be about to negotiate a treaty itself, there are obligations of cooperation which require Member States to act as what has been described as 'trustees' for the EU where the EU is not a participant in the negotiations, or to follow the EU's line of negotiation where the EU is an entity negotiating in parallel with its members.[132] Requirements for implementation, and mechanisms for the EU to ensure compliance with any applicable EU law if there are aspects on which the EU has competence, are the same as for other treaties to which Member States are parties.

IV Interpretation of Treaties in National Legal Systems

The same principle underlies interpretation of treaties in domestic law as guides the conduct of states under international law generally and in implementation of treaties in particular: states must abide by their international obligations and cannot plead their domestic law or legal machinery as a defence if they violate the law. This simple proposition, however, conceals the central questions in interpretation of treaties in domestic law:

(1) who is to interpret the provisions of treaties; and
(2) what principles of interpretation apply?

As treaties are instruments governed by public international law and set up mutual rights and obligations between states, their authentic interpretation could be expected to require use of interpretative mechanisms provided by international law and effective in relations between states. The actual situation is that innumerable treaties are taking effect through

---

[132] Schütze (n 121) 305–09; on mixed agreements generally see J Heliskoski, 'Mixed Agreements: The EU Law Fundamentals', ch 36 in R Schütze and T Tridimas (eds), *Oxford Principles of European Union Law*, vol 1 (OUP 2018).

domestic law every minute of the day and are necessarily interpreted within national legal systems. There are three obvious candidates for undertaking the latter task:

(1) the executive or government;
(2) the legislature; and/or
(3) the courts and judiciary.

1 Role of the Executive

Relations between states are generally the responsibility of an organ of state dedicated to that purpose (typically the Ministry of Foreign Affairs). Other government departments, however, are increasingly directly involved. International elements attach to almost every field of activity, from agriculture, fisheries, or health to trade, transport, and telecommunications. Thus government ministers and their officials participate in international conferences, work on development and implementation of multilateral treaties, and conduct bilateral activities of equivalent kinds with other states.

This is particularly significant in the context of treaty implementation and interpretation because the appropriate processes may involve regular or frequent consultations, and more formal negotiations for amendments if differences and disputes arise. The dynamics of resolution of disputes over the interpretation and application of treaty provisions include use of pressures available in international relations. For example, if a state considers that another party to a treaty is applying an incorrect interpretation of one of its provisions, the aggrieved state may legitimately withhold rights accorded under the treaty to the state which it perceives to be in default.[133]

Such action requires sensitive appreciation of relations between states, as well as a sound assessment of the legal case for adopting a particular interpretation. It is not surprising, therefore, that some legal systems acknowledge a significant role for the government in interpreting treaties rather than placing responsibility for this upon the legislature or the judges. Those who negotiate treaties and who are in touch with their implementation in the international relations of states are likely to be in the best position to work out the proper interpretation.

---

[133] See ch 6, section I below.

IV Interpretation of Treaties in National Legal Systems 155

2 Role of Governments and Legislatures

While this approach recognizes the position of governments as having the conduct of international relations, where treaties take effect in domestic law, there is clearly scope for some involvement of a Parliamentary or legislative assembly, reflecting its position as the law-giver. The role of a legislative assembly is generally, however, secondary to that of the government at whose behest it usually acts in these matters. For example, the US Senate may endorse ratification of a treaty with reservations it specifies, though these may simply be following the proposal of the President. This is not, however, really an exercise of an interpretative role, but rather establishing the basis on which the USA will participate in the treaty.[134] In contrast, Parliament in the UK may ascribe an interpretation when it implements provisions of a treaty by using different words from those in the treaty. Sometimes, indeed, it does so specifically to resolve an ambiguity by legislative provision.[135] In truth, however, the British Parliament almost invariably acts in such treaty matters at the behest of the government and provides little input of its own to interpretation of treaties. In some other states, legislatures have a role in the pre-negotiation phase and in the implementation and interpretation of treaties.[136]

3 Role of Courts

(a) General approach to Vienna rules

When it comes to interpretation of treaties by courts in national systems, the major questions are what rules of interpretation they will apply, whether they will take into account the decisions of courts of other parties, and how far they are guided by relevant international materials and processes. In the courts in countries which are viewed as taking a dualist approach, however, there is a logically anterior question. Will the courts interpret a treaty or will they only interpret legislation implementing a treaty? This distinction is of

---

[134] See text to nn 23 and 24 above.
[135] See eg s 2 of the Carriage by Air and Road Act 1979, which gave a legislative interpretation of the same provisions which were in issue in *Fothergill v Monarch Airlines Ltd*, and ss 53 and 100 of the Arbitration Act 1996, which reversed the decision of the House of Lords in *Hiscox v Outhwaite* (n 55).
[136] See Sloss (n 1) and works cited in n 18 above.

importance because it explains some of the difficulties encountered over interpretation of treaties in dualist systems.

The principle that a legal instrument should be interpreted according to its 'proper law' should lead to treaty provisions being interpreted according to the rules of public international law (now codified in the Vienna Convention's rules for interpretation of treaties).[137] International recognition of these rules as customary rules of international law has carried over into the domestic arena in many cases. National systems that are essentially monist in approach could be expected to apply the rules, especially if in a state party to the VCLT. Thus the view that international law's rules apply is accepted, for example, in Germany.[138] Many systems described as dualist also use the Vienna rules.

The simple sense of this is, however, displaced by several factors. Even where the executive is not given a decisive role in regard to treaties, there are commonly opportunities for the executive to make representations to the courts by giving a view on interpretation. There is no clear divide between the practice of states which follow the common law tradition and those which have a civil law basis, even though it might reasonably be posited that the former group tend to have a predominantly dualist complexion while the latter monist. There is not even a clear line between those which are parties to the Vienna Convention and those which are not, for some of the latter apply the VCLT's rules of interpretation as customary international law and therefore applicable to treaty interpretation without being treaty bound.[139]

The picture is yet more cloudy as even where courts purport to acknowledge the applicability of the Vienna rules they may not get beyond the first paragraph of Article 31 and, conversely, where they have not asserted that they are attempting to apply the Vienna rules they nevertheless take account of subsequent agreements, practice, other treaties, and preparatory work in a manner which approximates to a loose application of the Vienna rules. Some of the difficulty in evaluating practice, particularly in civil law jurisdictions is not simply that judgments are not expansive in their explanations but because interpretation of treaties was not traditionally viewed

---

[137] See arts 31–33; for the content of the rules see ch 4 above.
[138] See JA Frowein, 'Federal Republic of Germany' in FG Jacobs and S Roberts (eds), *The Effect of Treaties in Domestic Law* (Sweet and Maxwell 1987) 74 and cases cited in n 142 below.
[139] O Ammann, *Domestic Courts and the Interpretation of International Law: Methods and Reasoning Based on the Swiss Example* (Brill/Nijhoff, 2020) 231–33.

IV Interpretation of Treaties in National Legal Systems 157

as the province of the courts. Until 1990, the French Conseil d'État sent all matters of treaty interpretation to the Minister of Foreign Affairs except where the meaning was absolutely clear. Now the Minister is still consulted but courts are not bound by the response. However, insufficient time has elapsed from the change in practice for extensive case law to develop.[140] In contrast in Switzerland, another civil law country, some use was made by courts of the Vienna rules even before Switzerland became bound by the Vienna Convention. There has been extensive practice there referring to the Vienna rules, but this has not shown their consistent structured and comprehensive deployment, with some harking back to a former inclination to adopt purposive approaches.[141]

There are numerous examples of reference to the Vienna rules in the courts of parties to the Vienna Convention, with very variable accuracy in the extent of application and understanding of how those rules should apply. Among the most common limitations are the assumption that Article 31(1) VCLT is the whole of the general rule, failure to recognize the distinction between 'context' in that paragraph and the circumstances of conclusion in Article 32 VCLT, and a failure to appreciate the role of supplementary means of interpretation. However, the principle that the Vienna rules apply is widely acknowledged.

In states whose constitutions provide for automatic reception of treaties into domestic law on becoming a party to them (the so-called monist states), formal promulgation of the whole text in an official journal or equivalent publication is commonly required. This has the advantage that courts and tribunals more readily accept that they are interpreting the treaty itself rather than merely any implementing legislation. It is difficult to assess how much use is made of the Vienna rules by national courts in such states but there are quite a few examples. One such example is the German Federal Supreme Court (*Bundesgerichtshof*), which cited Articles 31–33 of the Vienna Convention when interpreting the Hague Convention on International Child Abduction 1980.[142] The Court used appropriate elements of the Vienna rules in deciding whether courts of a state could make a

---

[140] PM Eisemann and R Rivier, 'France', ch 8 in D Hollis, M Blakeslee, and B Ederington (eds), *National Treaty Law and Practice* (Martinus Nijhoff 2005) 270–71; note that France is not party to the Vienna Convention: see text to nn 145 and 146 below.
[141] Ammann (n 139) ch 7, where, in addition to detailed analysis of Swiss case law, there is a useful comparative study of the practice in many states.
[142] XII ZB 210/99, BGHZ 145, 97 (16 August 2000) 145,100, and see full text and summary by the Permanent Bureau of the Hague Conference on Private International Law, no 467

custody order notwithstanding a decision that a child was to be returned to another jurisdiction. The Court examined the text and the purpose of the Convention, the practice of several other states, and the Explanatory Report on the Convention, deciding that a decision on the merits of a custody application was not permitted by the Convention in the particular circumstances. There are numerous further examples showing references in national courts in states parties to the VCLT to the Vienna rules.[143]

(b) Interpretation in courts of states not parties to the Vienna Convention

A total of 116 states, out of a little over 190 states, are parties to the 1969 Vienna Convention.[144] From the nearly 40 per cent of states which are not parties to the Convention, no particularly distinctive or comprehensively different approach to treaty interpretation from the Vienna rules has emerged. This is to be expected since application of the Vienna rules as a statement of customary international law would not compromise any position taken in opposition to any other provisions of the Vienna Convention which are the basis for not accepting it. Thus, for example, France has not signed or ratified the Convention primarily because of continued opposition to the formulation of provisions on *ius cogens*.[145] Yet in *Re Société Schneider Electric*, the French Conseil d'État cited the conclusions of the

---

http://www.incadat.com. See also *Proceedings on The Constitutional Complaint* BVerfG, 2 BvR 1290/99 of 12 December 2000 http://www.bverfg.de/entscheidungen/rk20001212_2bvr12909 9en.html, where the German Federal Constitutional Court (*Bundesverfassungsgericht*), in a case concerning the interpretation of arts II and VI of the Convention on the Prevention and Punishment of the Crime of Genocide 1948 affirmed the applicability of arts 31 and 32 of the Vienna Convention to treaties generally.

[143] See eg *Attorney-General v Zaoui* [2006] 1 NZLR 289, where the New Zealand Supreme Court accepted arts 31 and 32 of the Vienna Convention as stating customary international law, acknowledged the rules to be part of the law of New Zealand, and followed their scheme systematically; see also *Crown Forest Industries Ltd v Canada* [1995] 2 SCR 802, where the Canadian Supreme Court referred to arts 31 and 32 of the Vienna Convention, and many later cases where the higher courts in Canada have referred to elements of the Vienna rules, eg *Gulfmark Offshore NS Limited v Canada* [2007] FCA 302; *Takeda Canada Inc v Canada (Health)* [2011] FC 1444; *Ezokola v Canada* [2013] SCC 40; and *Peracomo Inc v TELUS Communications Co* [2014] SCC 29; *Trinidad Cement Ltd v Co-operative Republic of Guyana* (Caribbean Court of Justice) (2009) 74 WIR 302. For Australia see text to nn 173 and 174 below.

[144] Multilateral Treaties Deposited with the Secretary-General of the UN, UN treaty database http://treaties.un.org (accessed 8 March 2023).

[145] See James Crawford, 'First Report on State Responsibility' [1998-II(1)] Yearbook of the ILC 1, 17, para 62, fn 26.

Commissaire du Gouvernement in which he recounted how since 1980 the Conseil as developed an approach to interpreting treaties guided by the general principles of public international law set out in Articles 31–33 of the Vienna Convention.[146]

Courts in the USA have long engaged with treaty interpretation, developing extensive practice and including references in judgments to the Vienna rules at every level except the Supreme Court.[147] The decision not to ratify the Vienna Convention was not because of the unsuccessful attempt by the US delegation at the Vienna Conference to adjust the ILC's draft rules on treaty interpretation.[148] To the contrary, the indication by the US State Department that it accepts the Vienna Convention as in large part 'the authoritative guide to current treaty law and practice' has been largely matched by the courts' general acceptance of the Vienna Convention and many judgments make specific references to the Vienna rules.[149]

The US Supreme Court has referred to the definition of 'treaty' in the Vienna Convention, contrasting it with the more limited meaning in the US Constitution's provision on the specific procedure in the Constitution before ratification of treaties.[150] Although the Court has not referred to the Vienna rules on interpretation, the American Law Institute has noted that, while the Court's terminology may not precisely track the Convention, 'it generally has applied an approach and principles of interpretation that are consistent with those set forth in the Vienna Convention on the Law of Treaties'.[151] Account should also be taken of the fact that briefs to the

---

[146] 4 ITLR 1077, 1106, 1115–16, judgment of 28 June 2002; other examples from states not at the time parties to VCLT include: *Jethmalani and Others v Union of India* (Supreme Court of India 14 ITLR 1, 26, para 60 (explicitly referring to art 31(1) of the Vienna Convention) and *Sølvik v Staten v/Skatt Øst* (Supreme Court of Norway) 11 ITLR 15, 34, para 47 (applying art 31(1) of the Vienna Convention as being 'generally accepted as the international norm').

[147] See American Law Institute, *Restatement of the Law (Fourth), The Foreign Relations Law of the United States*, § 306 'Interpretation of Treaties' (2018). For a list of early American cases see T-C Yü, *The Interpretation of Treaties* (Columbia University Press 1927) 81–82, n 1. See also Criddle (n 24) 435; and DJ Bederman, *Classical Canons* (Ashgate 2001), chs IX–X.

[148] See text to n 24 above.

[149] 'We therefore treat the Vienna Convention as an authoritative guide to the customary international law of treaties' 110 S Exec Doc L, 92d Cong, 1st Sess 1 (1971); and see *Chubb & Son Inc v Asiana Airlines* 214 F3d 301 (2d Cir 2000) 308 ff and cases cited there.

[150] See *Weinberger v Rossi* 456 US 25 (1982), 29, fn 5 and US Constitution, art II, para 2. Justice Blackmun mentions the Vienna Convention in a dissenting opinion in *Sale v Haitian Centers Council* 509 US 155, 191 (1993), using the Convention in support of the treaty interpretation element relying on 'ordinary meaning'.

[151] *Restatement* (n 147) comment a. See also HP Aust, A Rodiles, and P Staubach, 'Unity or Uniformity?: Domestic Courts and Treaty Interpretation' (2014) 27 Leiden J Intl L 75, 85.

Supreme Court sometimes refer to the Vienna Convention which is thereby brought to the court's attention.[152] Further, the Court pays considerable deference to the view of the executive on treaty interpretation which, in the light of the State Department's acknowledgement of the Vienna rules and the USA's reliance on them in international legal proceedings, reinforces the likelihood of the Court's interpretations being in accord with application of the rules.[153]

The leading case in the US Supreme Court, showing a generally internationalist approach, is *Abbott v Abbott*.[154] This concerned the extent of the right of custody in the Hague Convention on Child Abduction.[155] Among the briefs to the Court was that for the United States as amicus curiae, which noted that: '[a]lthough the United States has not ratified the Vienna Convention on the Law of Treaties, the United States generally recognizes the Convention as an authoritative guide to treaty interpretation'.[156] Similarly, the brief for the petitioner before the Supreme Court noted that: 'the Department of State' has indicated both that 'the [Vienna] Convention is already generally recognized as the authoritative guide to current treaty law and practice', and that: '[m]ost provisions of the Vienna Convention, including Articles 31 and 32 … are declaratory of customary international law'. It appears that these briefs helped steer the Court towards the approach of the Vienna Convention.

In summary, the case concerned a child who had been removed from Chile where there was a statutory prohibition and court order forbidding either parent from removing the child from the country without the other parent's consent (a '*ne exeat*' prohibition). The central issue was whether this prohibition gave the father a 'right of custody' within the Convention's definition of that term. The Supreme Court's analysis looked to the context which included in the definition a right to 'determine the child's place of residence'. The Court decided that 'place of residence' included the child's

---

[152] See eg Brief for the United States as Amicus Curiae in *Abbott v Abbott* 130 S Ct 1983 (2010).
[153] See eg *Award of Arbitral Tribunal for the Agreement on German External Debt (Belgium, France, Switzerland, UK and USA v Federal Republic of Germany)* ('Young Loan' case, 1980) 59 ILR 495, 529, para 16 and *Restatement* (n 147) Reporters' Note 1; for occasions on which the Court has declined to follow an interpretation of the executive branch see ibid Reporters' Note 10.
[154] See n 152.
[155] Convention on the Civil Aspects of International Child Abduction 1980.
[156] 2009 WL 3043970 (US) n 6, citing *Fujitsu Ltd v Federal Express Corp* 247 F3d 423, 433 (2d Cir), cert denied, 534 US 891 (2001).

country of residence, especially as the Convention's explicit purpose was to prevent wrongful removal across international borders.[157]

This initial examination of the ordinary meaning in context and in the light of the object and purpose of the treaty was thus precisely in line with the Vienna rules. The Court also looked at the practice in the decisions of courts of other parties to the treaty which showed 'broad acceptance of the rule that *ne exeat* rights are rights of custody'.[158] The Supreme Court also considered the history of the Convention, particularly through examination of an Explanatory Report published soon after conclusion of the Convention, adopting what might now be viewed as an 'evolutionary' interpretation.[159]

There remains, however, the occasional indication that the US Supreme Court retains some distinctively nationalist traits, at odds with its growing willingness to adhere to its professed recognition that treaties have an international character. In *BG Group Plc v Argentina* the Court treated the bilateral treaty as equivalent to a domestic contract citing a number of domestic cases to demonstrate how its interpretation should be approached, only later acknowledging that the instrument was a treaty but concluding that this made no difference.[160] The Supreme Court also adopts a wider notion of 'context', allowing reference to a broader range of evidence of a state's intent, including material revealing a party's own documentation, which may not amount to internationally accepted views of what constitutes preparatory work of the treaty. This is unsurprising as it is in line with the proposal made by the US delegation at the Vienna Conference to give the content of Article 32 of the Vienna Convention (supplementary means, including circumstances of conclusion and preparatory work) the same value as the other elements in the Vienna rules; but it goes rather further than that by extending the notion of preparatory work and surrounding circumstances to include, as indicated above, material of unilateral origin.[161] However, this does not substantially derogate from the trend in US case law to follow the Vienna rules.

---

[157] *Abbott v Abbott* (n 152) 1990–91.
[158] ibid 1993.
[159] ibid 1994, but see MK Madden, '*Abbott v. Abbott*: Reviving Good Faith and Rejecting Ambiguity in Treaty Jurisprudence' (2012) 71 Maryland LR 575.
[160] 134 S Ct 1198 (2014).
[161] See *Restatement* (n 147) Reporters' Note 11; see also CJ Mahoney, 'Treaties as Contracts: Textualism, Contract Theory, and the Interpretation of Treaties' (2006–2007) 116 Yale LJ 824.

(c) Interpretation of treaties in courts in the United Kingdom and other 'common law' countries

> The language of an international convention has not been chosen by an English parliamentary draftsman. It is neither couched in the conventional English legislative idiom nor designed to be construed exclusively by English judges. It is addressed to a much wider and more varied judicial audience than is an Act of Parliament.[162]

The description of the circumstances in which courts in the United Kingdom will consider treaties does not show in full the position which courts adopt when interpreting provisions originating in treaties. This is because the judges have not generally formulated a clear rationale for their approach to such provisions as part of the body of English law, or as recognized or received into English law, despite the recognition of treaties given by the judge in the passage quoted above. There are two main questions revealed by practice in this area. First, is a court which refers to a treaty simply using its text as an aid to interpreting a statute rather than interpreting the treaty itself? The significance of this is whether English rules of statutory interpretation are to be applied to the text of the treaty or the rules of public international law. If the latter, the second question is whether English courts use the Vienna rules to interpret treaties?

One senior English judge inclined towards interpretation being of the incorporating statute rather than the treaty, but with a nod to international obligations:

> [t]he metaphor of incorporation may be misleading. It is not the treaty but the statute which forms part of English law. And English courts will not (unless the statute expressly so provides) be bound to give effect to interpretations of the treaty by an international court, even though the United Kingdom is bound by international law to do so. Of course there is a strong presumption in favour of interpreting English law (whether common law or statute) in a way which does not place the United Kingdom in breach of an international obligation.[163]

---

[162] *Fothergill v Monarch Airlines Ltd* (n 48) 281–82 (Lord Diplock).
[163] *R v Lyons* [2002] UKHL 44, para 27 (Lord Hoffmann).

IV Interpretation of Treaties in National Legal Systems

There have, however, been numerous cases in which treaties have been considered and interpreted in the course of judgments without any indication that this is an exercise of statutory rather than treaty interpretation. Further, there has been growing willingness to apply the Vienna rules in courts in the UK and in other countries which follow the common law tradition. In the UK this started with *Fothergill v Monarch Airlines Ltd*,[164] In that case, three of the judges referred to the Vienna rules to support examination of the preparatory work of the relevant treaty (whose substantive provisions were scheduled in both English and French to an Act) when trying to determine whether the term 'damage' (*avarie*) included partial loss of contents of a suitcase slit open during performance of a contract for carriage by air.[165] The judgments gave considerable attention to the preparatory work of the Convention. Lord Diplock indicated that application of the Vienna rules was mandated, noting that, although it applied only to treaties after the Vienna Convention came into force, 'what it says in Articles 31 and 32 about interpretation of treaties, in my view, does no more than codify already-existing public international law.[166] He then quoted the rules in Articles 31(1) and 32, stating:

> [w]here the text is ambiguous or obscure, an English court should have regard to any material which the delegates themselves had thought would be available to clear up any possible ambiguities or obscurities. Indeed, in the case of Acts of Parliament giving effect to international conventions concluded after the coming into force of [the Vienna Convention], I think an English court might well be under a constitutional obligation to do so.[167]

These clear indications that the Vienna rules warranted attention were somewhat eclipsed by the attention given by the court to the possible role of preparatory work of a treaty. This may be why progress towards use of the Vienna rules in English courts has been somewhat uneven and incomplete. Courts in the UK now generally acknowledge that the Vienna rules govern interpretation, but they do not always correlate their actual

---

[164] [1981] AC 251.
[165] See art 26 of the amended Convention on Unification of Certain Rules relating to Carriage by Air 1929 (Warsaw Convention), as set out in the Schedule 1 to the Carriage by Air Act 1961.
[166] [1981] AC 251 at 282 (emphasis added).
[167] ibid 283.

approach very closely or comprehensively to the rules. The clearest recognition after *Fothergill v Monarch Airlines Ltd* that the Vienna rules apply *in toto* (though mirroring the weakness of international case law in not mentioning the provisions on differing languages) was voiced in *Sepet* by Lord Bingham who, in 2003, set out the whole of Articles 31 and 32 of the Vienna Convention, introducing them by stating:

> The task of the House [of Lords] is to interpret the 1951 [Status of Refugees] Convention and, having done so, apply it to the facts of the applicants' cases ... In interpreting the Convention the House must respect articles 31 and 32 of the Vienna Convention on the Law of Treaties 1969.[168]

Since then, cases in the UK Supreme Court have offered the same acknowledgement in several cases.[169] This acceptance is only marred by occasional but persistent harking back to propositions of earlier English case law that 'the interpretation of international conventions must not be controlled by domestic principles but by reference to broad and general principles of construction' and reliance on earlier cases (prominently *Fothergill v Monarch Airlines Ltd*).[170] This detracts from proper application of the Vienna rules and their downgrading by a statement such as 'while it may be difficult to know what are broad and acceptable principles, some principles are enshrined in articles 31 and 32 of the Vienna Convention'.[171] However, there has been considerable progress and the courts commonly apply particular Vienna rules without making specific reference to all of them.[172]

---

[168] *Sepet v Secretary of State for the Home Department* [2003] UKHL 15, para 6
[169] See eg *Moohan and Anor v The Lord Advocate* [2014] UKSC 67 (Lords Kerr and Wilson quoting arts 31 and 32 fully and specifically considering arts 31(2) and 31(3)(c); *Anson v Commissioners for Her Majesty's Revenue and Customs* [2015] UKSC 44 (at para 54 ff, quoting and applying arts 31 and 32 of the Vienna rules); *R v Reeves Taylor* [2019] UKSC 51 (quoting arts 31 and 32 and applying them systematically); and *Basfar v Wong* [2022] UKSC 20, para 17, regrettably stating there that the general rule is in art 31(1) VCLT (rather than constituted by the whole of art 31), but also quoting art 31(3) and stating the content of art 32.
[170] See eg *Warner v Scapa Flow Charters (Scotland)* [2018] UKSC 52, paras 14–16; and *Alize 1954 v Allianz Elementar Versicherungs AG* [2021] UKSC 51, para 37.
[171] *Gard Marine and Energy Limited v China National Chartering Company Limited* [2017] UKSC 35, para 73 endorsing this statement of the Courts of Appeal, and *Warner v Scapa Flow Charters (Scotland)* [2018] UKSC 52, paras 14 ff (giving grudging acceptance of the Vienna rules).
[172] See eg *Evergreen Marine (UK) Limited v Nautical Challenge Ltd* [2021] UKSC 6, where the Court treats art 31(1) as the general rule but nevertheless looks to practice without reference to art 31(3)(b) of the Vienna Convention; similarly, *Basfar v Wong* [2022] UKSC 20, where the Court espoused a bold notion of evolutionary interpretation.

Courts in some other 'common law' jurisdictions have adopted the Vienna rules in a somewhat similar fashion to those in the UK, or sometimes more comprehensively. For example, courts in Australia have long since made reference to the Vienna rules, and in principle apply them to issues of treaty interpretation. In 1983, in *Commonwealth v Tasmania* (The Tasmanian Dam), judges in the High Court of Australia accepted that the Vienna rules applied to treaty interpretation, though distinguishing their application from that in *Fothergill v Monarch Airlines Ltd* on the ground that the Australian case concerned interpretation of the Convention for the Protection of the World Cultural and Natural Heritage, Paris, 1972, as an international agreement, not as Australian law.[173] Later, the Full Court of the Federal Court of Australia set out Articles 31 and 32 of the Vienna Convention in *QAAH v Minister for Immigration & Multicultural & Indigenous Affairs*, with some further explanations of the approach taken by the Australian courts to treaty interpretation, characterized there as an ordered, yet 'holistic' one.[174] Other courts in states whose legal systems follow the common law tradition have similarly used the Vienna Convention's rules on treaty interpretation.[175]

(d) Interpretation in courts of civil law jurisdictions

Too numerous to explore extensively, decisions of courts of civil law jurisdictions raise some points to be noted. One feature which distinguishes civil law jurisdictions from the British common law tradition is clearer constitutional arrangements for treaties. This tends to attract the assumption that these are monist systems. This is only partly true and, as the American experience shows, a constitutional provision for treaties does not necessarily lead to complete clarity in how treaties are implemented and interpreted. In the case of France too the matter may not have always been clear:

> It must be recalled that international treaties to which France is a party, once agreed upon under the appropriate procedure and published in the *Journal Officiel*, have a legal value which, according to article 55 of the Constitution, supersedes ordinary statutory law. The question has

---

[173] (1983) 158 CLR 1, para 77 (Gibbs CJ).
[174] [2005] FCAFC 136; and see *Qenos Pty Ltd v Ship 'APL Sydney'* [2009] FCA 1090, paras 11–17; *Secretary, Department of Families, Housing, Community and Indigenous Affairs v Mahrous* [2013] FCAFC 75, para 55; and for systematic application of the general rule see *Li v Zhou* (Court of Appeal, NSW) [2014] NSWCA 176.
[175] See n 143 above.

been raised in doctrine whether the treaties thus introduced into the French legal order could be considered as 'transformed' into domestic law, or whether they are applied as part of international law, and to be interpreted by French courts, especially by the Conseil d'Etat, according to the customary rules of international law enshrined in articles 31 to 33 of the Vienna Convention on the Law of Treaties.'[176]

As indicated above, the French courts for a long time placed complete reliance on input from the Ministry of Foreign Affairs for interpretation of treaties. This has changed. The Court of Cassation granted the power of interpretation of treaties to judges in civil matters in 1995 and in 2004 the Criminal Chamber of the Court granted full power to the criminal judges to interpret treaties without distinguishing between matters of private interest and those related to the public interest or international public order (the latter being referred to the Ministry before 2004). The Criminal Chamber of the Court of Cassation has further underlined the significance of full account being taken of treaty relations so as to include consideration of reservations and declarations formulated by a state.[177]

As regards the means of interpretation, it has been reported that although France is not a party to the Vienna Convention on the Law of Treaties, French courts do consult the principles of interpretation contained in Articles 31–33 of the Vienna Convention, which they regard as codifying customary international law; but it is not their practice to refer explicitly to the Convention.[178] It has also been reported that, although France has no legal presumption of compatibility, its judges often try, as a matter of practice, to read statutes and treaties to conform with one another consistently.[179]

Professor Bjorge, in an analysis of the approach of French courts to treaty interpretation detects movement from earlier approaches characterized by what had been described as 'a certain preference for literal or minimalist interpretation' and a measure of 'timidity'.[180] He notes that the *Commissaire*

---

[176] GB Burdeau, 'France', ch 6 in A Reinisch (ed), *The Privileges and Immunities of International Organizations in Domestic Courts* (OUP 2013) 109.

[177] *X and Ors*, Appeal judgment, no 13-84.778, ILDC 2376 (2014): Court of Cassation, Criminal Division, analysis by S Jamal, paras A3–4.

[178] Rogoff (n 70) 455–56.

[179] Hollis (n 18) 50, 270–71.

[180] E Bjorge, '"Contractual" and "Statutory" Treaty Interpretation in Domestic Courts? Convergence around the Vienna Rules', ch 4 in HP Aust and G Nolte (eds), *The Interpretation of International Law by Domestic Courts: Uniformity, Diversity, Convergence* (OUP 2016) 55, text to nn 39 and 40.

IV Interpretation of Treaties in National Legal Systems   167

du Gouvernement (in later cases *Rapporteur Public*), who has the role of presenting an independent view to the French *Conseil d'État*, cited and summarized Articles 31 and 32 of the Vienna Convention in his conclusions in the 1990 *GISTI* case.[181] The decision of the Conseil did not expressly mention the Vienna Convention but, taking account of the Commissaire's conclusions, amounted to endorsement of interpretation according to the Vienna rules.[182] Bjorge contrasts approaches in two cases in the French Chambre Criminelle of the Cour de Cassation, noting that in the later *Erika* case the Court, which rarely makes express mention of the Vienna Convention, did refer to the Convention's requirement to interpret terms in the light of a treaty's object and purpose.[183] He concludes that: 'Both courts cite the Vienna rules and rely upon them in an internationalist fashion which does not deserve to be described as overly textualist or minimalist.'[184]

In Germany, provisions of a treaty are usually directly applicable if capable of being so applied and if formulated with sufficient precision, matters which are to be tested by applying the Vienna rules on treaty interpretation.[185] The German Federal Administrative Court (*Bundesverwaltungsgericht*, the highest federal court for administrative matters) has been explicit in its application of the Vienna Convention. This was confirmed in a case concerning compatibility of tuition fees in Higher Education with the UN's the International Covenant on Economic, Social and Cultural Rights 1966.[186] The Court alluded to its earlier jurisprudence, noting that for treaties concluded before Germany became a party to the Vienna Convention the Vienna rules were to be regarded as an expression of general customary

---

[181] Bjorge (n 180) 57, text to n 53.

[182] Conseil d'Etat, Assemblée, du 28 juin 2002, 232276, recueil Lebon, and see Bjorge (n 180) text to nn 51 and 52 and references to further conclusions of the Commissaire and the Rapporteur. It should be noted that decisions of the Conseil refer to documents whose content they have taken into account.

[183] Cour de cassation, criminelle, Chambre criminelle, 25 septembre 2012, 10–82.938, Publié au bulletin: '[q]*u'il ne s'agit pas ici d'interpréter une loi pénale, ce qui impliquerait de recourir à d'autres règles d'interprétation, mais une convention et celle-ci s'interprète, aux termes de la Convention de Vienne du 23 mai 1969, à la lumière de son objet et de son but*.'

[184] Bjorge (n 180) 62, text to n 90; cf *Cigna Insurance v Transport Nijs*, Cassation appeal, No C.97.0176.N, ILDC 38 (BE 2000) (30 March 2000), where the Belgian Court of Cassation held that failure to apply the Vienna rules would not lead to the lower court's judgment being overruled unless that failure had led to a breach of the treaty—a judgment which in effect recognizes the applicability of the Vienna rules.

[185] *Anonymous v (Former) Bitterfeld County*, Order of Federal Administrative Court, 7 B 64.10, ILDC 2418 (DE 2010), NVwZ 2011, 752 (13 December 2010).

[186] BVerwG 6 C 16.08, Judgment of 29 April 2009, and ILDC 1556 (DE 2009); see further AL Paulus, 'Germany', ch 5 in D Sloss (ed), *The Role of Domestic Courts in Treaty Enforcement* (OUP 2010) 222–23.

international law. This is in line with decisions in the UK and elsewhere. The Court took into account observations of the UN Committee on Economic, Social and Cultural Rights (the Social Committee), as reflecting practice in application of the treaty which, while not binding in international law, it viewed as an important means of interpretation of the Covenant showing consensual state practice.[187] One point, which has not received a great deal of attention in case law elsewhere, led the Court to consider Article 33 of the Vienna Convention. Noting that German was not one of the authentic languages described in that article, the Court compared the various authentic language provisions and, taking account of the object and purpose of the provisions, concluded that equality of treatment was what the Covenant required rather than free higher education.[188]

The German Constitutional Court (*Bundesverfassungsgericht*) has also engaged with the Vienna Convention on several occasions. This establishes the applicability in German courts of the Vienna rules on interpretation, although sometimes the application is eclectic rather than systematic. Thus, in the *East German Expropriation Case* (2004) the Court cited Article 31(2)(b) of the Vienna Convention to show that a joint letter sent on behalf of the two German entities prior to unification to the foreign ministers of the occupying powers was to be taken into account in interpreting the Treaty on the Final Settlement to show that the Federal Republic of Germany had accepted an obligation to leave expropriations made on the basis of sovereign acts by occupying powers untouched.[189] For the most part, however, that case paid little attention to the Vienna rules being more concerned with other aspects of international law and the provisions of the Vienna Convention on *jus cogens*.

A more substantial application of the Vienna rules is to be found in the *Jorgic Case*.[190] In holding that the Genocide Convention did not exclude exercise of German criminal jurisdiction on the basis of international law's acceptance of universality for prosecution of the crime of genocide, the Constitutional Court referred to Articles 31 and 32 of the Vienna Convention. The Court specifically took account of the object and purpose of the Genocide Convention as striving for effective criminal prosecution

---

[187] BVerwG 6 C 16.08 (n 186) paras 47–48.
[188] ibid paras 50–52.
[189] BVerfGE 112, 1, ILDC 66; see also *New Strategic Concept Case* 2 BvE 6/99, ILDC 134 (2001) para 148, considering subsequent agreement and practice (arts 31(3)(a) and (b)) as possible treaty commitments.
[190] *J (A Bosnian Serb)*, Individual Constitutional Complaint, 2 BvR 1290/99, ILDC 132.

IV Interpretation of Treaties in National Legal Systems   169

and, on the basis of Article 31(3)(b), took into account the Rome Statute and the history of its negotiation, to show that German jurisdiction was not excluded.[191]

A comprehensive study by Professor Ammann of the approach of Swiss courts to treaty interpretation shows that the Swiss Supreme Court, the Federal Court (*Bundesgericht*) first cited the Vienna Convention in 1971 (well before the UK decision in *Fothergill v Monarch Airlines Ltd* in 1979).[192] This was a case concerning a treaty on railway transport dating from 1858 which included a provision on exemption from imposition of taxes.[193] Citing various authoritative authors on international law, the judgment opened with the proposition that interpretation of a treaty must primarily be based on the text of the treaty, an approach which it noted corresponded, inter alia, with the rules of interpretation in Articles 31 and 32 of the Vienna Convention.[194] The judgment then in effect followed and applied Article 31(1) VCLT, giving attention to the literal meaning of the text but taking account also of the object and purpose of the treaty. Further, although not expressly linked to Article 31(3)(c), the judgment examined other relevant treaties in just the manner which the Vienna rules indicate. The Court also looked at French and Italian translations, remarking on some inexactitude in the former and observing that German was the only authentic language of the treaty.

Professor Ammann observes that, following this decision, the Federal Court continued to make references to the Vienna Convention, or to use its approaches to interpretation without express mention, even though Switzerland did not become a party until June 1990. However, she assesses the Court's use of interpretative methods as frequently lacking predictability, clarity, and consistency.[195] For the period after the Vienna Convention's entry into force for Switzerland, Professor Ammann provides a wealth of examples which show extensive reference to the Vienna rules; but she offers a somewhat critical assessment:

> While the Court's recent interpretative approach is – at least as a matter of principle – more predictable, clear, and consistent, it also displays signs of repetitiveness and superficial engagement with the various

---

[191] ibid paras 39–41.
[192] Ammann (n 139) 235–36.
[193] *Bundesrepublik Deutschland gegen Kanton Schaffhausen* BGE 97 I 359 S 359.
[194] BGE 97 I 359 S 359, 363–64.
[195] Ammann (n 139) 238.

interpretative methods. Moreover, the fact that the VCLT's methods are acknowledged as customary and that they are mentioned as the starting point of interpretation does not mean that they are followed in practice.

Art. 31(1) VCLT is the most frequently quoted provision of the VCLT in the Swiss case law. The Court often neglects the fact that the 'general rule' of art. 31 is not limited to its first paragraph.[196]

Further criticisms made by Professor Ammann are a tendency towards self-referentiality, reliance on Swiss practice and Swiss legislative materials, as well as often citing only Swiss judicial decisions.[197] Yet these, and the earlier quoted criticisms, are ones which could be levelled against the manner of use of the Vienna rules in most national jurisdictions. In contrast, the great number of examples given by Professor Ammann of the various Swiss courts paying some attention to the Vienna rules is at least evidence of their increasing familiarity, even if not of their precise application in a number of cases.[198]

4 Conclusion

Although there is room for improvement in understanding the proper deployment of the Vienna rules, their application, together with the use of other provisions of the Vienna Convention, is gaining ground in national courts. Even in the USA and France, which are not parties to the Convention, the rules have been applied by the courts. That there remain some difficulties in American applications, just as there are deficiencies in courts in other jurisdictions, is partly because the Vienna rules are expressed very economically. For their proper application they themselves require a considerable amount of interpretation. Thus the observation of Detlev Vagts on US practice may still have some force, albeit diminishing, and could readily apply to courts in other jurisdictions:

---

[196] ibid 242.
[197] ibid 243.
[198] See extensive case law from other Swiss Federal and cantonal courts in Ammann (n 139) 248–65.

Finally, it is concluded that the true difficulty with the practice of United States courts in treaty interpretation arises not from new theory, but from an old preference for reading treaties as fitting into the familiar landscape of American law, rather than facing the reality that treaties change national law.[199]

---

[199] DF Vagts, 'Treaty Interpretation and the New American Ways of Law Reading' (1993) 4 EJIL 472, 473.

6
Ensuring Treaties Work

> These gentlemen would do well to reflect that a treaty is only another name for a bargain, and that it would be impossible to find a nation who would make any bargain with us, which should be binding upon them *absolutely*, but on us only so long and so far as we may think proper to be bound by it.[1]

The optimism (which is likely to be viewed as misplaced) implied by the title to this chapter should be accompanied by noting that the majority of treaties in the modern age concern practical subjects. Because of their manifest utility no 'enforcement' mechanisms are actually required for them to be effective. There are frequently differences over how they are to be interpreted and applied, but discussion or institutional activities resolve most problems amicably. This chapter mainly concerns supervision of implementation of treaties, responses to breach, and methods for encouraging compliance where this is necessary. Discussions or negotiation, the pressures of reciprocity, and diplomatic action provide the traditional means for ensuring implementation, but increasingly international institutions have a role in this.

While negotiation remains the principal means of dealing with perceived breaches of a treaty, resort to arbitration or judicial settlement of disputes has been increasingly common, with use of proportionate measures in response to a breach such as denial of benefits under the treaty or withholding other rights as a further resort. Serving a notice of termination may be a form of pressure in negotiations but, if carried through, denotes failure to ensure or agree on compliance, although it can lead to renegotiation to produce terms acceptable to the parties.

---

[1] J Jay, *The Federalist*, No LXIV (T Fisher Unwin 1886) 405 (emphasis in original).

The possibility of countermeasures, where permissible, or their actual implementation, can provide an inducement to avoid aberrant behaviour or resume compliance. A systematic combination of a form of arbitration and subsequent allowance of measures in response has been part of the institutional framework of the dispute settlement mechanism under the treaty establishing the World Trade Organization. There has also grown up a significant industry of claims by individuals and corporations before international arbitral tribunals pursuant to bilateral investment treaties.

Some of the topics of this chapter are not viewed as part of the law of treaties. The 1969 Vienna Convention touches on breach of treaties in its Part V which is headed 'Invalidity, Termination and Suspension of the Operation of Treaties'. These provisions are of limited help in securing compliance. While many treaties include their own provisions for resolution of differences over their interpretation and application, and some set up bodies to monitor or supervise implementation and compliance, other measures are in the province of general international law.

Where there is a dispute between states which is likely to endanger the maintenance of international peace and security, the UN Charter offers a range of methods of peaceful settlement.[2] Effectively, these are also the means of settling lesser differences and those concerning treaties. They include 'negotiation, enquiry, mediation, conciliation, arbitration, judicial settlement, resort to regional agencies or arrangements, or other peaceful means of [the states'] own choice'.[3] Apart from negotiation and mediation, these means are likely to need a treaty as the specific basis for their operation, but even negotiation and mediation may be mandated and regulated in individual treaties.

I Reciprocity and Diplomatic Action

1 Simple Reciprocity

Where treaties contain reciprocal benefits or a balance of advantages, these factors are likely to be enough to encourage compliance. Treaty relations formed by bilateral treaties can produce this effect relatively simply. In the case of multilaterals, the situation may be more complex. Thus, for example,

---

[2] See art 33.
[3] ibid.

the multilateral Vienna Convention on Diplomatic Relations, 1961, requires a host state not to discriminate among other parties in their treatment under the Convention, but it permits a host state to apply any of its provisions restrictively because of a 'restrictive application' of that provision to its mission in the sending state, or where by custom or agreement two parties extend to each other more favourable treatment than is required by the Convention.[4]

2 Negotiated Arrangements

Countless are the treaties which require an attempt be first made by negotiation in order to settle any difference or dispute over their interpretation or application. In *Georgia v Russia* (2011) the ICJ considered what constitutes negotiations, what is their adequate form and substance, and to what extent they must be pursued before it can be said that a precondition requiring that disputing parties to negotiate has been met.[5] Citing extensively its own and its predecessor's case law, the Court observed that negotiations are distinct from mere protests or disputations:

> Negotiations entail more than the plain opposition of legal views or interests between two parties, or the existence of a series of accusations and rebuttals, or even the exchange of claims and directly opposed counter-claims. As such, the concept of 'negotiations' differs from the concept of 'dispute', and requires—at the very least—a genuine attempt by one of the disputing parties to engage in discussions with the other disputing party, with a view to resolving the dispute.[6]

That said, however, the Court further noted that no emphasis is to be placed on any rigid or formalistic construction of what constitutes negotiations, each case having to be considered on its facts. The absence of specific reference to a treaty during diplomatic discussions does not preclude the precondition of negotiations being met provided that the subject-matter of the discussions relates to the subject-matter of the dispute which, in turn,

---

[4] See art 47.
[5] *Application of the International Convention on the Elimination of All Forms of Racial Discrimination (Georgia v Russian Federation)* (Judgment) [2011] ICJ Rep 70, 132–34, paras 156–62.
[6] ibid para 157.

must concern the substantive obligations contained in the treaty in question.[7] Elsewhere the Court has stated:

> Precisely what periods of time may be involved in the observance of the duties to consult and negotiate ... are matters which necessarily vary according to the requirements of the particular case. In principle, therefore, it is for the parties in each case to determine the length of those periods by consultation and negotiation in good faith.[8]

3 Responding in Kind (*Exceptio Inadimplenti*)

While some treaties provide for a single transaction of a unilateral character, an underlying notion of many treaties is that a promise is given for a promise or that obligations are mutual (sometimes described as 'synallagmatic'). Why should one party implement a treaty or continue to perform their part of the bargain if the other is not performing? Performance can legitimately be withheld by the aggrieved party, at least until things are sorted out. This notion is graced with the Latin soubriquet *exceptio inadimplenti non est adimplendum*.[9]

Reciprocal non-performance looks simple enough where parties to a bilateral treaty have identical obligations and one fails to fulfil their treaty commitment. However, the place and scope of the principle in international law are uncertain because it has been located both in the law of treaties and in the law of state responsibility without clear and comprehensive rules placing it firmly in either category. The principle is reflected in the law of treaties, at least in part, by provisions of the Vienna Convention on suspension of operation of a treaty in response to a breach of the treaty. The relevant focus in the law of state responsibility is on permissibility of countermeasures by the aggrieved state in response to the breach of international law occasioned by a breach of a treaty, and the measures are thus outside the confines of the law of treaties. To the extent that international

---

[7] ibid para 161.
[8] *Interpretation of the Agreement of 25 March 1951 between the WHO and Egypt* (Advisory Opinion) [1980] ICJ Rep 73, 96, para 49.
[9] See M Fitzmaurice, 'Angst of the Exceptio Inadimplenti Non Est Adimplendum in International Law', ch 16 in L Bartels and F Paddeu (eds), *Exceptions in International Law* (OUP 2020); and D Azaria, 'Exception of Non-Performance', MPEPIL www.mpepil.com (subscription) (accessed 8 March 2023).

law is codified in these areas, its application and the link to the *exceptio* principle are considered below in the context of the Vienna Convention provisions on suspension of treaties.

II Supervision by International Institutions

Chapter VII of the UN Charter provides for action to be taken with respect to threats to the peace, breaches of the peace, and acts of aggression extending to the possibility of sanctions and the use of force. Few treaties have envisaged such possibilities but instead rely on more modest measures of encouragement to compliance through guidance, monitoring, supervision, or investigation. Some treaties provide for private parties to submit applications or complaints asserting non-compliance to an international body, leading to consideration of the issues, and sometimes to investigations and reports. Submission of reports and their publication with the relevant state or states' responses to them can exert a modicum of pressure towards conformity.

The term 'supervision' is used here in a very general sense to include monitoring and reporting on implementation. Professor Romano makes a helpful distinction between the function in international institutions of providing 'adjudicative means' for upholding the international rule of law and 'non-adjudicative means', the latter being the immediate focus of attention here.[10] He notes that while the reports and recommendations of institutions when providing non-adjudicative means are not binding, some non-binding outcomes carry significant weight and can be authoritative. He instances the advisory opinions of the ICJ, the findings of the Inter-American Commission on Human Rights, the World Bank Inspection Panel, and the implementation committee of any of the major environmental treaties.[11] The list of those providing non-adjudicative means extends to at least seventy-five bodies, some being global, others regional.[12] There is no standard system, but something of the various approaches can be seen from a few examples.

---

[10] CPR Romano, 'A Taxonomy of International Rule of Law Institutions' (2011) 2 J Intl Dispute Settlement 241, 253–61.
[11] ibid 253–54.
[12] ibid 256–61.

The International Labour Organization (ILO), founded in 1919, was one of the pioneers. Precise details vary in regard to its different conventions but, in principle, parties to each ILO convention are required to report regularly on measures taken for its implementation. Governments are required to submit copies of their reports to employers' and workers' organizations which may then comment. A Committee of Experts examines the reports and provides an impartial and technical evaluation of application of the Conventions' standards in member states. These reports set out 'observations' and the Committee may make direct requests for further information. The observations are published in an annual report.[13]

The ILO also provides 'supervision' in response to 'representations' and 'complaints'. Representations may be made by employers' or workers' associations and are examined by a tripartite examining committee which reports to the ILO Governing Council with recommendations. If the government concerned does not take appropriate measures in response the Council may set up a commission of inquiry if a complaint in made. Complaints alleging non-compliance can be made by member states, delegates to the ILO's Conference, or the Governing Council itself; but the resultant possibility of enforcement measures takes this procedure into the category of adjudicative means of supervision.[14]

That non-adjudicative means of supervision can have a significant impact on implementation of treaties is shown by the work of the UN Committee on Human Rights in its reports monitoring implementation of the International Covenant on Civil and Political Rights by its states parties. The Covenant empowers the Committee to include 'general comments' when transmitting reports submitted by parties to the Covenant.[15] General Comment no. 24 concerns the compatibility of reservations with the Covenant and their assessment by the Committee.[16] While the states were divided in their views on this comment, the General Comment played a considerable part in the development of the ILC's *Guide to Practice on Reservations to Treaties*.[17]

---

[13] ILO, *Monitoring Compliance with International Labour Standards* (ILO 2019) https://www.ilo.org; see also C Drake, 'ILO: The First Fifty Years' (1969) 32 Mod L Rev 664.

[14] ILO (n 13).

[15] International Covenant on Civil and Political Rights 1969, art 44(4). There is a separate process for dealing with individual complaints and inter-state complaints of violation of the Covenant in respect of states which have accepted the 1976 Optional Protocol to the Covenant.

[16] UN Treaty Bodies Database Doc CCPR/C/21/Rev.1/Add.6 https://tbinternet.ohchr.org/.

[17] Addendum to Report of the International Law Commission, Sixty-third session (2011), UN General Assembly Official Records, Sixty-sixth Session, Supplement No 10, A/66/10/

A further example, from an organization which originally was regional, is the evolved system of monitoring by the Organisation for Economic Co-operation and Development (OECD) of the Bribery Convention.[18] This is described by the OECD as 'a rigorous peer-review monitoring system' in which each country's implementation is reviewed in phases, with experts evaluating the adequacy of the country's legal framework to fight foreign bribery and implement the Convention, assessing the legislation as it is being applied in practice, and following up implementation of recommendations, with attendant publication of reports.[19]

III Resort to Arbitration, Courts, and Tribunals

Judicial or quasi-judicial determination of disputes arising from treaties depends on the agreement of states to accept the jurisdiction of courts and tribunals. Arbitration has two essential requirements: the agreement of states to arbitrate and identification or establishment of an arbitral tribunal (sometimes called a 'court of arbitration'). The former element imports acceptance of jurisdiction being conferred upon the tribunal. Before the establishment of permanent courts much of the focus of attention was on the composition of an arbitral tribunal, or at least the means of constituting one, and that remains an important consideration today even where a tribunal or dispute settlement mechanism has been institutionalized by treaty, as with disputes arbitrated under the aegis of the International Centre for Settlement of Investment Dispute or subject to recommendations of panels set up under the World Trade Organization's Dispute Settlement Mechanism.

Accounts of the modern history of arbitration commonly start with the 1794 treaty between the USA and Great Britain ('the Jay Treaty').[20] To

Add.1, 220–42 http://legal.un.org/ilc/reports/2011/english/addendum.pdf; see also ch 2, section III.2(a) above.

[18] Convention on Combating Bribery of Foreign Public Officials in International Business Transactions 1997, 2802 UNTS 49274.
[19] OECD, Country Monitoring of the OECD Anti-Bribery Convention, https://www.oecd.org/corruption/countrymonitoringoftheoecdanti-briberyconvention.htm; A Tyler, 'Enforcing Enforcement: Is the OECD Anti-Bribery Convention's Peer Review Effective' (2011) 43 Geo Wash Int'l L Rev 137 and E Bao and K Hall, 'Peer Review and the Global Anti-Corruption Conventions: Context, Theory and Practice' (2017) 35 Aust YBIL 67.
[20] Treaty of Amity, Commerce, and Navigation (London 1794) https://avalon.law.yale.edu/18th_century/jay.asp.

resolve issues arising from the American War of Independence—issues which it had not proved possible to settle by negotiation—this treaty provided for the establishment of mixed commissions. These commissions were composed of American and British nationals in equal numbers with an additional commissioner holding the balance and selected by agreement between the parties' nominated commissioners or, failing agreement, one chosen by lot from nominees of each side.[21] These mixed commissions functioned to some extent in the manner of judicial tribunals, the commissioners being sworn to decide impartially and according to the evidence. They stimulated interest in the potential of arbitration for settling international disputes.

The *Alabama Claims* arbitration in 1872, also between the United Kingdom and the United States, was founded on the 1871 Treaty of Washington, which set a much more judicial tone than the Jay Treaty and demonstrated how a mechanism could be agreed for achieving an arbitral tribunal which had a truly neutral controlling balance.[22] The tribunal was given powers to decide points of law, but in large measure the applicable law was specified in the treaty which propounded the rules on aspects of maritime neutrality. The arbitral award was binding.

The claims arose from breaches of neutrality which the USA asserted had been committed by Great Britain during the American Civil War. The treaty provided for a tribunal of five members, one nominated by each disputing party, the rest to be appointed respectively by the heads of state of three states entirely neutral to the case. Significantly, in the light of twentieth-century problems over effectiveness of treaty provisions setting up a tribunal (considered below), the treaty named fallback heads of state who could be asked to nominate arbitrators if the original named heads of state failed to nominate at all, or if they failed to nominate replacements for arbitrators who died or otherwise failed to fulfil their role. The arbitral tribunal confirmed the rules of neutrality and ordered the United Kingdom to pay compensation, which the United Kingdom did. The significance of this arbitration for present purposes is that it provided something of a template for the typical treaty provision on how to establish an independent tribunal to resolve disputes over the application of a treaty. It also showed how an arbitration could contribute to identification of rules of international law,

---

[21] ibid arts 5–8.
[22] *Alabama Claims of the United States of America against Great Britain* XXIX UNRIAA 125; and T Bingham, 'The Alabama Claims Arbitration' (2005) 54 ICLQ 1.

confirming those in the Treaty of Washington specifying maritime neutrality rules in respect of which Britain was found to be in breach.

The importance of having a watertight provision in any treaty for appointment of an arbitral tribunal was shown by the *Peace Treaties* cases in 1950.[23] Allegations had been made that various East European states were failing to comply with human rights provisions in certain peace treaties. A provision of these treaties for dealing with allegations of breaches stated:

> Any such dispute not resolved by them within a period of two months shall, unless the parties to the dispute mutually agree upon another means of settlement, be referred at the request of either party to the dispute to a Commission composed of one representative of each party and a third member selected by mutual agreement of the two parties from nationals of a third country. Should the two parties fail to agree within a period of one month upon the appointment of the third member, the Secretary-General of the United Nations may be requested by either party to make the appointment.[24]

In issue was whether the Secretary-General could appoint a 'third' member of the tribunal if a party to the dispute failed to nominate the 'second' member. The ICJ gave its opinion that a third arbitrator could not be appointed where no second member had been named. There was an obligation on the relevant party to appoint the second member, but the treaty had not been drawn up in such a way as to ensure appointment in default of this obligation being met. The tribunal could not, therefore, be constituted without the co-operation of the parties after the dispute had arisen. Hence, in treaties concluded after these cases arbitration clauses typically include provision for nomination of any missing tribunal members by an independent authority (such as the President of the ICJ).

Jurisdiction of a court or tribunal in any international arbitration or international judicial process for adjudication of a dispute between states is established by the agreement of the parties to the dispute, typically in a treaty or what has been described as a 'treaty-instrument'. In the prevalent French diplomatic language of yesteryear this was termed a 'compromis',

---

[23] *Interpretation of Peace Treaties with Bulgaria, Hungary and Romania (Second Phase)* (Advisory Opinion) [1950] ICJ Rep 221.
[24] ibid 226.

translated as 'special agreement' in the Statutes of the PCIJ and ICJ.[25] Where treaties include provision for jurisdiction of a permanent judicial institution or of a tribunal constituted specifically for any dispute arising under the treaty, the provisions are commonly described as a 'compromissory clause' with the term 'compromis' being generally used for an agreement to establish an ad hoc tribunal for a specific dispute or defining the issues to be submitted for adjudication.[26]

That the latter has been described as a 'treaty-instrument' suggests the question whether some forms of international agreement fall into a different category from treaties generally? Establishing the jurisdiction of an international court or tribunal to resolve a dispute between states requires agreement amounting to a treaty, but instituting proceedings before a court or initiating an arbitration engaging that jurisdiction may take a different form. Thus a 'declaration' accepting jurisdiction of the ICJ under the 'optional clause' (Article 36 of the ICJ Statute) is a means by which a state unilaterally completes its consent to the jurisdiction of the Court. States may, however, agree to accept jurisdiction for a particular case. This may be by an agreement equivalent to or constituting a treaty, as was found to be the case with the exchange of letters and minutes in *Qatar v Bahrain*.[27]

However, whether there is a treaty provision for compulsory jurisdiction, a declaration under the optional clause, or a treaty agreeing to arbitration over issues yet to arise, there may need to be a provision for how the court or tribunal is to be seized of a particular case, whether this is to be by unilateral notice or joint submission. Thus in the second phase of *Qatar v Bahrain* a key issue was whether the agreement identified in the first phase of the case envisaged unilateral seisin of the Court or whether a further compromis was required. The Court found that the case could be brought before it unilaterally, relying on the exchange of letters and minutes constituting a treaty; but had a compromis been required, following on from the agreement and jointly setting out the issues in dispute and submitting them to the Court, it seems it would have been apt to describe this document as a 'treaty-instrument'.[28]

---

[25] H Thirlway, 'Compromis', MPEPIL www.mpepil.com (subscription) (accessed 8 March 2023).
[26] ibid.
[27] *Maritime Delimitation and Territorial Questions between Qatar and Bahrain (Qatar v Bahrain)* (Jurisdiction and Admissibility) [1994] ICJ Rep 6.
[28] ibid.

There are now, of course, a fair number of international courts and tribunals which are established by treaty but whose processes are engaged by or in respect of individuals or companies. The means by which such parties initiate proceedings against states before human rights courts or arbitral tribunals for investment disputes are set out in the constitutive treaties, as are the processes for instituting criminal processes against individuals at the International Criminal Court.

IV Suspension, Termination, and Other Responses to Breach of a Treaty

Provisions of the Vienna Convention on the suspension of treaty commitments by a party aggrieved by another's breach of the treaty appear in the section on 'Invalidity, Termination and Suspension of the Operation of Treaties'.[29] Attempts to show invalidity based on the Vienna grounds have met with little success. Conversely, termination generally provides little scope for debate where this is by notice and clear provisions for that are usually included in final clauses, although the consequences may be more difficult to handle. Suspension, however, presents a much more controversial legal terrain.

1 Invalidity

Assertions of invalidity warrant only the briefest of accounts here because such assertions play no part in encouraging implementation of treaties.[30] However, occasionally and tangentially arguments are based on assertion of invalidity as a defence to attempts at enforcement. The grounds for invalidity are usually classified in terms of 'relative' and 'absolute' invalidity. Treaties in respect of which there are relative grounds of invalidity are voidable at the choice of an affected state. Grounds for voidability relate to absence of capacity to express the consent of a state to be bound or where consent is in some way vitiated. Where it is alleged that consent to be bound

---

[29] VCLT, Pt V, which includes general provisions in arts 42–5, such as that on separability of treaty provisions where relevant to this section (art 44).
[30] See M Schröder and A Schwerdtfeger, 'Treaties, Validity', MPEPIL www.mpepil.com (accessed 8 March 2023) and E Cannizzaro (ed), *The Law of Treaties Beyond the Vienna Convention* (OUP 2011) Pt IV.

by a treaty has been expressed in violation of a provision of a state's internal law, consent is only voidable if the violation was 'manifest and concerned a rule of its internal law of fundamental importance'.[31] Specific restrictions on authority of representatives to express the consent of a state can only be relied on if the restriction had been notified to the other negotiating states before consent was expressed.[32] The other relative grounds are error, fraud, and corruption of representatives of a state.[33] A relevant error is one which relates to a fact or situation which was assumed by a state to exist at the time when the treaty was concluded and which formed an essential basis of its consent.[34] Fraud and corruption are largely self-explanatory terms but international law is almost devoid of examples in the present context.[35]

In similar vein, suggestions of absolute invalidity for coercion of a state or its representatives in negotiating or concluding a treaty, or for violation of a peremptory norm (*ius cogens*), have not been widely evidenced by authoritative findings, although the subject of peremptory norms has received considerable attention academically and judicially subsequent to inclusion of somewhat controversial provisions in the Vienna Convention concerning treaties conflicting with existing and new peremptory norms of general international law.[36] However Shelton notes with reference to *jus cogens* that: 'In practice, the concept has been invoked largely outside its original context in the law of treaties'.[37]

2 Suspension, Termination, and Countermeasures

The general principle allowing responding in kind to breaches of treaties as an exception to the obligation to fully perform all treaty obligations (*exceptio inadimplenti*) has been briefly outlined above. Greater particularity has been provided by the codifications of rules in the Vienna Convention and in the provisions on countermeasures in the ILC's 'Draft

---

[31] VCLT, art 46.
[32] ibid art 47.
[33] ibid arts 48–50.
[34] Provision is made in VCLT, art 79 for procedures to correct errors in texts or in certified copies of treaties.
[35] See Schröder and Schwerdtfeger (n 30).
[36] VCLT, arts 53, 64: see Schröder and Schwerdtfeger (n 30); and D Shelton, *Jus Cogens* (OUP 2021).
[37] Shelton (n 36) 96.

Articles on Responsibility of States for Internationally Wrongful Acts'.[38] Immediate questions arising in this context are what are the differences between these sets of rules on broadly the same subject and what action do they permit?

Article 60 of the Vienna Convention differentiates its permitted reactions to breaches of bilateral treaties from those envisaged for multilateral treaties. A material breach of a bilateral treaty by one party entitles the other to invoke the breach as a ground for terminating the treaty or suspending its operation in whole or in part. A party specially affected by a material breach of a multilateral treaty may invoke the breach as a ground for suspending the operation of the treaty in whole or in part as between itself and the defaulting state.[39] In addition, a party other than the defaulting state may invoke the breach as a ground for suspending the operation of the treaty in whole or in part with respect to itself 'if the treaty is of such a character that a material breach of its provisions by one party radically changes the position of every party with respect to the further performance of its obligations under the treaty'.[40] As regards collective action, the parties other than the defaulter may by unanimous agreement suspend the operation of the treaty in whole or in part, or terminate it either as between themselves and the defaulting state or as between all the parties.[41]

Professor Fitzmaurice identifies three ways in which the Vienna regime differs from the customary law *exceptio inadimplenti* (the right to stop performing obligations in face of a breach).[42] The *exceptio* is potentially applicable to any breach whereas Article 60 provides for reactions only to a 'material breach', a term which is defined as 'a repudiation of the treaty not sanctioned by the present Convention' or 'violation of a provision essential to the accomplishment of the object or purpose of the treaty'. Second, the *exceptio* envisages responsive denial of the same right or nonperformance of the same obligation as that underlying the breach. Article 60 allows termination of the treaty or suspending its operation in whole or in part—hence a much wider range of possible responses. Third, the Vienna

---

[38] The Vienna regime is in VCLT, Pt V, s 3. The ILC draft on countermeasures are arts 22 and 49–54 (with commentaries), [2001-II(2)] Yearbook of the ILC ; and see successive UN General Assembly promulgation and endorsements as in Resolution 74/180 of 18 December 2019, accompanied by the Secretary General's compilation of citations of the draft articles by international courts, tribunals, and other bodies, Doc A/74/83 (2019).
[39] VCLT, art 60(2)(b).
[40] ibid art 60(2)(c).
[41] ibid art 60(2)(a).
[42] Fitzmaurice (n 9) 289.

Convention requires formal notification of termination or suspension with an indication of the exact measure proposed and the reasons for taking them.[43] Unless there is special urgency the proposed measures may only be taken if no objection is raised within three months. If an objection is raised the parties must seek a solution through the means indicated in the UN Charter.[44] Application of the *exceptio* does not call for such precise steps, although diplomatic notification and attempts at negotiation are likely and proper precursors to taking action.

There may be a conceptual difference between the *exceptio* as precluding wrongfulness under general international law—non-performance is justified by the other party's breach—as contrasted with suspension or termination where the treaty obligation no longer binds temporarily or permanently.[45] However, there is little in case law or records of practice to show whether this difference has significant consequences, except in the sense that the *exceptio* has a more temporary appearance to it. Several of the provisions of the Vienna Convention on termination and suspension of treaties were considered by the ICJ in the 'Danube Dams case', *Gabcíkovo-Nagymaros (Hungary/Slovakia)*.[46]

This case arose from a 1977 treaty under which Hungary and the former Czechoslovakia agreed on joint construction of a locks and barrage system on a stretch of the Danube for the development of water resources, energy, transport, agriculture, and other economic activities. Before its share of the construction work had been completed Hungary got cold feet. There were some uncertainties about the economic viability of the project and growing concern about its possible environmental consequences. Hungary stopped work and sought to terminate the scheme unilaterally; Czechoslovakia carried on with its own modified versions (Variant C) which it saw as 'approximate application of the treaty scheme'.

Although the Vienna Convention did not apply to the 1977 treaty as that treaty preceded the Convention's entry into force, the ICJ considered that

---

[43] VCLT, art 65; the provisions on termination and suspension in response to breach do not apply to breaches of 'treaties of a humanitarian character, in particular to provisions prohibiting any form of reprisals against persons protected by such treaties': VCLT, art 60(5).
[44] VCLT, art 65(3); UN Charter art 33.
[45] Fitzmaurice (n 9) 287.
[46] [1997] ICJ Rep 7 para 46; cf the judgment of the PCIJ in *Diversion of Water from the Meuse*, where the Court held that the Netherlands could not sustain its case that Belgium's construction and use of a lock for irrigation and other purposes was contrary to an 1863 bilateral treaty when the Netherlands was doing the same thing with a lock on its part of the river: [1937] PCIJ Series A/B, No 70, 50.

the termination and suspension provisions in the Convention's Articles 60–62 constituted a codification of customary international law.[47] Further, both parties in the case agreed that Articles 65–7 of the Vienna Convention, if not codifying customary law, at least generally reflected customary international law and contained certain procedural principles based on an obligation to act in good faith.[48]

Hungary accumulated various grounds in the Vienna Convention which it alleged provided a basis for termination of the treaty and justified its own non-performance. However, as regards termination for breach, the Court's judgment found Hungary's six days' notice of termination to have been premature. No breach of the treaty by Czechoslovakia had yet taken place and consequently Hungary was not entitled to invoke the subsequent breach of the treaty by Czechoslovakia's implementation of Variant C as a ground for terminating the treaty when it did. Czechoslovakia's argument of 'approximate application' by implementing its own Variant C, a version of the project favourable to it when faced with Hungary's wrongful refusal to proceed, was rejected by the Court as a justification for not complying with the treaty. Hungary's breach of the 1977 Treaty could not be remedied by creating a project not envisaged by the treaty.[49] However, the breach by Czechoslovakia in carrying out a modified version of the scheme when what was required was a joint scheme had not occurred before the Hungarian measures.

The ICJ did not accept any of the further Hungarian arguments, based on impossibility or fundamental change of circumstances, or any other grounds such as would justify termination by Hungary at the time it purported to effect such termination.[50] The treaty required the parties to take joint action, including agreed measures to protect the environment. The Court required the parties to attempt to reach agreement but, failing this, the matter was to be referred back to the Court for further consideration. Although negotiations did not result in an effective agreement, some twenty years after the judgment and after an application for a further judgment had been long pending, the case was withdrawn.

---

[47] *Gabčíkovo-Nagymaros Project (Hungary v Slovakia)* (Judgment) [1997] ICJ Rep 7, para 46; VCLT, art 4 provides for the Convention to be non-retroactive, although the case did also feature a 1989 Protocol to which the VCLT applied.
[48] *Gabčíkovo-Nagymaros Project* (n 47) para 109.
[49] ibid paras 76, 78.
[50] See VCLT, art 61 ('Supervening impossibility of performance') and art 62 ('Fundamental change of circumstances').

The Court stated in its 1997 judgment:

'Nor does the Court need to dwell upon the question of the relationship between the law of treaties and the law of State responsibility ... as those two branches of international law obviously have a scope that is distinct. A determination of whether a convention is or is not in force, and whether it has or has not been properly suspended or denounced, is to be made pursuant to the law of treaties. On the other hand, an evaluation of the extent to which the suspension or denunciation of a convention, seen as incompatible with the law of treaties, involves the responsibility of the State which proceeded to it, is to be made under the law of state responsibility.'[51]

This distinction between whether treaty obligations have been legitimately terminated or suspended and issues of responsibility arising from what has been done by way of, or in response to, a breach of a treaty may seem clear enough. As regards countermeasures, the ILC has commented:

Countermeasures involve conduct taken in derogation from a subsisting treaty obligation but justified as a necessary and proportionate response to an internationally wrongful act of the State against which they are taken. They are essentially temporary measures, taken to achieve a specified end, whose justification terminates once the end is achieved.[52]

However, the difficulty in separating out the regimes within the law of treaties for measures in response to a breach and that within general international law for countermeasures arises because the same facts and legal parameters may fall to be assessed from both points of view. This is particularly confusing in the case of suspension of treaty obligations which gives rise to consequences ostensibly matching, although more limited than, possible countermeasures. Some help can be found in the ILC Commentary on draft articles on state responsibility. Citing the *Rainbow Warrior* arbitration case, the ILC noted 'the tribunal held that both the law of treaties and the law of State responsibility had to be applied, the former to determine whether the treaty was still in force, the latter to determine what the consequences

---

[51] *Gabčíkovo-Nagymaros Project* (n 47) para 47.
[52] ILC, 'Draft Articles on Responsibility of States for Internationally Wrongful Acts, with commentaries' [2001-II(2)] Yearbook of the ILC, Pt III, ch II 'Countermeasures', comment (4).

were of any breach of the treaty while it was in force, including the question whether the wrongfulness of the conduct in question was precluded'.[53]

The Court in *Gabčíkovo-Nagymaros* referred to the explicit indication in Article 73 of the Vienna Convention that the provisions of that treaty are not to prejudge any question that may arise from the international responsibility of a state. It can be seen, therefore, that if countermeasures are loosely based on the *exceptio* principle—that is exemption from responsibility for what would otherwise be a breach of international law in failing to meet a treaty obligation—this suggests that countermeasures fall squarely within the ambit of general international law on state responsibility rather than the law of treaties.

A point in the codified law on state responsibility which marks a clear difference from the Vienna provisions on suspension is the extent of permissible measures. While it is a requirement of the law of state responsibility that countermeasures be proportionate, they are not limited to disapplying provisions of a treaty corresponding to any terms that have been breached.[54] Hence in the leading arbitral case on countermeasures before the ILC codification, France had refused to allow an American airline to switch to smaller aircraft in London on flights from the USA to France, asserting that such a switch was not permitted by the bilateral treaty between the two states.[55] The tribunal found that the USA's complete suspension of Air France's flights to Los Angeles was not a clearly disproportionate response, there being no exact, reciprocal equivalent to the limitation which France had imposed.

The aim of countermeasures is to encourage compliance and the rules therefore specify that proportionality takes into account 'the gravity of the internationally wrongful act and the rights in question'.[56] In *USA v France* the measures did relate to the same treaty, but this is not specified to be necessary in the draft articles. There are, however, specific limitations. Countermeasures are not to affect the UN Charter obligations in regard to: refraining from the threat or use of force, human rights, those of a humanitarian character prohibiting reprisals, peremptory norms of general

---

[53] ibid 71, Pt I, ch V 'Circumstances Precluding Wrongfulness', comment (3); *Rainbow Warrior (New Zealand/France)* (1990) XX RIAA 251–52.
[54] Draft art 51 and commentary; ILC, 'Draft Articles on Responsibility of States for Internationally Wrongful Acts, with commentaries' [2001-II] Yearbook of the ILC 134–35.
[55] *Case Concerning the Air Services Agreement of 27 March 1946 (USA v France)* 54 ILR 304 (1978).
[56] ibid draft art 51.

international law and inviolability of diplomatic or consular agents, premises, archives and documents.[57] Countermeasures are not permitted, or if already taken must be suspended, if 'the dispute is pending before a court or tribunal which has the authority to make decisions binding on the parties'.[58]

Thus, notwithstanding the differences in the applicability and content of the Vienna regime for termination or suspension of treaties and the ILC codification of rules on countermeasures, it can be seen that both can have a part to play in assisting compliance with treaty obligations.

V Further Avenues for Dealing with Differences over Implementation

Amicable progression of negotiations over implementation of treaties may be aided by various measures. The extreme measure of termination of a treaty under the provisions in the Vienna Convention for dealing with breach of a treaty may be inappropriate where the breach or disputed application is merely the result of a perceived imbalance in benefits and obligations that have been achieved over the lifetime of the treaty. Normal termination by notice may be used in these circumstances simply as a spur to renegotiation to produce an adjusted treaty, although termination may not actually have to be completed to achieve agreement to revision.[59]

The possibilities for adjusting a treaty include amendment, modification, or complete revision. While 'modify' in common parlance can be used loosely as a synonym for 'change', the 1969 Vienna Convention established a clear distinction between 'amendment' (broadly, a change to a treaty open to all parties and prospective parties to it) and 'modification' (a change to a treaty made by two or more parties as between themselves alone).[60] This differentiation between amendment and modification, which is useful in assessing changes to terms of a treaty, is not, unfortunately, systematically maintained in treaty parlance or academic analysis.

---

[57] ibid draft art 50.
[58] ibid draft art 52.
[59] See eg the 1977 termination of the UK–USA Air Services Agreement 1946: AF Lowenfeld, 'The Future Determines the Past: Bermuda I in the light of Bermuda II' (1978) 3 Air and Space L 2; C Pejovic and JN Pardede, 'Revising Bilateral Investment Treaties as a New Tendency in Foreign Investment Law: India and Indonesia in the Focus' (2020) 17 Indonesian J Intl L 253; and UNCTAD *World Investment Report* 2021, 122–23.
[60] VCLT, arts 40, 41.

Amendment of treaties is a good illustration of the dilemma that the split personality of treaties presents to international law. As a source of obligations to which states commit themselves by their free choice, treaties might appear equally to be open to amendment at choice. However, where a treaty operates in a quasi-legislative role, stating a general rule of international law, to what extent can it be changed by two or more states among themselves? This is essentially a problem of general international law and an issue in the formation of custom.[61] Here it is sufficient to note that the Vienna Convention does lay down some principles relevant to aspects of the problem, but it does not deal with the core of it.

The details of the Vienna Convention's provisions on amendment and modification can be found in Articles 40 and 41 respectively. These provisions are subject to any different provisions in the individual treaty under consideration. The underlying principle is that states may agree in treaties whatever they choose, provided what they choose does not conflict with any rules of international law from which it is not permissible to except oneself. In theory, therefore, states which agree upon a set of obligations in a treaty can equally agree to amend the treaty whenever they wish to do so. The principle that states are bound by a treaty only if they consent to it means that all those who are parties to a treaty must consent to any amendment to it unless the treaty provides otherwise. Absent such alternative provision, any one state which does not consent to amendment is entitled to have the treaty applied in its original form. Any state applying a changed rule would be breaching its obligations to states parties to the unamended treaty.

> Thus the most difficult of these Vienna provisions are those defining the circumstances for modification. This is permitted by Article 41(2), where:
> (a) the possibility of such a modification is provided for by the treaty; or
> (b) the modification in question is not prohibited by the treaty and:
>   (i) does not affect the enjoyment by the other parties of their rights under the treaty or the performance of their obligations;
>   (ii) does not relate to a provision, derogation from which is incompatible with the effective execution of the object and purpose of the treaty as a whole.

---

[61] See ch 2 above.

The difficult case arises under sub-paragraph (b). Where, for example, a multilateral treaty aims to provide uniform law (as is quite common), can some states change the uniform law among themselves only? The difficulty presents itself in interpreting the extent of required uniformity. There may be several factors to take into account. If such a treaty specifies how the Convention is to be given effect—as, for example, by defining a criminal offence to be introduced into each party's criminal law—it is clear that the definition cannot be changed among only some of the parties. If, however, the treaty allows reservations, that suggests that modification may be permissible.

Thus, conflicting commitments will arise only in the case of obligations of a kind which require uniform application under a multilateral treaty. In many cases it is possible to have treaty obligations in original and amended form applying in parallel. A state which is bound by the treaty in its original form and as amended simply applies the former in its relations with states which have not accepted the amendments and the latter to those that have. In the light of these dynamics of treaty making, the Vienna Convention makes the distinction indicated above between 'amendment' and 'modification'. Once a treaty has been amended or modified several times, complete 'revision' (meaning a new treaty) may be desirable.[62]

An example of a switch from amendment to successive revisions is the case of the International Convention for the Protection of Industrial Property, Paris, 1883, which established a 'Union' of states accepting obligations affecting their laws on intellectual property. The earliest amendments, when the number of participating states was small, entered into force only when ratified by all members of the Union. Later, however, revisions of the Paris Convention entered into force once a specified number of states had ratified the new instrument (described as a new 'Act' of the Union). States which ratified the new treaty but did not denounce earlier versions of the treaty remained in treaty relations with states which had not accepted a revised Act and were therefore bound by conflicting obligations.

It seems, however, that if the later treaties afforded their nationals better protection in states which had accepted the newer versions, those remaining only parties to an earlier version of the Paris Convention were unlikely to complain. In simple terms they got something for nothing, not

---

[62] For an examination of issues arising in amendment, modification, and revision see R Gardiner, 'Revising the Law of Carriage by Air: Mechanisms in Treaties and Contract' (1998) 47 ICLQ 278.

having assumed the more onerous obligations themselves. Nevertheless, the construct of a 'Union' of states, bound by uniform rules resulting from treaty relations, was broken. In the case of the Paris Union, this problem defeated the revision attempted in the 1980s as one proposal was to allow certain states to accord a lesser protection than previously guaranteed to members of the Union. States which were not prepared to accept this would no longer accept application of a later Act of the Union to which they were not party. Hence, agreement could not be reached.[63]

The Vienna Convention contains provisions on application of successive treaties, but these provisions do not solve all the problems of conflicting treaty relations just described. While the Convention's Article 30 sets out principles to apply in the case of successive treaties relating to the same subject matter, its provisions do not resolve the issues that can arise where not all parties to a previous treaty become parties to an amended or revised treaty on the same subject. Article 40 of the Vienna Convention states that unless a treaty otherwise provides, where a state becomes party to an amended treaty, if it does not express a different intention, it also becomes a party to the unamended treaty in relation to any party which has not agreed to be bound by the amended treaty. Where it applies, this ensures that a 'late' joiner in a sequence of amended treaties has treaty relations with all those states parties only to any earlier version; but the Vienna provisions cannot resolve the situations that can arise where a pair of states are parties to separate incarnations of the same treaty but do not share any one version in common.[64]

---

[63] On treaty relations within the Paris Union, cf GHC Bodenhausen: 'States party to the Convention have constituted a *Union* embodied in successive Acts of the Convention, as a consequence of which a State can only enter (and leave) the *Union as a whole* and must always be *bound*-albeit possibly by different Acts of the Convention-to *all other member States*.' Guide to the Application of the Paris Convention ... (BURPI 1968) 204 (emphasis in original), and see ch 3 above, text to n 19.

[64] An example of treaties which deliberately excluded automatic acceptance of unamended forms of the same treaty was the series of Protocols amending the 1929 Warsaw Convention on carriage by air, which attempted to avoid conflicting obligations where the amended treaties provided different regimes of liability and compensation for accidents and other events in air carriage. Courts have not always shown an understanding of the significance of treaty relations, but have sometimes fashioned provisions they consider appropriate where treaty relations derived from the same instrument have not been present: Gardiner (n 62).

7
Treaties at the Heart of International Law

This chapter seeks to make out the case that treaties are not merely a collection of mutual obligations between states but are the most substantial statement of the rules of international law. It draws together some of the material in earlier chapters. For the sake of coherence many of the examples are recapitulated rather than making a long list of cross-references.

There are several aspects of the contribution of treaties to international law which could be examined in assessing their role. Those outlined here are the development of general international law, the establishment and function of international institutions, and the foundations of specialist areas of international law. Various classifications are possible. Those treaties which make for formation and implementation of international law form a rather variegated collection. Some are fundamental to the conduct of international relations; others are on topics where the risk of abrasive international contact makes regulation by treaty particularly appropriate. A prominent class is formed by treaties which establish the international organizations associated with specialist areas of international law and which generate the greater part of modern international law.

I General International Law

1 Scope

The term 'general international law' has no authoritative definition but the ILC used the term repeatedly in its debates on the law of treaties and included it in some provisions of the Vienna Convention.[1] Tellingly, the ILC rejected the word 'general' from its reference to international law in Article

---

[1] See arts 53, 64, and 71.

31(3)(c) (on taking account of international law when interpreting a treaty provisions) because the Commission considered that this would exclude other relevant treaties.[2] Nevertheless, much of its work has been codification and statement in treaty form of rules of general international law.

In this chapter, however, 'general international law' is used simply to distinguish those areas which do not fall within what have come to be recognized as specialist fields of international law. Slightly confusingly, some of these specialist fields have been significant contributors to the development of topics which come within general international law as well as law in their own area.[3] The topics considered here, which are sometimes described as the general part of international law, include war and peace, statehood combined with state immunity and diplomatic law, general topics codified by the ILC, the law of spaces (sea, air, and outer space), and individuals' rights and obligations.[4]

2 War and Peace

In early international law a binary distinction was made between the law of peace and the law of war. Thus Oppenheim, following the division inherent in the title of Grotius' *De Jure Belli ac Pacis* (1625), produced two volumes, on 'Peace' and 'War' respectively, for his 1905 treatise *International Law*, which was a dominant work in the profession of international law through its nine editions in the twentieth century. As well as having a direct effect on particular wars, in the sense of relating to alliances in going to war and establishing peace at the end of war, treaties have had three more general effects. First, they have affected status in war, particularly by distinguishing neutrals from belligerents. Second, treaties have sought to control the conduct of belligerents to take account of humanitarian concerns. Third, treaties have attempted progressively to eliminate the unilateral resort to armed conflict and unilateral use of force except in self-defence.

While the 1928 Pact of Paris did not mark the end of formal declarations of war, still less war itself, it was a treaty which paved the way for Article

---

[2] [1966-I] Yearbook of ILC 190, 191, and 197.
[3] See eg M Wood, 'The International Tribunal for the Law of the Sea and General International Law' (2007) 22 Intl J Marine and Coastal L 351.
[4] See Martti Koskenniemi, 'Report of the Study Group on Fragmentation of International Law: Difficulties arising from the Diversification and Expansion of International Law', UN Docs (2006) A/CN.4/L.682 and A/CN.4/L.682/Corr.1, 254.

2(4) of the UN Charter which effectively marked the end of legitimate use of unilateral declarations of war, though unable to eliminate the illegal use of force and the establishment of hostilities.[5] While the Pact and Charter are directed to discouraging resort to war, treaties have established a whole body of law concerned with the conduct of hostilities and protection of individuals in the course of hostilities. That these treaties constitute a distinct body of law was confirmed by the ICJ in an advisory opinion addressing the question whether the threat and use of nuclear weapons are prohibited:

> A large number of customary rules have been developed by the practice of States and are an integral part of the international law relevant to the question posed. The 'laws and customs of war'—as they were traditionally called—were the subject of efforts at codification undertaken in The Hague (including the Conventions of 1899 and 1907), and were based partly upon the St. Petersburg Declaration of 1868 as well as the results of the Brussels Conference of 1874. This 'Hague Law' and, more particularly, the Regulations Respecting the Laws and Customs of War on Land, fixed the rights and duties of belligerents in their conduct of operations and limited the choice of methods and means of injuring the enemy in an international armed conflict. One should add to this the 'Geneva Law' (the Conventions of 1864, 1906, 1929 and 1949), which protects the victims of war and aims to provide safeguards for disabled armed forces personnel and persons not taking part in the hostilities. These two branches of the law applicable in armed conflict have become so closely interrelated that they are considered to have gradually formed one single complex system, known today as international humanitarian law. The provisions of the Additional Protocols of 1977 give expression and attest to the unity and complexity of that law.
>
> ...
>
> It is undoubtedly because a great many rules of humanitarian law applicable in armed conflict are so fundamental to the respect of the human person and 'elementary considerations of humanity' as the Court put it in its Judgment of 9 April 1949 in the *Corfu Channel case* (*I.C.J. Reports 1949*, p. 22), that the Hague and Geneva Conventions have

---

[5] One of the 1907 Hague Conventions, 'Convention (III) relative to the Opening of Hostilities', which sought to ensure that hostilities would not commence without previous warning by declaration or ultimatum, has thirty-six parties, all of which became bound before the First World War, save for Belarus (1962), Fiji (1973), South Africa (1978), and Ukraine (2015) (ICRC database 26 January 2022). For the Pact of Paris see text to ch 5, n 7 above.

enjoyed a broad accession. *Further these fundamental rules are to be observed by all States whether or not they have ratified the conventions that contain them, because they constitute intransgressible principles of international customary law.*'[6]

The one major product of the Hague Conferences mentioned in this extract which did not directly concern the conduct of war was a treaty on pacific settlement of international disputes.[7] The main outcome of this treaty (originally in 1899 and revised in 1907) was establishment of a Permanent Court of Arbitration which, although in no way living up to its grandiose title, has made a substantial contribution to the judicial settlement of disputes both by hosting arbitrations and by paving the way for the Permanent Court of International Justice (later the ICJ).

3 Statehood, State Immunity, and Diplomatic Relations

Statehood itself has not been exactly defined by treaties, although treaties can play a part in providing evidence that an entity is a state by application of established criteria and showing that other states regard it as such.[8] The areas of international law which are most closely connected with statehood are state immunity and diplomatic relations. Rules for protecting embassies and envoys date from ancient times, with obvious and practical justification for ensuring safe and reliable interaction. Sovereign immunity developed from national practice arising where one sovereign had contact with another. As a matter of mutual respect (or reciprocal self-regard), a sovereign, in the sense of a princely or royal personage, visiting the realm of another could only be treated as a sovereign and was therefore not subject to the jurisdiction which the host had over his or her subjects.

Although state immunity, as the successor to personal sovereign immunity, had its origins within the jurisdiction of states, developments in

---

[6] *Legality of the Threat or Use of Nuclear Weapons* [1966] ICJ Rep 226, paras 75, 79 (emphasis added to last sentence).
[7] Convention for the Pacific Settlement of International Disputes, The Hague, 1899 and 1907.
[8] Montevideo Convention, art 1 (Convention on the Rights and Duties of States 1933, 165 LNTS 19, no 3802) sets out the criteria commonly regarded as customary requirements for an entity to be a state, but statehood is often also subject to a political assessment.

the twentieth century took states increasingly into direct involvement with international trade and commercial activities. Shipping being a significant point of international contact, an early indication of the distinction between sovereign and commercial activities of states was a 1926 treaty drawn up under the auspices of the League of Nations relieving state-owned vessels of immunity unless warships or other listed types of non-commercial services.[9] Although only some thirty states became bound by this treaty, these states and many others have recognized the distinction between sovereign and commercial activities for purposes of immunity.

Codification of state immunity has taken treaty form on a regional basis in the European Convention of 1972 and, more recently, on a potentially global scale in a UN Convention.[10] Only eight states have become parties to the former, while the UN Convention has fewer than thirty signatories and only just over twenty parties. The ICJ has nevertheless paid considerable attention to the provisions of these Conventions in a case concerning private claims against Germany and German state property.[11] The Court cited Article 2(1) of the United Nations Charter as making clear the fundamental character of the principle of sovereign equality of states from which the Court saw state immunity to be derived.[12] References to the European and UN Conventions permeate the Court's judgment and the Court used the negotiating history of the latter treaty to show that in 2004 there was no established limitation of state immunity by reference to the gravity of the violation of international law or the peremptory character of a rule which has been breached.[13] Thus even treaties which have attracted limited participation but show a wide involvement in detailed negotiation can play a decisive role in international litigation.

No such restricted participation applies to diplomatic and consular law, where the relevant treaties have almost universal participation and clearly constitute a fundamental element of international law governing the active

---

[9] International Convention for the Unification of Certain Rules relating to the Immunity of State-owned Vessels 1926 and Additional Protocol 1934, 176 LNTS 199, no 4062 (Brussels Convention).

[10] European Convention on State Immunity 1972, (ETS) No 74 (Basel Convention) and United Nations Convention on Jurisdictional Immunities of States and Their Property 2004, UNGA Res 59/38 (2 December 2004); status as at 8 March 2023.

[11] In *Jurisdictional Immunities of the State (Germany v Italy, Greece intervening)* (Judgment) [2012] ICJ Rep 99, the litigating states were not parties to the Conventions. See also H Fox and P Webb, *The Law of State Immunity* (revised 3rd edn, OUP 2015).

[12] *Jurisdictional Immunities of the State (Germany v Italy, Greece intervening)* (Judgment) (n 11) para 57.

[13] ibid para 89.

conduct of relations between states as the very core of the system.[14] In the leading case concerning these treaties the ICJ observed:

> '[T]he Vienna Conventions, which codify the law of diplomatic and consular relations, state principles and rules essential for the maintenance of peaceful relations between States and accepted throughout the world by nations of all creeds, cultures and political complexions.
>
> The rules of diplomatic law, in short, constitute a self-contained régime which, on the one hand, lays down the receiving State's obligations regarding the facilities, privileges and immunities to be accorded to diplomatic missions and, on the other, foresees their possible abuse by members of the mission and specifies the means at the disposal of the receiving State to counter any such abuse.[15]

4 Codification of International Law

The functions of the UN General Assembly include 'encouraging the progressive development of international law and its codification'.[16] While codification could be achieved by publishing compilations of existing rules, 'progressive development' of the law has strong legislative overtones, which in international relations is most positively achieved by treaties rather than the vagaries of establishing customary rules. This distinction is, in effect, acknowledged in the Statute of the ILC: 'the expression "progressive development of international law" is used for convenience as meaning the preparation of draft conventions on subjects which have not yet been regulated by international law or in regard to which the law has not yet been sufficiently developed in the practice of States'.[17] No such indication of preparation of draft conventions is expected of the ILC in its work of codification which is simply defined as 'the more precise formulation and systematization of rules of international law in fields where there already has been extensive State practice, precedent and doctrine'.[18] In practice, however, some

---

[14] See E Denza, *Diplomatic Law* (4th edn, OUP 2016).
[15] *United States Diplomatic and Consular Staff in Tehran (USA v Iran)* (Judgment) [1980] ICJ Rep 3, paras 45, 86.
[16] See art 13 and see further ch 2 above.
[17] See art 15.
[18] ibid.

of the work of the ILC has combined codification and progressive development in its output and hence been the subject of treaties. Several of the treaties prepared by the ILC are mentioned elsewhere in this book, the most prominent in connection with treaties being the Vienna Convention on the Law of Treaties (VCLT) 1969.[19] It should be recalled that the early work of the ILC envisaged its work on the law of treaties as aimed at producing a code rather than a treaty. Fitzmaurice, the third Special Rapporteur on the law of treaties, produced his reports on that basis.[20] He saw it as inappropriate that a code on the law of treaties should itself take the form of a treaty.[21] This may have reflected the thought that any rules should be ones which were already, or would become, customary international law. However, that the law of treaties is now stated in treaty form has not prevented its rules being acknowledged as being of general application. On many occasions, states which are not parties to the Vienna Convention have relied on its rules to show formulations of customary law. Thus there is an increasing practice of courts and tribunals looking to treaties for formulations of international law applicable to states generally.

Where the ILC does not intend to change the law, it has in more recent times elaborated 'guides' or simply 'conclusions'. The most prominent example is the monumental Guide to Practice on Reservations to Treaties, which was self-evidently incapable of working as a treaty.[22] Similarly, the law of state responsibility, which is a major subject in international law, was largely codified in draft articles which were endorsed by the UN General Assembly but not formally adopted as a treaty.[23] Nevertheless, overall it seems reasonable to conclude that treaties based on work of the ILC have been a major driver towards codification, amplification, and development of international law.

---

[19] Topics which have resulted in draft texts of treaties and other outputs of the ILC can be found through its 'Analytical Guide to the Work of the International Law Commission': https://legal.un.org/ilc/research.shtml.
[20] See Report of GG Fitzmaurice [1956-II] Yearbook of the ILC 104 at 106, para 9.
[21] ibid.
[22] Addendum to Report of the International Law Commission, Sixty-third session (2011), UN General Assembly Official Records, Sixty-sixth Session, Supplement No 10, A/66/10/Add.1 http:// legal.un.org/ilc/reports/2011/english/addendum.pdf, See also ch 3, section III.2(a) above.
[23] See ch 6 above.

5 Law of Spaces

In his address to Congress on the declaration of the USA's entry into the First World War, President Woodrow Wilson stated: 'International law had its origin in the attempt to set up some law which would be respected and observed upon the seas, where no nation had right of dominion and where lay the free highways of the world.'[24] This acknowledged that areas outside the sovereignty of states have long been the arena for development of international law by reason of the possible competing interests of instrumentalities (ships, aircraft, and space objects) of states and their nationals. Early steps in making rules as regards use of the sea were by custom and parallel domestic legislation. However, later codification, consolidation, and expansion of the law of the sea has been by treaty. Air law and, to a less developed extent, the law of outer space, are wholly dependent on treaties for their specialist regimes, although general international law continues to apply where specific rules have not been adopted.

At is simplest, but most important in practical terms, in maritime law uniform regulations based on accepted customs of seafarers were needed to replace national laws for preventing collisions at sea. A distillation of customary practices as enacted by national laws of states which had substantial shipping interests became generally accepted as a body of international rules known simply as 'the Collision Regulations'. Just as international treaties were developed under the description Safety of Lives at Sea Conventions, the Collision Regulations were also embodied in treaty form.[25] Responsibility for updating these rules was placed with the Inter-Governmental Maritime Consultative Organization, which was later transformed into the International Maritime Organization.

Much more extensive have been the efforts to codify the whole law of the sea, defining and regulating sea areas (territorial sea, exclusive economic zone, high seas etc.). Once again, claims through national laws such as those on extent of territorial seas, fisheries, exploitation of the continental shelf, and a regime for the high seas ('the area') could only be effectively

---

[24] Declaration of War Message to Congress (2 April 1917): Records of the United States Senate; Record Group 46, National Archives (65th Congress, I Session, Senate Document No 5).
[25] International Convention for the Safety of Life at Sea 1974 and amendments, 1184 UNTS 2, no 18961; Convention on the International Regulations for Preventing Collisions at Sea 1972, 1050 UNTS 16, no 15824.

harmonized by treaty, and then only incrementally by states' acceptance of treaty rights and obligations.

Four conventions concluded at Geneva in 1958 were succeeded by the UN Convention on the Law of the Sea 1982.[26] This treaty represents a monumental effort to regulate use of the sea, the seabed, and subsoil and to protect them and the related environment. As well as dealing with navigation rights, jurisdiction, and economic exploitation, the Convention provides mechanisms for cooperation and resolution of disputes. While there are grounds to qualify the degree of success such a treaty can achieve by reason of significant absence from the body of parties (168 at 8 March 2023), and to question the effectiveness of the dispute settlement provisions, the Convention shows that the treaty form is the closest in this area that the international community can approach to law. This general convention does not exhaust the list of treaties which concern use of the sea. There have long been treaties regulating carriage of goods by sea, and other aspects of commercial maritime activity and liability are covered by separate treaties, as well as those concerned with environmental matters such as oil pollution and carriage of nuclear material.

While the codification and elaboration of the law of the sea and maritime law was the product of a long period of coalescence of customary laws and practice, there was no such substantial custom and practice in the case of aviation before the first treaties on air law. Only intensive academic interest in the thirty years preceded the main treaty which set the foundations of air law, save to the extent that the potential of military aviation revealed by the First World War produced acceptance that each state has complete sovereignty over the whole airspace above its territory at whatever height.[27] The Paris Convention on International Aerial Navigation 1919 ushered in the era of regulated international aviation and provided an almost complete code of public international air law, also establishing rudimentary machinery for its further development.[28] The current 'Chicago

---

[26] United Nations Convention on the Law of the Sea 1982, 1833 UNTS 3, no 31363 (UNCLOS).

[27] See A Roper, *La Convention Internationale du 13 Octobre 1919 portant Réglementation de la Navigation Aérienne* (Recueil Sirey 1930) 9–12, who lists the extensive literature for the period 1891–1911. Article 1 of the 1919 Paris Convention (see below) states: 'The High Contracting Parties recognise that every Power has complete and exclusive sovereignty over the air space above its territory.' Even though there had been little chance for any peace-time practice or *opinio juris* to develop, this is formulated as a declaration of customary law, recognition signifying acknowledgement of an existing status rather than creation of a new one.

[28] Convention relating to the Regulation of Aerial Navigation 11 LNTS 173, no 297. This was not ratified by the USA but broadly similar Conventions were drawn up at Madrid, Havana, and Bucharest.

Convention' was closely based on the principles of the early multilateral aviation Conventions.[29] The Paris Convention set up an International Commission on Aerial Navigation. One of its major tasks, and of its successor the Council of the International Civil Aviation Organization set up by the Chicago Convention, was to develop detailed regulation of international aviation through Annexes to the Conventions. Such use of Annexes, often with a simpler means of amendment than a formal protocol of the kind used to amend a treaty, is increasingly the preferred model for international regulation of technical matters.

Treaties have also been the means for linking up national systems of criminal law to control hijacking and sabotage of aircraft, as well as the 'air rage' of unruly passengers which has disrupted some flights in recent years.[30] These treaties have encouraged the exercise of criminal jurisdiction of states by requiring them to submit cases of offences defined by the treaties for prosecution by their own authorities or to extradite those accused of such offences to states who intend to prosecute them. A further treaty concluded at Chicago in 1944 and a very large number of mostly bilateral treaties have enabled the operation of international air services, defining routes and regulating air transport operations around the world.[31] In private law, the 1929 Warsaw Convention and its successor the 1999 Montreal Convention enabled the development of commercial aviation by unifying rules on carriage by air, particularly as regards contracts and tortious or delictual liability.[32]

The law relating to outer space (broadly speaking to be found beyond where airspace ends) is very rudimentary. The blueprint in the Outer Space

---

[29] Convention on International Civil Aviation 1944, 15 UNTS 295, no 102 (Chicago Convention).

[30] Convention on Offences and Certain Other Acts Committed on Board Aircraft 1963 (Tokyo Convention, 187 parties); Convention for the Suppression of Unlawful Seizure of Aircraft 1970 (The Hague Convention, 185 parties); Convention for the Suppression of Unlawful Acts against the Safety of Civil Aviation September 1971 (Montreal Convention, 188 parties, with 46 states parties to 2010 Beijing revised Convention); parties as at 8 March 2023 https://www.icao.int/secretariat/legal/Lists/Current%20lists%20of%20parties/AllItems.aspx.

[31] International Air Services Transit Agreement 1944, 84 UNTS 389, no 252 (Chicago Convention, 134 parties); most bilateral agreements were modelled on, or developed from, the UK–USA 'Agreement Relating to Air Services' 1946, 3 UNTS 253, no 36 (Bermuda Agreement).

[32] Convention for the Unification of Certain Rules Relating to International Carriage by Air 1929 (and amendments) (Warsaw Convention, 152 parties) and Convention for the Unification of Certain Rules for International Carriage by Air 1999 (Montreal Convention, 139 parties), parties as at 8 March 2023 https://www.icao.int/secretariat/legal/LEB%20Treaty%20Collection%20Documents/composite_table.pdf.

Treaty 1967 is very sketchy and, as with the few other space law treaties—the 'Rescue Agreement', the 'Liability Convention', the 'Registration Convention', and the 'Moon Agreement'—does not enjoy the participation of all states having capabilities activities in outer space.[33] There is, nevertheless, a particular significance of this treaty in that its formulation follows almost verbatim a UN General Assembly Declaration, particularly in its Article II, which states: 'Outer space, including the moon and other celestial bodies, is not subject to national appropriation by claim of sovereignty, by means of use or occupation, or by any other means.'[34]

This statement is formulated as an existing rule—that is as customary international law, rather than as a new treaty obligation. Why did a statement of law in a resolution of the UN General Assembly which had been adopted unanimously need to assume treaty form?[35] This may have been because the treaty also reflected a UN resolution calling on states to refrain from placing in orbit nuclear weapons or weapons of mass destruction on celestial bodies, propositions which were not statements of customary law but would constitute obligations for states becoming parties to a treaty when formulated as undertakings.[36]

Whether treaty obligations are more effective than statements of customary international law in a General Assembly resolution is not simply an academic question—although academic questions can be very useful for finding and meeting future problems! On 3 December 1976, a number of equatorial states adopted a Declaration at Bogota stating their claims to the segments of the geostationary orbit above their territories. This was based on the assertion that this particular area of outer space (the geostationary geosynchronous orbit) can be defined by its characteristic that satellites

---

[33] Treaty on Principles Governing the Activities of States in the Exploration and Use of Outer Space, including the Moon and Other Celestial Bodies 1967 (112 parties); Agreement on the Rescue of Astronauts, the Return of Astronauts and the Return of Objects Launched into Outer Space 1968 (99 parties); Convention on International Liability for Damage Caused by Space Objects 1971 (98 parties); Convention on Registration of Objects Launched into Outer Space 1974 (72 parties); and Agreement Governing the Activities of States on the Moon and Other Celestial Bodies 1979 (18 parties): status of international agreements relating to activities in outer space as at 1 January 2022, UN Office for Outer Space Affairs Doc A/AC.105/C.2/2021/CRP.10.

[34] cf Declaration of Legal Principles Governing the Activities of States in the Exploration and Use of Outer Space, UN GA Res 1962 (XVIII), para 3.

[35] On the political background and on the legal status of declarations in Resolution 1962 (XVIII) see Bin Cheng, 'United Nations Resolutions on Outer Space: 'Instant' International Customary Law?' (1965) 5 Indian JIL 23, reprinted in Bin Cheng, *Studies in International Space Law* (OUP 1997) ch 7.

[36] Outer Space Treaty, art IV and UNGA Res 1884 (XVIII).

positioned there remain in a constant relationship to an area of the Earth's surface. This synchronicity is a particularly valuable attribute for broadcasting and telecommunications as it enables constant coverage of most populated territory with suitably located satellites. The equatorial states asserted that as the geostationary geosynchronous attribute was a consequence of gravity, and since the orbit had a limited capacity for positioning satellites, it fell within the concept of natural resources recognized as under the permanent sovereignty of these developing countries in accordance with certain UN resolutions.[37]

The difficulty with any such reasoning lay in the effect of the Outer Space Treaty's prohibition of acquisition of sovereignty over portions of outer space. As a code of general international law very closely based on the Declaration in a UN General Assembly resolution, the proposition in this provision of the treaty defeats the claims of even those states that are not parties to it. States which are parties are clearly estopped from making any claim of sovereignty over outer space. The argument that the geostationary orbit is not in outer space is too implausible in view of the functional operation of satellites there, and the orbit is plainly outside airspace. That the orbit is a shared limited resource has been acknowledged by the international community through the allocations of the International Telecommunications Union rather than by claims to national sovereignty.[38] In this manner, treaties play an important role in modern communications even though their presence and influence is not widely apparent.

6 Rights and Duties of Individuals

That the ultimate beneficiaries of international law should be individuals has had limited reflection in international law until recently:

> [T]he fact [is] that, in relation to both rights and duties, the individual is the final subject of the law … recognition of the individual, by dint of the acknowledgement of his fundamental rights and freedoms, as the ultimate subject of international law, is a challenge to the doctrine which

---

[37] UNGA Res 2692 (XXV) and Res 3281 (XXIX), and see ch 2, section II.2 above.
[38] See CQ Christol, *The Modern International Law of Outer Space* (Pergamon 1982) 463, 588–90; Cheng, *Studies in International Space Law* (n 35) 564–67; and for a modern assessment see M Mejia-Kaiser, *The Geostationary Ring: Practice and Law* (Brill/Nijhoff 2020), esp chs 3 and 4 on the Bogota Declaration and the role of the ITU, respectively.

in reserving that quality exclusively to the State tends to the personification of the State as a being distinct from the individuals who compose it, with all that such personification implies.[39]

Acknowledgement that individuals and entities incorporated under national laws can hold and assert rights and obligations under international law has been achieved (if only haltingly) as a result of treaties. Treaties on international humanitarian law in the second half of the nineteenth century marked the start of clear recognition that states must afford decent treatment to prisoners of war and to others. Claims commissions afforded a means by which individuals and corporate losses could to some extent be remedied. However, that individuals have their own rights under international law and may (in some circumstances) have access to international courts and tribunals are rather more recent developments.

(a) Consular law

Although consular law had long guaranteed access by nationals to their consular representatives in foreign lands, that this was a right directly accruing to individuals under international law, as codified by treaty, has only become clear with judgments of the ICJ, albeit that where an individual has been denied this right by a 'host' state it is for their state of nationality to make good their claim:

> The Court recalls that 'Article 36, paragraph 1 [of the Vienna Convention on Consular Relations] creates individual rights, which, by virtue of Article I of the Optional Protocol, may be invoked in this Court by the national State of the detained person' (*LaGrand (Germany v. United States of America), Judgment, I.C.J. Reports 2001*, p. 494, para. 77).[40]

(b) Human rights

The historic starting point of the widespread protection of human rights is commonly taken as the UN General Assembly's Universal Declaration of Human Rights in 1948.[41] Although not a treaty, the Universal Declaration

---

[39] H Lauterpacht, *International Law and Human Rights* (Stevens 1950) 69–70.
[40] *Jadhav (India v Pakistan)* (Judgment) [2019] ICJ Rep 418, para 116.
[41] Universal Declaration of Human Rights, General Assembly Resolution 217A (III) of 10 December 1948.

was rooted in one, that is the UN Charter's mandate for the organization's work in this area.[42] The Declaration listed the rights but their effective protection demands legal machinery to interpret, to adjudicate, and to order enforcement. The legal means for putting these attempts into practice has been treaties, although resolutions of international organizations have provided a political accompaniment and some soft law for the treaty institutions to work with.

The UN's own list of rights has found extended treaty form in two grandly named 'Covenants': the International Covenant on Civil and Political Rights[43] and the International Covenant on Economic, Social and Cultural Rights.[44] There are also other treaties which deal with particular sectors within the general area of human rights. These include: the Convention on the Elimination of All Forms of Racial Discrimination,[45] the Convention on the Elimination of All Forms of Discrimination Against Women,[46] the Convention Against Torture and Other Cruel, Inhuman or Degrading Treatment or Punishment,[47] and the Convention on the Rights of the Child.[48] Regional human rights treaties include the European Convention for the Protection of Human Rights and Fundamental Freedoms 1950, the American Convention on Human Rights 1969, and the African Charter on Human and Peoples' Rights 1981.[49]

While the UN's treaties on human rights have wide participation globally, the institutions to give effect to the rights suffer from the political character of the organization.[50] Institutions which have more effective legal components are those established by regional treaties. At the start of a book on the European Court of Human Rights, Judge Nussberger identifies as one of the features of treaties that they are 'durable', but also notes that 'even if they seem to be carved in stone they are full of life and aptly adapt to new times and new challenges'.[51] While some of the changes and adaptations

---

[42] See UN Charter, preamble and arts 1(3), 55, 56, 63, 76.
[43] New York, 1966, 999 UNTS 171, no 14668.
[44] New York, 1966, 993 UNTS 3, no 14531.
[45] New York, 1966, 660 UNTS 195, no 9464.
[46] New York, 1979, 1249 UNTS 13, no 20378.
[47] New York, 1984, 1465 UNTS 85, no 24841.
[48] New York, 1989, 1577 UNTS 3, no 27531.
[49] Respectively: Rome, 213 UNTS 221, no 2889; San José, 1144 UNTS 143, no 17955; and Nairobi, 1520 UNTS 217, 26363.
[50] See eg UN Covenant on Civil and Political Rights, which has 173 parties (as at 13 January 2022), but only 116 are parties to its first Optional Protocol which provides for communications from individuals to the UN Human Rights Committee, a body of rather limited competence.
[51] A Nussberger, *The European Court of Human Rights* (OUP 2020) 3.

occur through the evolutionary content and application of the European Convention on Human Rights, the sixteen amending protocols attest to the role of treaties in bringing about changes that are considered necessary. It must be readily acknowledged that, even on a regional basis, securing participation in amending instruments can be difficult; but the continued functioning of human rights organs provides evidence of the significance of treaties in their creation and development as components of a specialist area of international law.

(c) Investment law

One of the most active areas of international law in recent times has been in arbitration of investment disputes. A substantial network of bilateral investment treaties has been established in the last fifty years. These treaties attempt to codify international standards for protection of investments of foreign nationals, individual and corporate, usually with provision for arbitration between the individual and 'host' state if an aggrieved investor asserts that the standards have not been met. The most common provision for arbitration is through the International Centre for the Settlement of Investment Disputes (ICSID), although alternatives are sometimes available.[52] A significant feature is that the governing Convention requires all ICSID members, whether or not parties to the dispute, to recognize and enforce ICSID arbitral awards.[53] Thus uncertainty about whether international arbitral awards involving states can be registered under other arrangements for recognition and enforcement of arbitral awards is circumvented.[54] The whole system is based on treaties.

(d) International criminal law

In the development of international law in the second half of the twentieth century, the concept of international criminal law has developed in four main ways. First, there were war crimes, a concept established long before the Nuremberg trials of Nazi criminals and the Tokyo trials of the Japanese equivalents but brought into prominence by these proceedings. Second,

---

[52] ICSID is governed by the Convention on the Settlement of Investment Disputes between States and Nationals of Other States 1965, 575 UNTS 159, no 8359 (the Washington Convention). It was set up under the aegis of the World Bank with an Administrative Council and a Secretariat. More than 150 states are parties to the Convention.
[53] See Washington Convention 1965, art 54.
[54] cf the Convention on Recognition and Enforcement of Foreign Arbitral Awards 1958 (the New York Convention).

the International Law Commission (ILC) embarked on development of a concept of international crime as a category of state responsibility. Third, a disparate body of multilateral treaties has defined crimes of international concern (torture, hijacking, bribery of officials, and several others) that are punishable within national legal systems pursuant to rules on jurisdiction laid down in the treaties. Fourth, international tribunals have been developed specifically to provide jurisdiction to try individuals charged with international crimes. The first two of these topics have been touched on earlier in this book.[55] While the ILC's work provided some preliminary approaches to international criminal jurisdiction, the main development has been through treaties, that is indirectly by the UN Charter empowering the Security Council to establish criminal tribunals and directly by the Rome Statute of the International Criminal Court.[56]

The International Criminal Court is at an early and precarious stage of its existence, but one of the features of the treaty by which it was established is the procedure for amending its provisions. These include amendment by a highly qualified majority vote (but coupled with express provision for immediate withdrawal by a non-accepting party). Not free from controversy, such provisions show how a treaty regime has potential for acting in a quasi-legislative capability. A prominent and historic illustration of this was the adoption of amendments defining the crime of aggression in 2010.[57]

II International Organizations

International organizations are corporate institutions whose relations with one another and with states are governed by international law. They are established by treaty. Such treaties are bespoke, there being no international law governing the form of their constitutive instruments. However, some are in grouped relations, such as the United Nations specialized agencies; but these, like all international organizations, have treaties tailored to the needs of their particular functional area.[58]

---

[55] See eg the Nuremberg Charter and loose link to the Pact of Paris at text to ch 5, n 7 above, crimes against aircraft at text to ch 5, n 9.

[56] 2187 UNTS 3 and 90, no 38544, 90, 123 states parties as at 8 March 2023 https://asp.icc-cpi.int/states-parties.

[57] But see A Zimmermann, 'Amending the Amendment Provisions of the Rome Statute: The Kampala Compromise on the Crime of Aggression and the Law of Treaties' (2012) 10 J Intl Crim Just 209.

[58] UN Charter, arts 57, 63, and see the list of agencies at https://www.un.org/en/about-us/un-system.

1 Historical Development

The modern wave of treaties establishing international organizations started in the nineteenth century, although there were some forms of earlier collective bodies which had features loosely comparable to today's organizations (such as the Hanseatic League).[59] The role of major rivers as inland waterways led to the establishment of river commissions, some of which, such as the Rhine Commission (1831), have continued to the present day. Developments in international communications, technology, and commerce spurred the establishment of several organizations which, with some changes in structure (and changes of name in a few cases), have maintained a continuous existence to become specialized agencies of the UN.[60] Examples of these are the International Telegraph Union (ITU 1865, with 'Telecommunications' later replacing 'Telegraph' in its name and combined with the former International Radiotelegraph Union), the General Postal Union 1874 (now the 'Universal' Postal Union (UPU)) and the Bureau for Protection of Industrial Property 1883 (now the World Intellectual Property Organization (WIPO)). The International Committee of the Red Cross (1863) is another early organization which, although essentially a non-governmental organization, has subsequently received treaty recognition with its unique structure and role.[61]

The treaties which set up the nineteenth-century commissions, unions, and bureaux were mainly concerned to establish uniform rules and to achieve some continuity in their development and monitoring through an international secretariat. The secretariat would provide the necessary administration, arranging premises for conferences and committee meetings, drawing up preparatory papers, keeping records, and taking follow-up action for groups of states having an interest in developing common policies through international law and through regulations carried over into their national systems of law. The work of these organizations was in specific

---

[59] Although founded earlier, this league of medieval merchant towns assumed formal origins in treaties following that of 1241 between Lübeck and Hamburg for mutual protection of trading interests. Its irregular assemblies at Lübeck were a precursor of the plenary meetings typical of modern international organizations, with small groups of more powerful cities taking the lead (Britannica Academic, https://academic-eb-com.libproxy.ucl.ac.uk/levels/col legiate/article/Hanseatic-League/). That its decisions were subject to review by the individual towns before taking effect is also not dissimilar to the international law-making mechanisms in some organizations today.
[60] Some of the specialized agencies, or their precursors, predate the UN itself.
[61] See further below.

fields of activity, often involving technical matters, and did not centre on general political work or stem from strategic alliances which became a role of later organizations. What is particularly significant about this stage in the development of international organizations is the link between the developing substance of international rules and the recognized need for permanent structures to carry on this development. International law, in the form of treaties, came to provide the means for producing more international law.

2 The International Telecommunications Union

A good example of the role of treaties in both the organization and substance of international telecommunications is in the constitution and work of the International Telecommunications Union (ITU). When telegraphy became available to the general public some ten years after Morse sent the first message over a telegraph line in 1844, international communication by this means was not readily possible because each country used a different system, and each had its own telegraph code to safeguard the secrecy of its military and political telegraph messages. States therefore made bilateral or regional agreements governing 'telegraph relations'. In the International Telegraph Convention of 1865, twenty European states accepted common rules to standardize equipment to ensure general interconnection, adopted uniform operating instructions, and set a common international tariff and accounting rules. They simultaneously set up the ITU to enable agreement on subsequent amendments to this initial treaty.[62]

The history of the ITU shows it embracing the advances which have been made from telegraphy to telephony and modern radio communications (including both sound and television broadcasting), accommodating them within appropriate treaties and regulations. An example of the development of organization and substantive law moving ahead together is the International Frequency Registration Board (IFRB) of the ITU. The IFRB was set up to manage the frequency spectrum as it became increasingly complicated. A 'Table of Frequency Allocations' was introduced in 1912 and its allocations became mandatory. This table sets out specific frequency bands allocated to each type of service using radio waves, with a

---

[62] Convention télégraphique internationale de Paris (1865).

view to avoiding interference between transmitting stations. This allocation now has to take account of advances in mobility to include communications between aircraft and control towers, mobile telephones, ships at sea and coast stations, and spacecraft and Earth-based stations. The ITU also works with other specialist organizations, such as the International Telecommunications Satellite Organization (ITSO) and the International Mobile Satellite Organization (IMSO).[63]

Comparable development of functional organizations, linked with substantive development of international law through treaties and regulations established by the organization itself, can be seen in the case of the UPU, the WIPO and many other specialist bodies established since these early ones. Viewed historically, this link between constitutional process and substantive rules is not surprising given the way in which multilateral treaties are drawn up. Although the practice persists of diplomatic conferences for adoption of such treaties being 'hosted' by a single state, the number of potential participants, the need for continuity in preparation and co-ordination of expertise, and the secretariat demands for circulation of treaty information all combine to make involvement of an international organization with a permanent secretariat a much more effective proposition. Further, responses to more urgent needs are less haphazard, whether it be coping with some new type of potential environmental pollution, an epidemic, the need to standardize equipment reflecting a scientific advance, or whatever.

3 Non-governmental Organizations

Since non-governmental organizations (NGOs) have legal status, if any, as bodies acting under municipal law, they are not usually directly governed by treaties or specifically the subject of treaty provisions, their major contribution to international law notwithstanding. One exception, which has a hybrid status because of its major involvement with humanitarian law in armed conflict, is the Red Cross (ICRC). The Red Cross (or Red Crescent) is a widely recognized symbol of one of the earliest surviving NGOs and of the humanitarian work associated with it, particularly in time of war.[64] The

---

[63] Formerly the International Maritime Satellite Organization (INMARSAT).
[64] The symbols of a red cross and a red crescent are internationally protected under the provisions of the Paris Convention on Industrial Property 1883, as revised. Another example of

Geneva Conventions are synonymous in public awareness with ensuring minimum standards of decent treatment for prisoners of war, and many people will have encountered the work of national committees of the Red Cross. Both the organization and the specialist area of 'international humanitarian law' are far more extensive and complex than these fundamental features reveal. The Red Cross is a form of federal institution, centred on a Swiss committee. International humanitarian law is (principally) a group of treaties, some of which acknowledge a particular role for the Swiss committee. The Red Cross lists some sixty treaties relevant to humanitarian law since the middle of the nineteenth century.[65]

A committee, formed in 1863 in response to maltreatment of the wounded in the battle of Solferino 1859, which was initially called the International Committee for Relief to the Wounded, rapidly became known as the International Committee of the Red Cross (ICRC, and now also Red Crescent). The underlying notion was of neutral status being given to medical services and volunteer nurses, who could be distinguished from combatants and ordinary civilians by adoption of a distinctive emblem and who were to be given protected status in the fighting. The Committee opened the way for a conference whose participants included government delegates, delegates of various organizations, and private individuals. The 1863 conference ended with the adoption of resolutions which provided for the establishment of societies to arrange relief for wounded soldiers. This led to a more complex federal arrangement, which is laid out in its 'Statutes' governed by Swiss law.[66] While the national societies are described in the Statutes as forming the basic units and constituting the vital force of the movement, the central body for humanitarian law work is the ICRC. The ICRC, as an independent humanitarian organization, has a status of its own. It co-opts its members from among Swiss citizens. Although not an inter-governmental organization, it is recognized in treaties and enters into international agreements in the form of treaties with governments wherever it works. In its Headquarters Agreement, the Swiss Government grants the organization privileges and immunities of the same kind as other international organizations, and:

---

an NGO recognized in a treaty is the International Olympic Committee, Nairobi Treaty on the Protection of the Olympic Symbol, 1981, 1863 UNTS 367, no 31732.

[65] https://ihl-databases.icrc.org/ihl (accessed 8 March 2023).
[66] Statutes of the International Red Cross and Red Crescent Movement, adopted on 21 December 2017.

[r]ecognizes the international juridical personality and the legal capacity in Switzerland of the International Committee of the Red Cross (hereinafter referred to as the Committee or the ICRC), whose functions are laid down in the Geneva Conventions of 1949 and the Additional Protocols of 1977 and in the Statutes of the International Red Cross and Red Crescent Movement.[67]

In 1990, the UN General Assembly gave observer status to the ICRC.'[68] Thus, through a combination of treaty provisions and practical recognition, the ICRC has a form of 'functional international personality'.[69] Although this conclusion is not without controversy, the agreements which the ICRC makes with states, its observer status at the UN, and its role under humanitarian law treaties provides evidence of recognition of this functional status in the development and application of law.

III Specialist Areas

Several areas of international law that are viewed as the concern of specialists have already been mentioned in this and other chapters above. All are treaty based and many are associated with international institutions which operate to produce further treaties. The International Labour Organization, for example, functioning in matters now subsumed under the heading of the economic and social area of human rights has produced, in its 100 years of functioning, 190 conventions and several protocols.[70]

International economic law and international trade law embrace shoals of treaties in the form of commodity agreements, bilateral investment treaties, and bilateral taxation agreements, as well as the major compilations of treaties established through the World Trade Organization in succession to the General Agreement on Tariffs and Trade.[71] The International

---

[67] Agreement between the International Committee of the Red Cross and the Swiss Federal Council to determine the legal status of the Committee in Switzerland, 1993.
[68] GA Resolution 45/6: see C Koenig, 'Observer Status for the International Committee of the Red Cross at the United Nations' https://www.icrc.org/en/doc/resources/documents/article/other/57jnwj.htm .
[69] Koenig (n 68) and ICRC Statutes, art 2(2) asserting: 'In order to fulfil its humanitarian mandate and mission, the ICRC enjoys a status equivalent to that of an international organization and has international legal personality in carrying out its work.'
[70] See ILO list https://www.ilo.org/dyn/normlex/en/f?p=NORMLEXPUB:12000:0::NO::P12000_INSTRUMENT_SORT:4.
[71] See WTO legal texts https://www.wto.org/english/docs_e/legal_e/legal_e.ht.

Centre for Settlement of Investment Disputes (ICSID) reports that there are more than 3,300 treaties providing for dispute settlement between investors and states.[72] While one of the aims of this vast array of treaties is to codify or establish clearer principles and procedures for compensation for expropriation of foreign investment which had only become settled in rather vague terms in customary international law, the major development in compulsory international adjudication of disputes between private parties and states could only be effectively established by treaties.

In a similar vein, modern environmental law was foreshadowed by a few principles of customary law, such as liability for transboundary harm, but modern developments have been through treaties: 'The vast bulk of environmental law is contained in treaty texts which are given dynamic force in part because they usually provide an institutional mechanism for their implementation.'[73] Almost by definition such treaties are global in potential, although some have only regional participation. Thus, imperfect though the system is, and incomplete the participation in it, the Antarctic Treaty has kept sovereignty claims on hold and maintained a fragile restraint on development in the Antarctic of activities that would be highly detrimental to the environment.[74]

Although declarations of Stockholm (1971) and Rio (1992) produced principles which may be broadly equated in status to the Universal Declaration of Human Rights, effective progression in environmental protection has been more by sectoral treaties than by codification of general principles.[75] Thus, balancing commercial interests in whaling with conservation of stock has been an environmental concern for a number of states at least since the 1931 Geneva Whaling Convention (and later treaties), while the even earlier regional Fur Seal Treaty (Washington, 1911), which had clearly commercial content, also reflected what would now be viewed as environmental concerns of the four states parties to it as shown by the indication in its long title that it was for the 'Preservation and Protection of Fur Seals'.[76]

---

[72] 'Introducing ICSID' (ICSID publication of 17 December 2021): https://icsid.worldbank.org/resources/publications/introducing-icsid.
[73] C Redgwell, 'International Environmental Law', ch 22 in M Evans (ed), *International Law* (5th edn, OUP 2018) 682 (citations omitted).
[74] Antarctic Treaty 1961, 402 UNTS 71, no 5778.
[75] Redgwell (n 73) 680.
[76] M Fitzmaurice, *Whaling and International Law* (CUP 2015); the 1911 Convention on Seals expired at the outbreak of the Second World War but was later replaced by more extensive treaty arrangements.

The marine environment began to engender treaty protection with prominent examples being the Oil Pollution Convention (1954) and the London Dumping Convention (1972).[77] Development of similarly widely applicable provisions in the UN Convention on the Law of the Sea 1982 and movement towards universality in the 1989 Hazardous Wastes Convention and the 1992 Biological Diversity Convention stand out among the plethora of treaties emerging on environmental matters.[78] In picking out an example of the effectiveness of treaties, the Montreal Protocol on the Ozone layer is probably the best known.[79] However, while one or two principles can be shown to constitute rules of customary international law, because international environmental law is composed of so many treaties, further consideration here is limited to those provisions which illustrate the use of quasi-legislative procedures.[80]

Thus, the Convention for the Prevention of Pollution from Ships (MARPOL) includes provisions for amendment of the practical rules in its annexes similar to those of aviation's Chicago Convention, by which an amendment comes into force for all parties unless a specified number object within a certain time (although with some individual 'opt-out' possibilities).[81] There are further examples of environmental law treaties with flexible arrangements for amendment and adaptation of their provisions and regulations to take account of scientific and other developments, as well as treaties which take account of the different capabilities and circumstances of states parties to them.[82]

---

[77] International Convention for the Prevention of Pollution of the Sea by Oil 1954, 327 UNTS 3, no 4714 and Convention on the Prevention of Marine Pollution by Dumping of Wastes and other Matter 1972, 1046 UNTS 120, no 15749.

[78] Convention on the Transboundary Movement of Hazardous Wastes 1989, 1672 UNTS 57, no 28911 and Convention on the Conservation of Biological Diversity 1992, 1760 UNTS 79, no 30619.

[79] Protocol on Substances that Deplete the Ozone Layer 1987 being a protocol to the Convention for the Protection of the Ozone Layer 1985: see *Handbook for the Montreal Protocol on Substances that Deplete the Ozone Layer* (14th edn, UNEP 2020).

[80] On customary environmental law see Redgwell (n 73) 683–85.

[81] International Convention for the Prevention of Pollution from Ships 1973, as modified by the Protocol 1978, 1340 UNTS 61, no 22484 (with many later amendments), art 16, and cf Convention on International Civil Aviation 1944, 15 UNTS 295, no 102, arts 38, 90.

[82] See Redgwell (n 73) 683.

IV Private International Law

Private international law, or conflict of laws as it is historically but less accurately or usefully described, would not usually be regarded as a separate specialist area of international law but as a distinct field contrasting with public international law. It is not an inherently unified field of law but is the characterization of reference to the internal rules of each state for deciding choice of law and allocating jurisdiction in any matter which affects private individuals and corporate entities where there are international aspects to a legal relationship or situation. For present purposes, the most helpful explanation is that: 'Private international law rules, although formally part of national law, constitute a type of distributed network of international ordering.'[83] While some general features of this ordering can be discerned in, for example, accepted principles for the exercise of jurisdiction (not entirely explained by the notion of 'comity'), there has been a distinct trend towards making rules of private international law uniform and concrete. The means for achieving this has been through treaties.

In some areas, unification or harmonization has been ad hoc or unassociated with any international organization, at least initially. Thus, the 1883 Paris Convention for the Protection of Industrial Property (now 'intellectual' property) had its origins in the practical need for protection of inventions and industrial designs in national laws revealed by the international exhibitions in London 1851 and Vienna 1873. Protection was required to assure potential exhibitors that their inventions and designs would not be filched.[84] The 1883 treaty was the foundation for the now greatly extended international arrangements for protection of intellectual property.

On a similar worldwide scale, without overcoming the parade of differing national laws on contractual, tortious, and delictual liability, international carriage by air could not have been developed. This need led to the 1929 Warsaw Convention on Unification of Certain Rules relating to Carriage by Air. Amended by several Protocols and reissued in substantially revised form at Montreal in 1999, that treaty has found a 'home' in the International Civil Aviation Organization. Nearly all states are parties to one or other versions of this treaty.

---

[83] See A Mills, *The Confluence of Public and Private International Law: Justice, Pluralism and Subsidiarity in the International Constitutional Ordering of Private Law* (CUP 2009) 24.

[84] M Blakeney, 'The International Protection of Industrial Property: from the Paris Convention to the Agreement on Trade-Related Aspects of Intellectual Property Rights (the TRIPS Agreement)' (2004) Doc WIPO/IP/UNI/DUB/04/1 2–6.

IV Private International Law 217

Three international bodies are the leaders in producing treaties harmonizing private international law. These are the Hague Conference on Private International Law (HCCH—derived from 'Hague Conference' with 'Conférence de La Haye', its working languages being English and French), the International Institute for the Unification of Private Law (UNIDROIT), and the United Nations Commission on International Trade Law (UNCITRAL).

The HCCH started work in 1893 and has a membership of ninety-one states and the European Union.[85] The Hague Conference has been particularly noted for its treaties on family law and on civil procedure.[86] Conventions listed by the HCCH as among the most widely ratified are Conventions on: the Civil Aspects of International Child Abduction 1980 (103 parties); Protection of Children and Co-operation in Respect of Intercountry Adoption 1993 (105 parties); Civil Procedure 1954 (49 parties); the Service Abroad of Judicial and Extrajudicial Documents in Civil or Commercial Matters 1965 (80 parties); and on the Taking of Evidence Abroad in Civil or Commercial Matters 1970 (65 parties).[87]

UNIDROIT is approaching its centenary. Its focus has been on preparatory work for conventions, principles, and model laws on a wide range of mainly commercial matters, with some of the conventions completed in conjunction with other organizations or through traditional diplomatic conferences.[88] Its most prominent treaty in recent times has been the Convention on International Interests in Mobile Equipment 2001 with eighty-two states parties to its Protocol on Aircraft Equipment (2001) and other Protocols (not yet in force) on railway rolling stock, space assets, and mining, agricultural, and construction equipment.[89]

The UNCITRAL produces both treaties and model laws, thus illustrating the link between private international law and national laws. The

---

[85] As at 8 March 2023: https://www.hcch.net/.

[86] See T John, R Gulati, and B Köhler (eds), *The Elgar Companion to the Hague Conference on Private International Law* (Edward Elgar Publishing 2020) 25–26.

[87] As at 8 March 2023, the HCCH lists nearly forty conventions: for current status see https://www.hcch.net/; most HCCH conventions allow non-member states to become parties after a convention has entered into force, but subject to acceptance of an acceding state by members which are already parties in many instances.

[88] See L Peters, 'UNIDROIT' in *Max Planck Encyclopedia of International Law*: UNIDROIT lists its area of interest as agency, agricultural land, capital markets, civil procedure, commercial contracts, contract farming, cultural property, factoring, franchising, international sales, international wills, leasing, reinsurance, contracts, security interests, transport: https://www.unidroit.org/.

[89] https://www.unidroit.org/instruments/security-interests/cape-town-convention/.

most widely accepted treaty with which the organization is now associated (through its 'Model Law on International Commercial Arbitration') is the Convention on the Recognition and Enforcement of Foreign Arbitral Awards 1958 (172 parties). Its 'own' most successful Convention is the UN Convention on Contracts for the International Sale of Goods 1980 (95 parties), but the UNCITRAL has also produced what it describes as 'legislative texts' (conventions and model laws) on diverse commercial, trade, and transport topics.[90]

V Conclusion

Can all these treaties, and the very much greater number which have not been mentioned here, be described as law? A few years ago Wolfgang Friedmann wrote:

> It is obvious that, in the fast-moving articulate and complex international society of today, the international treaty increasingly replaces custom as the principal source of international law.[91]

The passing years have confirmed that progression in the role of treaties. That treaties as such are only binding on states which have become parties to them limits the extent of their applicability unless their provisions can be shown to state customary international law. Nevertheless, the cogency of a rule reduced to writing lends it a force of attraction which tends to outweigh the need for consistency of practice and evidence of a widespread sense of obligation (*opinio juris*), which are the prerequisites to identification of a rule as customary international law. From a standpoint of theory, it could be said that only those rules in treaties that are universally binding, whether as codifications or because all states are parties, constitute law. That is not a very informative proposition. Many laws affect only particular groups of people or particular activities but are nevertheless law. That aside, the main point made here is that the majority of effective international rights and obligations that constitute the daily fare of international law and of lawyers encountering international issues are found in provisions of treaties.

---

[90] As at 8 March 2023 and see lists at https://uncitral.un.org/.
[91] W Friedmann, *The Changing Structure of International Law* (Stevens 1964) 123–24.

Selective Bibliography

This short bibliography lists substantial works which will provide extensive leads to material on treaties.

Barrett, J, and RC Beckman, *Handbook on Good Treaty Practice* (CUP 2020)
Bowman, MJ, and D Kritsiotis (eds), *Conceptual and Contextual Perspectives on the Modern Law of Treaties* (CUP 2018).
Boyle, AE, and CM Chinkin, *The Making of International Law* (OUP 2015)
Bradley, CA (ed), *The Oxford Handbook of Comparative Foreign Relations Law* (OUP 2019)
Brölmann, C, and Y Radi (eds), *Research Handbook on the Theory and Practice of International Lawmaking* (Edward Elgar Publishing 2016)
Cannizzaro, E (ed), *The Law of Treaties Beyond the Vienna Convention* (OUP 2011)
Corten, O, and P Klein (eds), *The Vienna Conventions on the Law of Treaties: A Commentary* (OUP 2011)
Dinstein, Y, 'The Interaction Between Customary International Law and Treaties' (2006) 322 RdC 243
Dörr, O, and K Schmalenbach (eds), *The Vienna Convention on the Law of Treaties: A Commentary* (2nd edn, Springer 2018)
Gardiner, R, *Treaty Interpretation* (OUP 2015)
Hill, J, *Aust's Modern Treaty Law and Practice* (4th edn, CUP 2023)
Hollis, DB (ed), *The Oxford Guide to Treaties* (2nd edn, OUP 2020)
Hollis, D, M Blakeslee, and B Ederington (eds), *National Treaty Law and Practice* (Martinus Nijhoff 2005)
Klabbers, J, *The Concept of Treaty in International Law* (Kluwer Law International 1996)
Kolb, R, *The Law of Treaties* (Edward Elgar Publishing 2016)
Nolte, G, *Treaties and Their Practice: Symptoms of Their Rise or Decline* (Brill Nijhoff 2019)
Roberts, I (ed), *Satow's Diplomatic Practice* (7th edn, OUP 2017)
Shelton, D (ed), *International Law and Domestic Legal Systems: Incorporation, Transformation, and Persuasion* (OUP 2011)
Sloss, D (ed), *The Role of Domestic Courts in Treaty Enforcement* (OUP 2010)
Villiger, ME, *Commentary on the 1969 Vienna Convention on the Law of Treaties* (Martinus Nijhoff 2009)

Index

For the benefit of digital users, indexed terms that span two pages (e.g., 52–53) may, on occasion, appear on only one of those pages.

accession
    as consent to be bound 67–68
    by non-signatory state 16
    definition of 67–68
adoption of treaty text 59
aggression 51, 176, 208
aircraft *see also* Chicago Convention 1944
    collisions, avoidance of 6n.4
    Hague hijacking convention 202, 207–8
    Montreal sabotage convention 111–12
    prohibition of using weapons against civil 31n.3
    Protocol on international interest in 6
    Tokyo Convention on crimes on board 202
Alaska, US-Russia treaty 14, 15
Allott, P
    sceptical definition of 'treaty', 13
amendment 189
    different from modification 189
    provisions of VCLT on 188
Amman, O, 156n.139, 157n.141, 169, 170
Aust, A, 20n.41, 42n.25
authentication of treaty text 59
aviation *see* Chicago Convention 1944
    bilateral transport agreements 202
    regulation by ICAO 201–2
Azaria, D, 29n.74, 43–44, 175n.9

Barrett, J, 53n.1, 55n.5, 121n.25
Bentham, J.
    treaties as main element of international law 5
Bjorge, E, 166–67
Bowman, MJ 12n.20
breach of treaty
    countermeasures 173, 175–76, 183–89
    ILC's conclusion on 187
    Danube Dams case 185–88
    negotiation as first response to 172
    ICJ's description of 174–75
    Pt V of Vienna Convention 173
    reciprocal non-performance (*exceptio inadimplenti*) 175–76, 183–85
    suspension of treaty 183–85
    terminating in response to 184
Bribery Convention (OECD) 113n.10, 178
    monitoring implementation 178

Cannizzaro, E, 12n.20, 182n.30
Cheng, B, 40–41, 76n.10, 203, 203n.35, 204n.38
Chicago Convention *see* Convention on International Civil Aviation
circumstances of conclusion *see* supplementary means
codification *see also* customary international law
    contrasted with progressive development 32, 38
    of customary law through treaties 33–34
    Outer Space Treaty as 39–41
    Paris Convention 1919 on airspace sovereignty as 41
    role of ILC in 32
collisions at sea
    Convention on Prevention of, 1972, 6n.4, 200
compliance
    reciprocity 173–74
    resort to arbitration, courts and tribunals 178–82
    supervision by international institutions 176–78
components of treaty *see* final clauses; negotiating states; preamble; testimonium; title
conclusion of treaty 58, 70

222 Index

Confidential Memorandum of Understanding *see* Memorandum of Understanding
consent to be bound *see* accession; ratification; signature
contracting state
  'contracting country' contrasted with 79n.18
  definition of 66–67
  not yet party 67
convention
  as synonym for treaty 7
Convention on International Civil Aviation, 1944
  Amended to prohibit force against civil aricraft 31n.3
  Annexes to, as regulations 201–2
  Rules of the Air 6
  Transit Agreement 202n.31
Corten, O, 12n.20, 26n.62
countermeasures, *see* breach of treaty
crystallization *see also* customary international law
  meaning of 33
customary international law
  codification or progressive development 38–39
  ILC conclusions on formation of 31–32, 41
  practice and opinio juris 31, 40–41
  role of treaties for 31–37

Denza, E, 148n.123, 198n.14
depositary
  functions of 64–65
  organization as 27
  retention of treaty original text 27
diplomatic relations
  convention on 33, 173–74, 196–98
Dörr, O, 12n.20, 75n.6
dualism *see* implementing treaties

effectiveness principle
  achieving object and purpose 77–78
  as maxim of interpretation 102
  (*ut res*) preferring a meaning to none 77–78
entry into force 68–70
environmental law 6, 144–45, 201, 214–16
European Court of Human Rights 80, 88, 206–7

European Union *see* implementing treaties
  treaty relations in 150–53
exceptio inadimplenti see breach of treaty
Exchange of Letters *see* Exchange of Notes
Exchange of Notes 17–18, 55

final act
  authenticating treaty text 59
  Helsinki, CSCE 1975, 22
  interpretative declarations in 83, 84–85
  Meridian Conference 1884, 23
  record of diplomatic conference 22, 28–29, 53n.2, 62
  resolutions in 57
  Vienna conference 1968-9, 28–29, 55n.4
final clauses 15, 17–18, 65, 68, 127, 151–52
  role establishing treaty relations 8, 11–12
  termination provision in 182
Fitzmaurice, M, 18n.37, 175n.9, 184–85, 185n.45
Fitzmaurice, Sir G, 42–44, 48, 199
France
  Conseil Constitutionnel, role in relation to treaties 137–42
  Conseil d'Etat, role in relation to treaties 138–39, 142–46, 165–67
  treaties in legal system of 132–37
Friedmann W
  treaties replacing custom 218n.91
full powers 21–22, 56–57, 66

general international law 193–94
genocide 45, 50, 51, 168–69
Germany
  VCLT in legal system of 167–69
good faith 7, 76–78, 106–7
  imports effectiveness 77–78

Hague Conference on Private International Law *see* private international law
Hill, J, 70n.46
Hollis, DB 12n.20, 62n.20, 117n.18, 157n.140
human rights 6, 115–16, 205–7, *see also* European Court of
  effect in France of treaties in 136–37, 139, 141, 143, 144–45
  Inter-American Commission on 176
  UN committee on 177
Hunter-Henin, M, 139, 139n.87
Hutchinson, DN 19n.40

Index   223

ICAO *see* International Civil Aviation Organization
ICSID *see* International Centre for Settlement of Investment Disputes
implementation of treaties
  in a civil law system 132–46
  distinguishing international and municipal effects 107–9, 111–12
  domestic authorisation distinct from international consent 118
  dualism and monism inadequate analysis 107
  in a dualist system 122–32
  'incorporating' a treaty 122
  national requirements 117–53
  self-executing provisions and direct applicability 114–15
  UK methods of 122–27
  UN Charter 110–11
International Centre for Settlement of Investment Disputes 178, 207, 213–14
International Civil Aviation Organization 6n.4
  Council of, making regulations 201–2
  as treaty depositary 115
international criminal law 6, 10, 207–8
International Labour Organization 177, 213
International Law Commission *see also* codification
  created by UN General Assembly 9
  statute of 38–39, 198–99
international organizations 208–13
  International Telecommunications Union 6n.3, 23n.51, 210–11
  legal status 26–27
  1986 Vienna Convention on treaties of 7, 26
  treaty establishment of 5–6, 27
interpretation of treaties
  agreements on conclusion 83
  art 31 of VCLT as general rule for 74–76
  'crucible' approach 75–76, 96
  good faith in 76–78
  as 'giving' meaning 71–72
  interpretative declaration 82, 84–85
    responses to 84–85
  meaning given by parties 81–90
  in national legal systems 153–71
  ordinary meaning in context 78–81
  'rules' in VCLT 1969, 74
  text of 72–74
  special meanings 96
  subsequent agreements as to 85–86
  subsequent practice in 86–90
  supplementary means 73, 97–102
    meaning of 74–75
  at Vienna Conference 1968–9, 48–49
interpretative declaration *see* interpretation of treaties
invalidity 173, 182–83
investment law *see* ICSID

jus cogens see peremptory norms

Klingler, J, 102n.78

languages 61–62
  choice of 61–62
  role in interpretation 102–3
law of treaties *see* Vienna Convention on
  distinguished from treaty law 11–12

Maine, H, 30n.1
McDougal, MS 13–14, 78
mandatory language 18–20
  examples of 43n.29
Memorandum of Understanding
  indiscriminate usage of term 20–22
  similar miscellaneous documents 22–24
  tribunals' differing as to status of 21–22, 23–24
modification 89, 189, 190–91
  distinguished from amendment 189
monism *see* implementing treaties
MOU *see* Memorandum of Understanding

negotiating states
  accepting reservation 45–46
  agreeing signature to be binding 66
  consenting to provisional application 69
  at diplomatic conference 57
  listed before words of agreement 16
  nominating depositary 64
  recital of 16
negotiating treaties 56–57
  see also full powers
Nicolson, H, 53
Nolte, G, 82n.27, 166n.180
Non-Governmental Organizations 211–13
  International Olympic Committee 211–12n.64
  Red Cross 212–13

224 Index

oil pollution 201, 215
Outer Space Treaty 1967 *see* codification

Pact of Paris 1928, 84, 109–10
pacta sunt servanda
   obligation to perform treaties 7–8, 42–43, 152–53
Paris Convention on Industrial Property 1883, 14, 60–61, 209, 211–12n.64, 216
   progenitor of the WIPO 14n.27
party
   capacity to make treaty 26–27
   definition of 56, 56n.7
   international organizations as 26
Pellet, A *see* reservations: Guide to Practice
peremptory norms (*jus cogens*) 32, 49–52, 124n.35, 183, 188–89
   debated at Vienna conference 49
   French opposition to provisions on 158–59
Poland
   Polish constitution 1997, 106–7
preamble
   in French constitution 133–35, 140
   identifying object and purpose for interpretation 72
   object and purpose in ICJ Whaling case 81
   reciting motivations and objectives 16
preparatory work (*travaux préparatoires*) 97–101
   confirming a meaning 98–99
   determining the meaning 99
   as legislative history 28–29
   meaning of 97–98
   use for general understanding 98
private international law 216–18
   Hague Conference (HCCH) on 28n.70, 54, 102n.77, 217
progressive development *see* International Law Commission; *see also* customary international law
Protection of Industrial Property *see* Paris Convention 1883
Proust 53–54
provisional application 63, 69
   of the GATT 69
   ILC Guide to 69n.38

ratification 59, 67–68
   accompanied by reservation 62
   bilateral exchange of instruments of 67–68
   definition of 67–68
   expressing consent to be bound 67–68
   instruments lodged with depositary 27, 65
   international process, not domestic 67–68, 119
   need for stated in testimonium 17
   process preceding in France 133, 134–35
   process preceding in UK 121
   process preceding in USA 120
registration
   compulsory at UN 27–28
   not conclusive of treaty status 19
   publication in UNTS 27–28
   UN Charter art 102, 19n.39
reservations 45–48
   consideration at Vienna Conference 1968-9, 45
   (Pellet) Guide to Practice on 47–48, 83–84, 85n.36, 177, 199
   reservation defined 45
revision 3, 14, 61, 189, 191–92
Roberts, I, 18n.36, 55n.4

sea
   Collision Regulations 6n.4, 11, 200
   Conventions on Safety of Life at 200
   Geneva Conventions on law of, 1958, 201
   law of the 42, 200–2
   UN Convention 1982 on Law of 201
Shelton, D, 32n.8, 49, 50, 183
ships 6, 200, 210–11, 215
signatory state
   not same as party 17, 66–67
   obligations of 63–64
signature *see also* testimonium
   ad referendum requiring ratification 59
   as consent to be bound if so specified 66–67
   as consent, mostly bilateral 59
   effects of 63
   most often now subject to ratification 67
   opening for, at end of conference 62
   as part of 'testimonium' (*qv*) 17
   place of, as part of formal citation 15
   with reservation 62
   as signifying conclusion 58

Index 225

Sloss, D, 105, 111, 115–6, 155, 167
state immunity 196–97
successive treaties *see* treaty relations
supplementary means of interpretation
 see also preparatory work
 circumstances of conclusion 97–101, 157, 161
 distinguished from context 97
 maxims or canons as 102
 use of 97, 98–101
 value of preparatory work as 99
suspension of treaty *see* breach of treaty
Switzerland 156–57, 169, 213

telecommunications *see* International Telecommunications Union (ITU)
termination *see also* breach of treaty
 Pt V, Vienna Convention 101
testimonium 15, 17–18, 23, 58
title
 citation by, with place and date of conclusion 15
 as designation, not conclusive of status 15
 MOU indeterminate indicator of status 20
 not always identified by negotiators 15
torture convention 51, 207–8
travaux préparatoires see preparatory work
treaty *see* final clauses; negotiating states; preamble; testimonium; title
treaty implementation *see* implementation of treaties
treaty law
 distinguished from law of treaties 11–12
treaty relations 8, 11–12, 13, 30, 69–70, 127, 173–74
 avoidance of 22
 modification of 47
 role of final clauses in 11–12
 in successive treaties 70, 191, 192
treaty definition of 5n.2, 13, 14–15
 McDougal's policy-oriented 13
 Phillip Allot's sceptical 13
 VCLT 1969, 13, 17, 24, 25, 121

Ukraine 24n.54, 195n.5
UNCITRAL 217–18
UNIDROIT 54, 217
uniform rules from treaty 6, 191, 209–10
United Kingdom
 approval before ratification 121
 claims of, against Russia 14
 implementing treaties in 122–25
 interpretation of treaties in courts of 162–65
 legislating treaty text 126–27
 long delayed treaty ratification by 63n.22
 transforming treaty's terms 126
 Treaty Series in Command Papers 121
UN Treaty Series
 publication of registered treaties 27–28
unwritten agreements 24–25
USA
 Alaska purchase treaty 14, 15
 arbitrations with UK 21, 178–80
 constitution's provision on treaties 110–11
 counter-measures in dispute with France 188–89
 non-ratification of VCLT 120
 not proceeding to ratify Rome Statute 64n.25
 proposal on interpretation rules 48
 recognition of VCLT as guide to treaty law and practice 159
 Supreme Court of
 referring to VCLT definition of treaty 159–60
 on treaty interpretation 159–61
 treaties concluded as executive agreements 120, 121
ut res magis valeat see effectiveness

VCLT *see* Vienna Convention on Law of Treaties 1969
Vienna Convention on Law of Treaties 1969
 amendment and modification, provisions on 189
 as codification 33, 42
 definitions in 8n.12
 accession 67–68
 contracting state 66–67
 full powers 56
 negotiating state 57
 party 56n.7
 ratification 67–68
 treaty 13, 14–15, 17, 24, 25
 full text of 7
 history of 42–52
 invalidity, termination and suspension, provisions on 173, 182–89
 meaning of 'conclusion' in 17–18, 56, 58
 rules of, on treaty interpretation 72–74

226 Index

Vienna Convention on Law of Treaties 1986 (International Organizations), 7, 7n.8, 11, 26
Vierdag, VW 58n.13
Villiger, ME 12n.20, 42n.27

Waldock, Sir H
  architect of 1969 Vienna Convention 44–45
  expert consultant at Vienna Conference 1968–9, 97–98
  on interpretation
    'giving' meaning to treaty 71–72
    maxims or canons, not rules 102n.79
    rules as principles or guidelines 74
  use of preparatory work 98–99
  Special Rapporteur for Law of Treaties 44
war 194–96
  Hague and Geneva law distinguished, 195–96
  humanitarian law in armed conflict 6, 195
  Red Cross and Red Crescent 211–12
whaling 81, 90, 214
Wood, M, 32, 41, 194
World Intellectual Property Organization *see* Paris Convention 1883
World Trade Organization 69, 99, 150, 173, 178